Sources,
processes and methods
in Coleridge's
Biographia Literaria

Sources, processes and methods in Coleridge's *Biographia Literaria*

KATHLEEN M. WHEELER

Fellow of Jesus College, Cambridge

CAMBRIDGE UNIVERSITY PRESS

Cambridge

London   New York   New Rochelle

Melbourne   Sydney

Published by the Press Syndicate of the University of Cambridge
The Pitt Building, Trumpington Street, Cambridge CB2 IRP
32 East 57th Street, New York, NY 10022, USA
296 Beaconsfield Parade, Middle Park, Melbourne 3206, Australia

© Cambridge University Press 1980

First published 1980

Printed in Great Britain by
Western Printing Services Ltd, Bristol

British Library Cataloguing in Publication Data
Wheeler, Kathleen M.
Sources, processes and methods in Coleridge's
'Biographia literaria'.
1. Coleridge, Samuel Taylor. 'Biographia literaria'
I. Title
808.1   PR4476   79-41683
ISBN 0 521 22690 2

Contents

Preface

This book is an examination of the *Biographia Literaria*, the prose work of Coleridge's which is of the greatest interest to students of literature, both in its value as a piece of elevated prose writing innovatory for its time, and for the insights into poetry, criticism, and the faculties of mind (especially the imagination) which it offers. The title of the book, when explained, will indicate the nature of the study.

By 'sources', two things are meant. First, there are certain philosophical and aesthetic issues which Coleridge was trying both to explicate and to demonstrate in writing the *Biographia*. These philosophical undercurrents, which at times are quite overt, embrace German, English, and Greek origins, and are intimately connected with the aesthetics which emerge from the *Biographia*. Briefly, Coleridge's roots in Plato lie in his emphasis upon dialectic and that idealism 'which is the truest form of realism'. This grounding in dialectic and idealism has particular import both for a general theory of literary criticism and for a critique of the way in which the *Biographia* interacts – and is meant to interact – in experience. On the other hand, Coleridge's close 'practical' coincidences with Plato (as opposed to these predominantly theoretical ones) are through Plato's Socrates, and through those methods of irony and midwifery which are not a method of communication accidental to a Platonic ontological commitment, but which are necessary to it. Coleridge, who, like the Germans, absorbed the Platonic–Socratic tradition far more profoundly than did the English, with the exception of Berkeley and the Cambridge Platonists, assimilated this method into the *Biographia*, and it emerges (if not fully articulated) in a reading of the work.

The investigation of these sources is far from exhaustive, its intent being not to give a detailed account of borrowings and parallels, but rather to discuss the way in which Coleridge's understanding of the philosophical tradition upon which he drew functions in the *Biographia*. Hence that tradition is examined in chapter two with an emphasis upon how Coleridge understood it and used it to unite his metaphysics and his aesthetics. A further effort has been made in chapters two and three with respect to these sources to place Coleridge in a tradition of philosophizing which reaches back through the seventeenth century to Greek philosophy. To suggest that the German corpus upon which he drew is continuous with this longer tradition is to emphasize what Coleridge himself said in a marginal note to W. G. Tennemann's *Geschichte der Philosophie*, in ironic criticism of the author's failure to understand and appreciate the achievement of the ancients: 'Never, surely, was a Ph. History composed under a stronger *Warp* of Predetermination, that the elder Philosophers *must have* been – ignorant of Kant's Cr. d. r. Vernunft!!!' He adds, 'But the Kanteans are always afraid of allowing for much to the old Philosophers lest there should not be enough for Kant remaining.' (Marginal notes to 1, 181 and 158–9.) While it would be inappropriate to minimize Coleridge's debts to his German sources, it seems appropriate to keep in mind the longer tradition upon which both Coleridge and the Germans drew, and which provides an indispensable perspective upon the nature of Coleridge's relation to Kant, Schelling, and others.

It is well to state here what may be only implied in chapters two and three, namely that Coleridge was far more profoundly influenced by Kant than by Schelling. It was Kant who was the occasion for Coleridge's working out of a creative theory of mind in all its ramifications, and who thus taught Coleridge how to read the ancients more appreciatively and to realize the implications of their wisdom, which he had perhaps only dimly perceived before. It was Kant who brought about the complete and final rejection of associationism and passive theories of mind, and who showed how to move beyond Locke's representative theory of perception to a more creative idealist posture. The Platonic philosophy later provided Coleridge with his 'completion of Kant', and Coleridge's reading of Schelling worked more to confirm than to revolutionize, as Kant had done for Coleridge in 1800. By comparison, Coleridge's enthusiasm for Schelling is brief and quickly qualified in important ways, though the 'mythology' which for example Naturphilosophie provided, as Friedrich Schlegel was to suggest, was undoubtedly of immense value as a source of ideas.

This longer tradition is less directly important with regard to the actual working out of Coleridge's aesthetics and his relation to his German counterparts, such as Schiller, the Schlegels, Tieck, and Karl Solger (except in so far as the aesthetics is grounded in the metaphysics). Thus these German 'sources' and parallels are more explicitly discussed than those relating to the metaphysics, and because they are somewhat less familiar than the others. But the discussion of German aesthetics is limited to the Romantic Ironists, since Coleridge's irony is the point to be elucidated. The debts to Schiller, Lessing, and Herder are only evident by implication; that is, this triumvirate form the basis of the German Romantic Ironists' aesthetic.

The word 'sources' is used in another sense, to suggest the gradual growth over a period of some thirteen years or more of a work which was eventually to become that 'fragmentary miscellany' and original genre which achieved a synthesis of the whole man in his philosophical, poetic, critical, psychological, religious, and personal strivings. This growth of the *Biographia* is to a large degree illuminated by recently published notebooks and letters. What these recurring passages tell of the development of the text as well as of Coleridge's own attitudes towards it, may act to quicken our responses. For these passages often turn out to be examples of those metaphoric situations which are primary constituents of the structure of the *Biographia*.

By 'processes' and 'methods' two modes of composition – and analogously, of reading – are suggested, which are more easily distinguished in theory than in fact. By the former word patterns and events going on throughout the *Biographia* are described which are not necessarily the products of conscious interaction or control on the part of the author. Rather they may emerge from the material as legitimate and illuminating formulations pointing to 'depth' designs which may escape the conscious scrutiny of even the most reflective author. Or they may reflect the richness and inexhaustibility of a work of art as it is reinterpreted by succeeding readers. These designs are acting not according to (though probably not contrary to) the author's conscious will and judgment, but are emerging from the nature of the material as the artist transforms it, in so far as he is free to do so. 'Methods', on the other hand, suggests those procedures which seem likely to have been a result of a preponderance of judgment and intention in the author's composition of his book. Additionally, 'processes' can be understood as the level of discourse in the *Biographia* which seems to refer the reader to his own process of reading and interacting with the text. 'Methods', in these terms, would suggest the related level of discourse which refers to the author's consciousness of his composition of an aesthetic whole. Whether irony and metaphor constitute processes, methods, or both is a question implicit throughout, and which may be more problematic in the case of irony than of metaphor. In this context the profound nature of the relationship between irony and metaphor is indicated to be a relationship expressive of the mind's way of categorizing the world. Equally importantly, the crucial role of the fancy/imagination distinction in any philosophy or aesthetic which formulates its issues with irony and metaphor as the germinal principle is examined. Why the distinction was dropped from the rest of Coleridge's published writings, to be subsumed under the reason/understanding distinction, is a question which invites consideration of the relationship between the *Biographia* and these other works, and which suggests further confluences between source, process and method.

Acknowledgements

My warmest thanks are due to John Beer for several years of advice and criticism during the writing of this book, which began as a thesis. To John Wright of Ann Arbor, Michigan, I owe the earliest inspiration for the idea of the role of the reading process as central to Coleridge's method in the *Biographia*. I also owe much to Howard Erskine-Hill for informal criticisms of my analysis of the method and of the role of irony in Coleridge's work generally. Stephen Prickett made some helpful criticisms of the work for which I am grateful. To George Whalley I am indebted for making much of the marginalia of Coleridge on German writers available. I would also like to express my appreciation to Gillian Beer for her support.

To Girton College I am obliged for a two-year research bye-fellowship during the writing of this book, and to Jesus College, Cambridge I am indebted for a further research fellowship and for a research grant which has seen the work through to its final form. Finally, the librarians and staff of the University Library in Cambridge and at the British Library also deserve my thanks for various kinds of help.

Without the support of my mother this work would not have been possible.

K.M.W.

Abbreviations

❧❧

The following abbreviations of some of Coleridge's works are used in references:

AR   *Aids to Reflection in the Formation of a Manly Character*, ed. Thomas Fenby. Edinburgh: 1905.

BL   *Biographia Literaria; or Biographical Sketches of my Literary Life and Opinions*, ed. J. Shawcross. 2 vols. London: 1907.

CL   *Collected Letters of Samuel Taylor Coleridge*, ed. E. L. Griggs. 6 vols. Oxford: 1956–71.

C & S (CC)   *On the Constitution of Church and State According to the Idea of Each with Aids towards a Right Judgement on the late Catholic Bill*, ed. John Colmer. Vol. 10 in *The Collected Coleridge*. London and Princeton: 1977.

Friend (CC)   *The Friend. A Series of Essays in Three Volumes. To Aid in the Formation of Fixed Principles in Politics, Morals, and Religion, with Literary Amusements Interspersed*, ed. Barbara E. Rooke. 2 vols. Vol. 4 in *The Collected Coleridge*. London and Princeton: 1969.

T of L   *Hints towards the Formation of a more Comprehensive Theory of Life*, ed. S. B. Watson. London: 1848.

LS (CC)   *Lay Sermons*, ed. R. J. White. Vol. 6 in *The Collected Coleridge*. London and Princeton: 1972.

LR   *Literary Remains*, ed. H. N. Coleridge. 4 vols. London: 1836–9.

Misc. C   *Miscellaneous Criticism*, ed. T. M. Raysor. London and Cambridge, Mass.: 1936.

CD   *The Notebooks of Samuel Taylor Coleridge*, ed. Kathleen Coburn. Three parts in 6 volumes published so far. London and New York: 1957– .

P Lects.   *Philosophical Lectures of Samuel Taylor Coleridge*
               1818–19, ed. Kathleen Coburn. London: 1949.

Sh. C   *Shakespearean Criticism*, ed. T. M. Raysor. 2 vols. London:
               1930.

TT   *Specimens of the Table Talk of the late Samuel Taylor*
               Coleridge, ed. H. N. Coleridge. London and New York:
               1835.

In quoting from Coleridge's notebooks I have adopted in the main the
conventions used by Miss Coburn. Passages from her edition of the notebooks, of which volumes one, two, and three have now appeared, are
reproduced as she prints them. The explanation of her editorial symbols is
as follows:

<word>   a later insertion by Coleridge

[?word]   an uncertain reading

[?word/wood]   possible alternative readings

[word]   a reading editorially supplied

⌈word⌉   a tentative reading

[. . .]   an illegible word

†word†   a deletion by Coleridge

Introduction

⋘⧫⧫⧫⧫⧫⧫

Diverse readings of the *Biographia Literaria*

Coleridge's *Biographia Literaria* has been characterized by readers in different ways. Some read it as a work pre-eminently valuable for its critical insights, particularly into Wordsworth's poetry. Others see it as Coleridge's own *Prelude* or growth of a poet's mind. The *Biographia* can also be read as an analysis of the theoretical foundations of idealism. None of these strands is uppermost at all times in the *Biographia*. When a different purpose intrudes, a reader who has in view one of these aspects will be unable to see such intrusions as anything but gaps and crevices in the progression of the narrative. If he is aware of the integration of these several concerns into a single metaphysical and aesthetic foundation, on the other hand, he can advance beyond the impression of fragmentation and miscellany.

Coleridge's works, particularly the *Biographia*, are often said to lack 'a beginning, middle and an end',[1] that is, a unified structure and development. Such assessments are characteristic of critics sympathetically disposed to Coleridge as well as of those unable to enter into any genial relationship with him. Humphry House, for example, said of Coleridge in his Clark Lectures, 'It is one of the ironies of his life that he who saw so clearly, and expounded more fully than any English critic before him, the principle of organic unity of a work of art, should have achieved that unity so rarely.'[2] House did not specify exactly which of Coleridge's works are at fault or in what sense they lack unity. In the following sympathetic, impartial 'observation', Basil Willey's opinion that Coleridge's general achievement was fragmentary has delegated to itself the status of knowledge without corroborating evidence or principles of procedural demonstration: '*We all know* that the results of it [his life's task] remained fragmentary and incomplete; but remembering how he was thwarted by ill-health, personal unhappiness, and self-reproach for his weakness of will, the wonder is that he achieved so much.' (My italics.)[3] The presupposition upon which these and similar observations may perhaps be based is that unless the fundamental unity and structure of a

I

work are immediately discernible on the literal level of narration, its unity is deficient. This principle is sometimes associated with the theory that art is a copying or a metaphorical mirror of nature. In Coleridge's view on the other hand, an imitation is a reproduction of the profound internal principles of organization or the essence of the thing.[4]

This criticism of Coleridge's writings as fragmentary often appears as an assertion that the works lack any system and any precise doctrine, as, for example, Stephen Potter remarks in *Coleridge and S.T.C.*[5] This presupposition that a work ought to present a 'precise doctrine' or a system if it is to be unified and fully intelligible, rests upon the theory of knowledge as dogmatic and doctrinal, the market-coin of intercourse ridiculed by Socrates: knowledge is directly exchangeable. A more Coleridgean and a more Platonic view asserts that knowledge (and art) is experience and is only indirectly communicable.[6] Dorothy Emmet offers some important suggestions for this more profitable way of approaching Coleridge's thought. She writes of Coleridge, 'He is most illuminating in the occasional apparently throw-away remark.' She correctly rejects Coleridge as a 'professional philosopher' but nevertheless says that 'few professional philosophers have seen as far as Coleridge into the powers of the human mind'.[7] Moreover, 'his metaphysics was an attempt to hold these two faiths (moral and imaginative) together, not so much by clear abstract argument as by claims to insight in experiences where the inner and outer worlds met in symbolizing vision'.[8] Coleridge seems to embrace a theory of knowledge and experience which would not only encourage but require this non-dogmatic, 'non-professional philosopher' approach.

J. H. Muirhead, in *Coleridge as Philosopher*, has tried to supply the 'defects' of systematization which Coleridge assiduously avoided.[9] Muirhead characterizes Coleridge's philosophy as transcendental idealist voluntarism. He systematizes the main dogmas of such a philosophy and over-determines what was designed originally to be an open-ended and indeterminate dialectic. But Muirhead also seems to assume that without a dogmatic system there is no method. This presupposition is based on a mistaken notion of metaphysics as dogmatic instead of critical. A systematic exposition is designed to show what is negative or erroneous, but it can never lead to a 'positive waking knowledge', which Coleridge attempts to stimulate his reader to experience: 'For the writings of these mystics (George Fox and Boehme) acted in no slight degree to prevent my mind from being imprisoned within the outline of any single dogmatic system...all the products of the mere *reflective* faculty partook of DEATH.'[10] Of Muirhead's book Kathleen Coburn explains that it 'was one of those books of which the failure is almost more instructive than success...

Coleridge could not be reshaped by the mould of late nineteenth century idealism.'[11]

George Whalley takes up the criticism of Coleridge's philosophy as immethodical and suggests an alternative way of looking at what Coleridge was offering his readers:

his work does not reward us primarily with the formulated conclusions that we are perhaps too inclined to expect of philosophy and theory; rather his work – though by no means devoid of substantial and well-thought-out theory – stands for that more nourishing and hazardous order that is 'tentative and exploratory', and is no less positive or philosophical for that. For he was determined, as he noted at mid-night on 5 April 1805, to 'write as truly as I can from *Experience* – actual individual *Experience* – not from Book-knowledge.'[12]

Professor Whalley suggests in these lines the approach which seems necessary for an appreciation of Coleridge. Those conclusions which we are 'too inclined to expect' are the signs of closure and abstraction. They are the 'fixities' of the reflective faculty which 'partake not of productive thought but of death'. Professor Whalley indicates in his quotation from the notebooks the distinction between 'facts', or data of experience which are mistaken for knowledge, and that experience of relations and connections discoverable only by the individual, which truly constitutes knowledge. Coleridge seeks in his works not to overload the reader with another body of 'book-knowledge', as Muirhead's book tends to do. Coleridge strives to stimulate in his reader that crucial 'actual individual *Experience*' which is the sole source of knowledge. The effort to stimulate experience constitutes his method while a view of knowledge as experience defies the closure involved by definition in any system.

A system strives to contain the all within itself. Coleridge's works act in the opposite direction as symbols, as parts representative of a whole, which cannot be contained in any formulation. Experience is always more than the signs which seek to express it. In this larger sense his works are fragmentary, though not in the literal sense of needing more development or saying less than they might have said.[13] Professor Whalley says of Coleridge:

As he himself notices, the principle of unity in multeity obtains – not ideally to be sure, or in every instance, but as a constant dynamic interanimation that makes every fragment at least potentially reverberant . . . as though every item were 'seeking, as it were asking' for the self-realising relation that can declare that particular part an integral element in the whole. In the sense that not every item is self-subsistent, the manuscript material is fragmentary; in another and more profound sense, the separate items are facets rather than fragments, germs implying growth rather than broken pieces that bespeak disorder or death.[14]

Coleridge reiterates this attitude when he describes the difference between a 'quibbler in mock-logic' and the 'Reasoner, who *seeks* to understand, and looks into himself for a sense, which my words may excite in him, not *to* my words for a sense, which they must against his own will *force* on him.'[15] In seeking to understand Coleridge, the reader can discover a method and unity which is deliberately not immediate, and which is not forced upon him at the narrative or literal level of the text. It is Coleridge's contention that no improvement or completion of the system will produce a dogmatic system which is intelligible from the text alone: method is discoverable, and exists, only in and through experience.

Professor Whalley is one of the few critics to insist that the *Biographia* does have an integrity of its own, though his analysis seems to favour the second volume over the first:

That the *Biographia* contains nothing beyond a perplexing (and unsatisfactory) distinction between Fancy and Imagination, and some interesting biographical reminiscences is a view so commonly held that one of the most obvious 'uses' of the book has not been nearly as widely recognized as it should be: an unsurpassed critical analysis of the art and poetry of Wordsworth.[16]

Professor Whalley accurately describes the critical opinion of the *Biographia* which prevails and he has won for the work some added appreciation for its analysis of Wordsworth in volume two. His account of the integrity of the *Biographia* still however leaves it open to criticisms such as those of J. A. Appleyard, that the *Biographia* 'appears to fall into two parts: the account of Coleridge's literary opinions in the first volume, and the extensive criticism of Wordsworth in the second'.[17] The notion that the *Biographia* falls into two essentially unrelated parts is based partly upon the literal division of the work into two volumes with an emphasis in the one on philosophy and in the other on poetry. To suggest however that the work has two unrelated parts simply because one emphasizes philosophy and the other poetry is to assume that there is no integral relation between the two. This was not Coleridge's opinion, a point which he repeated throughout the *Biographia*, the notebooks, and the letters.[18]

Mr Appleyard's account of the *Biographia* is characteristic and tends to hinder a fresh reading of the work. For example, he complains:

Coleridge seems to realize himself that his ideas were dying under the weight of the theory which was supposed to elucidate them. He interrupts his exposition in the thirteenth chapter with 'a letter from a friend . . .' After thirteen chapters of preliminaries we are left to make our own way with the aid of these puzzling remarks [about primary and secondary imagination and fancy].[19]

There is no indication from Mr Appleyard that these puzzling remarks may be set in a context of irony; Coleridge's letter from a friend, which we

know was written by Coleridge himself, is taken with complete seriousness, in spite of all the signs in chapter twelve that a literal and serious
reading may hinder the aesthetic perception.[20] Mr Appleyard goes on to
complete his view of the *Biographia*:

Coleridge does not immediately move to an explanation of his notion of
imagination. He wants to proceed more or less chronologically, and so he
devotes four chapters to a criticism of associationist psychology and an account
of his own extrication from its grasp. Another chapter follows, on the influences
he has undergone from the idealist philosophers. This brings him to Schelling,
to a rather terse expression of his indebtedness to the German philosopher and
some defensive remarks about plagiarism, and finally to a profoundly complex
and obscure attempt to render the substance of Schelling's metaphysics of
absolute consciousness.

Mr Appleyard contrasts this with the second volume in which 'the point
of view is remarkably free of the speculative *obscuritie*s of the final chapters
of volume one. The notion of imagination is *simpler* and recalls the earlier
explanation of the imagination/fancy distinction.'[21] Mr Appleyard then
concludes that, because the distinction between primary and secondary
imagination is dropped from Coleridge's later terminology, it must be
unimportant.

The interpretation which Mr Appleyard has given seems little more
than an account of the narrative surface; his interpretation of Coleridge's
principle of organization is that it is merely chronological. This view
seems peculiarly dissonant with Coleridge's entire discussion of association,
which hinges upon the thesis that time does not constitute the *law* of
association, but is merely a *condition* of it for finite thinking minds.[22]
Furthermore, Coleridge treats association as a preliminary to the fancy/
imagination distinction not for chronological or biographical reasons. He
does so because his distinction is the essential core of the refutation of
materialist associationism. Its elaboration is prompted by the currency of
this 'psilosophy'. Coleridge's exposition of the chronological development
of the growth of the philosophic mind ought moreover to interest us not
primarily as biographical material, the order of which may be accidental.
It ought to be valuable in so far as the philosophic development of an
individual mind suggests essential interconnections amongst various
philosophies. Coleridge suggests that ontogeny recapitulates phylogeny.[23]
One might also wonder whether the chronology of events of the
growth of Coleridge's mind may not be analogously a sign of a more
essential organization of the *Biographia*, which is less immediately
obvious since 'surface always meets the eye before depth'.[24] Mr Appleyard,
in the two remarks above, complains of speculative obscurities, and

praises the simpler notion of imagination set forth in volume two and in chapter four of volume one. His faculty critical principle suggests that what is simple and obvious is good; what is not direct and literal is obscure and consequently poor writing. This canon of simplicity is at the root of the other presuppositions which were mentioned above. Coleridge seeks to address himself to this sort of lazy-mindedness when he sets himself his task: ' <to> rouse and stimulate the mind – to set the reader a thinking – and at least to obtain entrance for the question, whether the <truth of the> Opinions in fashion †are† is quite so certain as he had hitherto taken for granted'.[25]

One might also question Mr Appleyard's charge of 'metaphysical obscurities'. 'Obscurity' has a pejorative connotation, but Coleridge frequently points out that the charge of obscurity is problematic:

Heraclitus...was proverbially entitled the Dark (ὁ σκοτεινός). But it was a darkness which Socrates would not condemn, and which would probably appear to enlightened Christians the darkness of prophecy... But obscurity is a word of many meanings. It may be in the subject; it may be in the author; or it may be in the reader; – and this again may originate in the state of the reader's heart; or in that of his capacity; or in his temper; or in his accidental associations. Two kinds are especially pointed out by the divine Plato in his Sophistes. The *Beauty* of the Original is beyond my reach... 'One thing is the *Hardness-to-be-understood* of the Sophist, another that of the Philosopher. The former retreating into the obscurity *of that which hath not true Being*, ... and by long intercourse accustomed to the same, is hard to be known on account of the duskiness of the place. But the philosopher by contemplation of pure reason evermore approximating to the idea of true Being ... is by no means easy to be seen on account of the splendour of that region. For the intellectual eyes of the Many flit, and are incapable of looking fixedly toward the God-like.'[26]

Most readers fail to consider these alternative sources of obscurity, and act unconsciously upon the presupposition that if a meaning is not obvious it is the fault of the author. But an author may legitimately require a certain philosophical commitment.

In the next few chapters we will try to indicate the epistemological foundations of Coleridge's theory of perception as a prerequisite for a coherent interpretation of the unity of the *Biographia*. An application of the philosophy of polarity (or the reconciliation of opposites) to critical procedure will suggest how the reader may integrate in various ways the strands of thought and purpose which run through the *Biographia*. In chapter one the early sources of the *Biographia* in notebooks and letters are outlined, and in chapters two and three a general account is given of the philosophical sources which informed Coleridge's thought previous to the writing of the *Biographia*. In the fourth chapter the crucial distinction between 'common' and 'higher' irony will be drawn and some of the German (and Greek foundations of the) sources of Coleridge's aesthetics will emerge. The question of the sources will be in evidence throughout the book, whether dealt with directly as in the first few chapters, or indirectly as in the last.

The distinction between method – a conscious element of design and a tool of purpose – and process – a depth design or principle of art which emerges from the work by virtue of the nature of artistic creation – further divides the analysis. In chapters five, six, and seven, the method of metaphor and the process of irony operating in the *Biographia* which proceed directly from the philosophical foundations drawn out in chapters two, three, and four will be examined. In chapter eight our concern will be to discuss the issues of imagination and irony, which seem to be left unresolved in the *Biographia*. These issues we can schematize as three basic polarities, imagination/fancy, reason/understanding, and irony/ literal expression. How the imagination/fancy and reason/understanding distinctions are related, why the former was replaced by the latter in Coleridge's subsequent writings, and how problematic the imagination as a concept became for Coleridge, will be discussed below. The problematic nature of this pre-eminently vital faculty returns us directly to the issue of irony and indirectness of communication.

Irony (conceived of as a principle of art both for the artist and for the spectator, as opposed to irony as a verbal or dramatic technique) is in this analysis approached as a process, as distinguished from the conscious method of metaphor. But this distinction does not imply an essential division between process and method, for irony may be understood as the necessary consequence of a pre-eminently metaphorical mode of com- munication. Irony was however an aspect of Coleridge's work which remained unresolved. Like imagination it seems to have been suppressed in later works, however successfully both were used in the most lasting of Coleridge's works, 'The Ancient Mariner' and 'Kubla Khan'. Irony, as a principle of art, whether or not it is used intentionally by Coleridge or with awareness, may well have emerged almost in spite of his conscious purposes and designs. If the German conception of irony as a creative principle is coherent, such an indeterminacy of intention would not militate against an ironic interpretation of the *Biographia*; it would only indicate the possible or even necessary limitations of any artist's conscious- ness about his creative activity.

I

Sources of the *Biographia Literaria*
in notebooks and letters

However exaggerated Mr Appleyard's estimation of the *Biographia* as 'unread and largely unreadable',[1] his general characterization of it as an 'immethodical miscellany'[2] is a fair account of how both critics and readers tend to respond. He cites Coleridge himself as having rejected the *Biographia*, but the force of this rejection is tempered when the remark is placed within the context of his more characteristic statements.

An apparently significant type of evidence for the view that the *Biographia* has no aesthetic unity is the history of its conception. According to Coleridge the *Biographia* began as a preface to the edition of poems he was preparing in 1815 and which eventually became *Sybilline Leaves*.[3] E. L. Griggs explains:

On 29 July he announced that the preface to the poems had been extended to 'an Autobiographical literaria', containing his opinions on 'Poetry and *poetical* Criticism' and an account of the 'Controversy concerning Wordsworth's Poems & Theory'. A disquisition on the 'powers of association' and on the 'generic' difference between fancy and imagination he did not 'altogether insert'. By 17 Sept., when his work was complete, the 'philosophical Part', which in August he 'meant to comprise in a few Pages', had become 'a sizeable Proportion of the whole'. As a result, he suggested a more comprehensive title: 'Biographical Sketches of my LITERARY LIFE, Principles, and Opinions, chiefly on the subjects of Poetry and Philosophy'. (Letters 963–4, 969, 974, 980–1, and 993).[4]

The argument that because the *Biographia* began as a preface the continuation of it into a 'work per se' must have taken on the character of an increase by addition, and not by any inherent principles of growth and unity, is obviously weak. But the more popular claim is not so immediately erroneous, namely, that the *Biographia* falls into two *separate* parts, the disquisition on philosophy and that on poetry.[5] This claim gains support both from the account given by Griggs above, and especially from the information that the *Biographia* did begin as a preface on *poetry*; the philosophical half seems to be a later, unconnected addition, even though the general Preface was said to be on the principles of '*philosophic* and genial criticism' especially relating to poetry.[6] Moreover, the volume on poetry has long been considered to be the more organized and the more important of the two, with the single exception of the 'Satyrane Letters', which were included to 'fill out' the *Biographia* once it was realized that the printer's estimate, that there was enough material for a full two volumes, was inaccurate.[7]

The opinion that the *Biographia* is not an artistic unity but falls into two parts (the most interesting and most well-conceived of the two being the second half on poetry), gains strength from external considerations as well as from the nature of the text. The two-volume structure fosters a sense of separateness. But the information Griggs offers adds to this conviction, for it not only implies that the philosophical part was simply 'inserted', but also that it took on proportions not calculated in the original conception, and hence is somehow not a 'proper' part of a unity.

But this second argument is inadequate, for just as a preface could 'grow' into a whole larger than originally expected, so could the philosophical sections *blossom* into an integral part.[8] That the philosophical part was merely *inserted* is an assertion of altogether more seriousness. But if one examines the original context of Coleridge's remark about this 'insertion', it takes on a very different meaning from the impression given by Griggs's paraphrase. In this letter Coleridge describes both 'halves' of the *Biographia* as follows:

I have given a full account (raisonné) of the Controversy concerning Wordsworth's Poems & Theory, in which my name has been so constantly included – I have no doubt, that Wordsworth will be displeased – but I have done my Duty to myself and to the Public, in (as I believe) completely subverting the Theory & in priving that the Poet himself has never acted on it except in particular Stanzas which are the Blots of his Compositions. – One long passage – a disquisition on the powers of association, with the History of the Opinions on this subject from Aristotle to Hartley, and on the generic difference between the faculties of Fancy and Imagination – *I did not indeed altogether insert, but I certainly extended and elaborated, with a view to your perusal* – as laying the foundation Stones of the Constructive or Dynamic Philosophy in opposition to the merely mechanic – . But I am running on as usual and shall not leave space enough for the purpose of this note if I do not, like a Skaiter, strike a Stop with my Heel. – (My italics.)[9]

Note how the context alters the meaning of the phrase, 'I did not altogether insert': clearly Coleridge is *not* implying, as Griggs seems to indicate, that the philosophy was more or less 'stuck in' as an afterthought,
indeed a highly developed afterthought. Coleridge is making a generous
gesture of respect to Brabant's philosophical abilities and interests by
suggesting *only* that he 'extended and elaborated' that section, *with a view*
to Brabant's perusal, not that the section itself was inserted. A rephrasing
of this sentence better conveys the full import: 'I did not indeed altogether
insert this passage with a view to your perusal (i.e., there were *other*
reasons for its inclusion), but I certainly extended and elaborated it with
you in mind.' It can be further understood from the tone of the comment
that even the elaboration and extension were not without their inherent
reasons; Coleridge is merely being gracious in suggesting to his friend
that an awareness of his friend's perceptive and critical eye or his desire to
learn encouraged Coleridge to develop and expand his thesis. The whole
tone is one of understatement with a view toward showing a friendly
respect, beginning with the 'altogether' as the first understatement, up to
the final note.[10]

   This particular external evidence for the lack of unity of the *Biographia*
is then tenuous, if not wholly spurious.[11] Yet it is this 'external evidence'
which has created a climate for such a view, and may have actually
precluded the probability of the *Biographia* being approached without such
a preconception, by predisposing the reader and critic to assume the
same.[12] A passive and acquiescing reading will serve to substantiate and
justify the charge of disunity, and is thus actually encouraged by the
critical climate.

   In the Brabant letter it is also clear that Coleridge himself does not
consider that the diverse aspects of the *Biographia* form two unrelated
parts, nor even two wholly distinguishable parts. Indeed he refers to the
philosophical matter as 'one long passage', the choice of the word 'passage'
suggesting a related part. And Coleridge's criticism of Wordsworth's
theory that poetic language is best taken from the language of the low and
rustic way of life ties in very precisely with a criticism of fancy as the
prime activity of the poetic mind. Fancy is characterized, like low, rustic
speech, as lacking any true method of thought, any organic unity; it is the
merely mechanical.[13] Coleridge had criticized Wordsworth in volume one
of the *Biographia* for failing to make the distinction between the words,
and the second volume is an extended analysis of Wordsworth's theoretical,
if only occasionally practical, error, in Coleridge's rejection of the 'low,
rustic speech' as the model for the poet. The connection between fancy
and low rustic speech (the immethodical) and Coleridge's criticism of this
model as precisely analogous to his criticism of Wordsworth's failure to see

the fancy/imagination distinction, has not been fully appreciated, a matter which has helped to obscure the connection between the two volumes.[14]

Further 'external evidence' which has fostered the response to the *Biographia* as immethodical is the suggestion that it was written hastily and was completed in a few months. Still more persuasive is the claim that it was dashed off at a time of Coleridge's life when he was particularly despondent and in bad health, hence incapable of anything significant.[15] It is true that in April 1814 he had put himself under the medical care of Dr Daniel, but that the disturbances were such as in the long term to paralyse and preclude thought and reflection preparative to composition is not borne out by the evidence, for the years preceding the *Biographia* were not unproductive. The year 1811 saw contributions to the *Courier* and lectures on literature.[16] The lectures continued through 1812, which saw a reissue of *The Friend*, and in 1813 *Remorse* opened at Drury Lane and Coleridge lectured in Bristol on Shakespeare. More lectures were given in 1814, *Remorse* opened at Bristol, and the essays 'On the Principles of Genial Criticism' were written, not to mention more contributions to the *Courier*.[17] 1815 saw the preparation of *Sybilline Leaves*, and then the writing of the 'preface' which turned into the *Biographia*.[18]

In order to appreciate the place of the *Biographia* in Coleridge's literary productions, one may take further note of his productions subsequent to it. In 1816 'Christabel' and the *Statesman's Manual*, two of Coleridge's major works, were published. Although 'Christabel' had been written long before 1816, the task of preparing it for publication was not a formality. And the *Statesman's Manual* contains some of Coleridge's richest philosophical material. In 1817 the *Second Lay Sermon* was published, and in 1818, the 'Treatise on Method', the new *Friend*, lectures on poetry and drama, and the lectures on the history of philosophy running conjointly with more literary lectures all took place.[19]

This chronology suggests that the writing of the *Biographia* did not occur in a period of intellectual vacuum, nor as a lone and solitary flash in the midst of years of barrenness. Though preceded by some literary activity, the year 1815 does seem to mark a decisive upswing in production which was then followed by four more years of intense activity.[20] Hence the conclusion that Coleridge could not have carried out a definite project even if he had had one in mind does not coincide with the facts. If he was less healthy than usual, a point by no means well established, one is still not justified in assuming that one can know the effect it would have had upon his creative activity.[21]

The second claim, that Coleridge wrote the *Biographia* too quickly to have carefully formulated a structure of unity, is immediately suspect. From all that can be ascertained, the *Biographia* was composed in the summer and early autumn of 1815. A few months seems unusually short for a work as substantial as the *Biographia*; there is considerable evidence, on the other hand, that Coleridge spent a long time in the detailed conception of it, however compressed the final execution. The notebooks and letters give some clues to the works which he was planning in the early 1800s before the trip to Malta, a trip which seems to have had a seriously detrimental effect upon his hopes of writing. Amongst the several major works mentioned, the plans for a *Biographia* are very evident.[22] As early as 1803 he writes a note: 'Seem to have made up my mind to write my metaphysical works, as *my Life*, & *in* my Life – '.[23] In view of this statement it is hardly likely that the philosophical portion is an improper insert or a cumbersome afterthought. Only a few months later he mentions a work which in certain respects suggests the *Biographia*:[24]

the Title [is] – 'Consolations & Comforts from the exercise & right application of the Reason, *the Imagination*, and the Moral Feelings'. The 'Consolations' are addressed to all in adversity, sickness, or distress of mind/ the first part entirely practical – the second in which I consider distress of mind from gloomy Speculation will, of course, be speculative, & will contain a new Theodicee. (My italics.)[25]

In the same year Coleridge writes of his 'Great Work' and says: '2nd Vol – Soother of Absence. – My Life & Thoughts.' Here again a literary life seems to be intertwined with a work on 'Soothing' or Comforting, i.e. 'Comforts and Consolations'.[26] A few months later, Coleridge mentions a literary life again. On this occasion it does not seem difficult to determine that it was becoming in his mind a distinct work from the 'Consolations and Comforts'. In any case, he was clearly becoming convinced that the biographical mode was the right medium for the expression of his metaphysics:

Of it's Contents the Title will in part inform you – Consolations and Comforts from the exercise and right application of the Reason, the Imagination, and the moral Feelings, addressed especially to those in Sickness, Adversity, or Distress of mind, *from speculative Gloom*, &c ... The whole Plan of my literary Life I have now layed down – & the exact order, in which I shall execute them [it?], if God vouchsafe me Life & adequate Health – & I have sober tho' confident Expectations that I shall render a good Account of what may have appeared to you & others a distracting Manifoldness in my Objects & Attainments – .[27]

It seems that this 'Plan' was interrupted by the trip to Malta, as were the other projected works, and was not picked up again until 1815, some eleven years later:[28] 'The whole Plan of my literary Life I have now layed down' may not be exaggerated, for Coleridge admits in the same breath that he has 'executed' none of it as yet. This is evidence of how seriously he took the idea of a *Biographia*, and a hint that it may already have been well thought out by 1804. It is still more plausible in view of the fact that all of the issues, from the most major to minor ones, had already been read about, mulled over, and written about in letters and notebooks, from associationism and the fancy/imagination distinction to long reflection upon Wordsworth's poetry and the interpenetration or reconciliation of the opposites of philosophy and poetry.[29] The changes which Coleridge describes his 'preface' as undergoing in 1815 were not, it seems, conceptual or structural, but expansive and elucidatory.

The next important reference to a 'literary life' occurs only some ten years later (though materials for the *Life* are evident throughout the years). Coleridge, in describing his 'Great Work', which became the *MS* Opus Maximum, the Logos, or the 'Communicative Intelligence', says:

The Title is: Christianity the one true Philosophy – or 5 Treatises on the Logos, or communicative Intelligence, Natural, Human, and Divine: – to which is prefixed a prefatory Essay on the Laws & Limits of Toleration & Liberality illustrated by fragments of *Auto*-biography.[30]

Here the 'Literary Life' is described in an early conception as a preface not to the *Sybilline Leaves* but to a philosophical and religious work. This coincides with the earlier comment in 1803 that Coleridge had decided to write his metaphysics as a *Life*.[31] Thus the projected *Literary Life* was from its first tentative genesis connected with a metaphysical, philosophical work, and not primarily with a collection of poetry, to which it would be a preface on poetical criticism It almost seems as if the *Life* as a preface to *Sybilline Leaves* constituted the actual change in plans, not the addition of the philosophical half. The philosophical disquisition clearly has claim to priority in the long term, the poetical section growing out of a connection with its fancy/imagination distinction.

How closely the philosophy and poetry are interrelated will be discussed fully later. But Coleridge gives early indications of this interaction in a letter in which he writes:

I fear, let me work as hard as I can, I shall not be able to do what my heart within me *burns* to do – that is, *concenter* my free mind to the affinities of the Feelings with the Words & Ideas under the title of 'Concerning Poetry & the nature of the Pleasures derived from it.' – I have faith, that I do understand this subject/ and I am sure, that if I write what I ought to do on it, the Work would supersede all the Books of Metaphysics hitherto written/ and all the Books of Morals too.[32]

It is crucial to notice that although the work is to be entitled 'Concerning Poetry' etc., that it is to be a *metaphysical* and moral work, and the connection between the two is this affinity of 'Feelings with the Words & Ideas': it is this unity which constitutes the truly metaphysical for Coleridge. Words and ideas unconnected with feelings are the objects of speculative reason, while the connection (the 'humanization') of words and ideas with feelings implies the practical reason, that is, speculative reason in conjunction with the will. Reason operating philosophically seeks to grasp and formulate the general laws of these connections; reason acting poetically as imagination seeks not to formulate in the most general and all-encompassing language possible (such as the 'law of polarity') but seeks to express the laws in their infinite diversity or to embody them in all possible forms while at the same time the correlative idea shines through.

THE GENESIS OF THE 'BIOGRAPHIA'S' CONTENT

Throughout this ten to twelve year gap between the first vague soundings and the actual completion of the *Biographia* Coleridge was collecting material and reading with a view toward such a work, as the notebooks and letters show. As early as May 1799 he was transcribing a passage from a German book in Göttingen which was eventually to end up in *The Friend* as the metaphor of the castle appearing through the gloom in the reflection on the lake.[33] Then in 1801 comes a specific entry which relates to the *Biographia*:

The soil is a deep, rich, dark Mould on a deep Stratum of tenacious Clay, and that on a foundation of rocks, which often break through both Strata, lifting their back above the Surface. The Trees, which chiefly grow here, are the gigantic Black Oak, Magnolia, Fraxinus excelsior, Platane, & a few stately Tulip Trees. – Bart. p. 36, *I applied this by a fantastic analogue & similitude to Wordsworth's Mind*. March 26 1801. Fagus exaltata sylvatica. (My italics.)[34]

This entry may be compared to the corresponding passage in the *Biographia*:

The following analogy will, I am apprehensive, appear dim and fantastic, but in reading Bartram's Travels I could not help transcribing the following lines as a sort of allegory, or connected simile and metaphor of Wordsworth's intellect and genius.

Coleridge prints the rest of the passage as quoted above and concludes: 'What Mr. Wordsworth *will* produce it is not for me to prophesy: but I could pronounce with the liveliest convictions what he is capable of producing. It is the FIRST GENUINE PHILOSOPHIC POEM.'[35] Here Coleridge is using the organic metaphor to describe not a work of art, but the nature of genius and intellect: Genius is *like* Nature.

A prominent theme of the *Biographia* first emerges in another notebook entry close to the entry on Bartram's Travels, in which Coleridge records his initial confusion upon reading Giordano Bruno:

It was far too numeral, lineal, & pythagorean for my Comprehension – it read very much like Thomas Taylor & Proclus &c. I by no means think it certain that there is no meaning in these Works, nor do I presume even to suppose, that the meaning is of no value – /but it is <till I understand a man's Ignorance, I presume myself ignorant of his understanding> for others, at present, not for me – [36]

A typical passage of the *Biographia* which obviously derived from this early germ occurs in chapter twelve. What is most appealing about this opening to chapter twelve, the most difficult chapter only in a strictly philosophical sense, is Coleridge's gracious effort to prepare his reader for the initial trials of comprehension of the *Biographia* which will be necessary. In relating this anecdote, he is instructing his audience in the proper procedure of reading:[37]

In the perusal of philosophical works I have been greatly benefited by a resolve, which, in the antithetic form and with the allowed quaintness of an adage or maxim, I have been accustomed to word thus: '*until you understand a writer's ignorance, presume yourself ignorant of his understanding*'.[38]

Having described the experiences of reading the works of a bewildered visionary,[39] Coleridge describes the reaction he had to the *Timaeus*, which was a mixture of reverence with insight but confusion from many other parts. He explains the possible responses that he might make to these incomprehensible sections, such as passing them off as 'Platonic Jargon', which he says would be the fashionable thing to do. Instead he explains:

I have no insight into the possibility of a man so eminently wise using words with such half-meaning to his readers. When in addition to the motives thus suggested by my own reason, I bring into distinct remembrance the number and the series of great men, who after long and zealous study of these works had joined with me in honoring the name of PLATO with epithets, that almost transcend humanity, I feel, that a contemptuous verdict on my part might argue want of modesty, but would hardly be received by the judicious, as evidence of superior penetration. Therefore, utterly baffled in all my attempts to understand the ignorance of Plato, I CONCLUDE MYSELF IGNORANT OF HIS UNDERSTANDING.[40]

There can be no doubt that Coleridge is gently persuading his own readers to take this maxim to heart when reading the *Biographia*. This is another instance of indirect communication by means of analogy which is a frequently used technique for awakening the reader to a consciousness of the nature of the activity of reading in which he is engaged.

Two years later, a jotting in a notebook which proves to be another germ for one of the most frequently expressed threads in the *Biographia* and *The Friend*, comes up almost as an aside to the question which Coleridge is discussing, that of evil; it occurs to him that many people will find it an uninteresting question, and he complains about the need for superficial novelty:

No! forsooth! – the Question must be new, *new spicy hot* Gingerbread, . . . Something new, something *out* of themselves – for whatever is *in* them, is deep within them, must be *old as* elementary Nature. To find no contradiction in the union of old & novel – to contemplate the Ancient of Days with Feelings new as if they then sprang forth at his own Fiat – this marks the mind that feels the Riddle of the World, & may help to unravel it.[41]

This passage occurs almost verbatim in *The Friend* and later in the *Biographia*, a few words only being changed, though the idea is significantly expanded to connect it with the well-known image of 'Truths [which] . . . lie bed-ridden in the dormitory of the soul.'[42]

One of the finest passages in the *Biographia* can be traced in its development throughout these years. The passage in chapter four which, significantly, occurs immediately before the distinction between imagination and fancy and occurs in a footnote, discusses both the state of mind which Coleridge calls the *bull* and also the antithetical state.[43] Coleridge had toyed with the phenomenon of the bull in notes to himself on several occasions as well as in letters. His first explanation of the bull occurs as a comment to an anecdote on a man listening to a clock strike four: 'as it struck, he counted the four, one, one, one, one; and then he exclaimed, why, the clock is out of its wits; it has struck one four times over'. Coleridge comments: 'It has struck *one* four times. Bulls almost always confusion between Logic & Metaphysics, a science of things as they *are* out of the mind. – '[44] Two years later, in 1803 he again takes up the subject of the bull on two separate occasions and remarks: 'that curious modification of Ideas by each other, which is the Element of *Bulls*'. Coleridge then describes Derwent:

His Passion had compleatly [*sic*] confounded his Sense of Time, & its consequences – He saw that it was done; & yet he passionately entreated you not to do it – & not for the time to come/but for the Present & the Past. 'O but you have! O but don't now!' – This Mem. for †my† the effect of the Passions on the reasoning power imprimis in producing *Bulls*.[45]

The interest in the bull took its final form in the focus upon its *opposite* state, and this also is well formulated eight years before the *Biographia* was written down:

Sudden Connection of the Understanding in a very quick mind before the Imagination & general Habit of Thought & Sensation are reconciled thereto makes a man feel as if he stood on his Head. His State is the direct Antipode of *a Bull* – the †one† latter is the feeling with<out> the sense of connection, the former the perception without the Feeling.[46]

The passage on the bull in the *Biographia* incorporates this latest insight and not only explains it but is also one of the many occasions for making happen in the reader's mind the state described. In this case the bull passage is certainly a sort of preparation and 'practice session' for the really important point in chapter four – the imagination/fancy distinction.[47]

About the same time that the two examples of bulls occur in the notebooks, another entry occurs which was later incorporated into the *Biographia*. In distinguishing the discursive from the intuitive, a distinction not unrelated to the fancy/imagination distinction, Coleridge quotes a passage from the fifth book of the fifth *Ennead* which he had long ago entered into his notebook, with only a few minor changes in phrasing. It is once again, like all the passages noted above, an example of a sentence which explains and at the same time demonstrates its meaning; that is, unlike the bull or its opposite state, and unlike merely discursive writing, these passages *require* and stimulate the coincidence of understanding and feeling. Coleridge quotes Plotinus speaking of the inward Light:

It is not lawful to enquire from whence it originated, for it neither approached hither, nor again departs from hence to some other place, but it either appears to us, or it does not appear. So that we ought not to pursue it, as if with a view of discovering its latent †Abode† Original, but to abide in Quiet, till it suddenly shines upon us; preparing ourselves for the blessed Spectacle, like the eye waiting patiently for the rising Sun.[48]

In the same section of the *Biographia*, several more quotations from Plotinus are added to this one, all of which are about intuition.[49]

Another beautifully poetic passage which occurs in chapter twelve immediately after the Plotinus quotations also seems to have origins reaching as far back as 1804. In describing the generative conditions for philosophic imagination, the 'sacred power of self-intuition', Coleridge compares the mind to the symbol expressive of the relation of the potential to the actual:

They and only they can acquire the philosophic imagination . . . who within themselves can interpret and understand the symbol, that the wings of the air-sylph are forming within the skin of the catepillar; those only, who feel in their own spirits the same instinct, which impels the chrysalis of the horned fly to leave room in its involucrum for antennae yet to come.[50]

Some eleven years earlier he was already impressed with the caterpillar image not simply as the symbol of transformation of the soul from its prison in the body into a winged and free state, but primarily in the relation of the potential to actual, that is, as suggestive in men of a spiritual state working '*in* them, even as the *actual* works on them'. Coleridge writes:

O dear Sir! I am heart-sick and stomach-sick of speaking and writing concerning myself – nay, let me be proud, not my self – but concerning my miserable carcase – the Caterpillar Skin which, I believe, the Butterfly Elect is wriggling off, tho' with no small Labor and Agony.[51]

In this same letter Coleridge writes at length about Wordsworth and his poetry, and finally announces his imagination/fancy distinction in connection with his idea of poetry at its highest level as the complete synthesis of thought and feeling.[52] But 1804 was not the date of his conception of this distinction; much earlier, in 1802, he was writing about it, once again in connection with the unification of 'Heart & Intellect' necessary for great poetry; here occurs the first statement of the familiar definition of 'Fancy, or the aggregating Faculty of the mind – not *Imagination*, or the *modifying*, and *co-adunating* Faculty.'[53] Two parts of this letter are highly instructive for the distinction between imagination and fancy, and in view of the lack of general critical acceptance of the distinction, from Wordsworth to Eliot and beyond, they are of considerable interest. First, in comparing Greek to Hebrew poetry, Coleridge explains:

It must occur to every Reader that the Greeks in their religious poems address always the Numina Loci, the Genii, the Dryads, the Naiads, &c &c – All natural Objects were *dead* – mere hollow Statues – but there was a Godkin or Goddessling *included* in each – In the Hebrew Poetry you find nothing of this poor Stuff – as poor in genuine Imagination, as it is mean in Intellect – At best, it is but Fancy, or the aggregating Faculty of the mind – not *Imagination*, or the *modifying*, and *co-adunating* Faculty. This the Hebrew Poets appear to me to have possessed beyond all others – . . . each Thing has a Life of it's own, & yet they are all one Life.

Again in relation to Bowles the same distinction, though unspoken specifically, becomes quite apparent:

every Thing has a Life of it's own, & . . . we are all *one Life*. A Poet's *Heart* & *Intellect* should be *combined*, *intimately* combined & *unified*, with the great appearances in Nature – & not merely held in solution & loose mixture with them, in the shape of a formal Similies. I do not mean to *exclude* these formal Similies – there are moods of mind, in which they are natural – pleasing moods of minds, & such as a Poet will often have, & sometimes express; but they are not his highest, & most appropriate moods . . . The truth is – Bowles has indeed the *sensibility* of a poet; but he has not the *Passion* of a great Poet . . . he has no native Passion, because he is not a Thinker – [54]

Here the connection between imagination and religion is anticipated, as well as the definition of symbol ('each Thing has a Life of it's own, & yet they are all one Life') in the first quotation.[55] In the second passage, the theme which holds the *Biographia* together, the unity of thought and feeling, or passion, is intimately involved with the fancy/imagination distinction.[56]

In the examination of the early origins of the *Biographia*, and particularly of the origins of those passages which, as will be discussed in a later chapter, are examples of metaphoric situations, only the notebooks and letters up to about 1808 have been drawn upon. But throughout the next few years many jottings in the notebooks show that Coleridge was not only thinking during this time about the topics with which he would deal in the *Biographia*, but that a number of the jottings were virtually copied from their notebook origins into the final draft of the work. The most important and striking coincidences of these post-1808 entries can be profitably compared with the final version of the *Biographia*. These may be still more helpful in corroborating the thesis that the *Biographia* was in no sense the product of a summer's writing. It was certainly not a product of a summer's thought, but of some fifteen or more years of thinking and writing on that explicit work which Coleridge early referred to as his 'Life'.

In volume two of the *Biographia* Coleridge uses a metaphor of the movement of a serpent as an emblem for the movement of the mind in the act of thinking:

The reader should be carried forward, not merely or chiefly by mechanical impulse of curiosity, or by a restless desire to arrive at the final solution; but by the pleasurable activity of mind excited by the attractions of the journey itself. Like the motion of a serpent, which the Egyptians made the emblem of intellectual power; or like the path of sound through the air; at every step he pauses and half recedes, and from the retrogressive movement collects the force which again carries him onward.[57]

The significance of this metaphor is also discussed in chapter five below. What interests us here is its connection with a similar passage from the notebooks of 1810. The metaphor in this notebook passage is quite

different from that in the *Biographia*, but the idea certainly seems to be
the same:

The fibrous Integument that surrounds the Cocoa-nut Shell called *Coir* – Capt[n]
Thomas Forrest thus praises it – for *cables* – 'Being elastic, it gives so much
play to a ship that rides hard at Anchor, that with a cable of 120 fathoms, the
Ships retire or give way, sometimes half their length, when opposed to a heavy
sea – and instantly shoot ahead again: the coir-cable, after being fine-drawn,
recovering its size an*d spring*. Hempen Cables are strong & stubborn, and ships
often founder that ride by them, because nothing stretches or gives way: the
Coir yields and recovers. – ' [58]

Coleridge's interest in this passage is related to the idea of the fulcrum
expressed by the serpent metaphor in volume two, and by the metaphor of
the insect 'winning its way up the stream' in volume one[59] (quoted in full
and discussed below in chapter five). The importance of such an isolated
notebook entry would undoubtedly be missed if its significance as a source
or an instance of a metaphor for the idea of the fulcrum were not understood. Yet the idea of the fulcrum is only another variation of the theme of
the interaction of two opposite forces as the means of progression, such as
the active/passive dichotomy.

Elsewhere in the *Biographia* Coleridge draws out a characteristic of
Shakespeare's poetry which once again expresses the active/passive relation
and which applies equally well to the method of the *Biographia*:

The reader is forced into too much action to sympathize with the merely passive
of our Nature. As little can a mind thus roused and awakened be brooded on by
mean and indistinct emotion, as the low, lazy mist can creep upon the surface
of a lake, while a strong gale is driving it onward in waves and billows.[60]

The source of this passage seems to be a notebok entry of Oct.–Nov. 1811,
and again Coleridge is using the description in reference to Shakespeare:

The reader's Mind & †heart† Fancy are forced into too much action to sympathize with the merely *Passive* of our Nature – As little can the mind thus
roused & awakened doze †under the† and be brooded on by indistinct †Dreams
& enfeebling Emotions† Passions, as the low lazy Mist can creep upon the
†Lake† surface while a strong Gale is driving the Lake on in waves and
billows before it – /[61]

This entry is also an illustration of Coleridge's method of using metaphoric situations to give the sensation as well as the sense of an idea:
he explicitly and discursively mentions the active versus the passive
intellective activity, and then he *demonstrates* it for the reader by creating
a metaphor, by means of which the reader's mind is activated to reproduce
the experience referred to and validate the distinction in his own mind.

Thus these metaphors become the point toward which the preceding discursive material moves for demonstration and verification on behalf of the reader.

We will suggest below in chapter eight the importance of Coleridge's rejection of the once-admired Hartleian view of association for his distinction between these active and passive faculties, such as imagination and fancy. The following notebook entry shows that Coleridge was thinking and writing in 1810 about this inadequate account of association as the essential activity of the mind, several years before actually completing a draft of the *Biographia*, a year however when many other issues later to be dealt with in the *Biographia* were absorbing his mind. His rejection of Hartley stems back of course to the late 1790s:

I had been talking of the association of Ideas, and endeavoring to convince an Idolater of Hume & Hartley, that this was strictly speaking a law only of the memory & imagination, of the *Stuff out* of which we make our conceptions & perceptions, not of the thinking faculty, by which we make them – that it was as the †power† force of gravitation to leaping to any given point – without gravitation this would be impossible, and yet equally impossible to leap except by a *power* counteracting first, and then using the *force* of gravitation. That Will, strictly synonymous with the individualizing Principle, the 'I' of every rational Being, was this governing and applying Power – And yet to shew him that I was neither ignorant, nor idle in observing, the vast extent and multifold activity of the Associative Force I entered into a curious and tho fanciful yet strictly true and actual, exemplification.[62]

This passage once again caps a discursive, philosophical point with a metaphor, and illustrates the idea of fulcrum, which has been at the basis of many of the quotations examined in this post-1808 period. It, like the entry quoted above on 'Coir', is closely related to the insect 'winning its way up the stream' in volume one, and to the metaphor of leaping (see below chapter five, for a quotation of this passage for comparison).[63] All of these entries discussed so far as originating in early notebooks and letters have been instances of extended metaphors and are thus interesting not only as evidence that the *Biographia* was growing in Coleridge's mind in explicit and detailed ways for some fifteen years. They are interesting for the *type* of material which he was aware from the beginning would be the most effective for communicating his ideas. And they suggest significant points about the way in which he used his sources, both his own ideas and those of others, not as discursive information incorporated into his work, but rather as situations for imaginative response which gained their integrity from the context in which they were placed and for the metaphorical level of discourse about thinking which they invariably display.

Whatever controversies surround the *Biographia*, one of the few areas of agreement about its worth is the critical analysis in volume two, both of poetry in general and of Wordsworth's poetry specifically as illustrating the principles of poetry which Coleridge is there evolving. The analysis of poetry is not however confined to volume two, for the *Biographia* begins with Coleridge's discussion of his own early experiences as a poet, the pitfalls he stumbled into, and the dangers of authorship. Thus the two volumes at least begin with obviously similar purposes, and this purpose, an analysis of the nature of poetry, is clearly one of the central strands holding the two volumes together. Even the long discussion of associationism is designed to show the necessity of the fancy/imagination distinction. And as will be discussed in chapter four, the material on Schelling and self-consciousness in chapter twelve of the *Biographia* has explicit connections with an aesthetic of irony.

In the notebooks and letters of the 1809–15 period, not only rough drafts or notes for future elaboration are in evidence. Long passages occur of several pages each, which clearly delineate the development of Coleridge's ideas about poetry and which state these ideas in the notebooks in a form almost identical with statements in the *Biographia*. All the aspects of poetry which are examined by Coleridge in the *Biographia*, with all their corresponding sources in the notebooks particularly, cannot be discussed because they are too numerous. That would require reproducing long passages from both for comparison, which the reader can easily do by consulting the entries mentioned below. In order to compare the *Biographia* and the notebooks, it is necessary to focus upon one of the characterictics of poetry which is most relevant to our more general discussion of the unity of the *Biographia*, the distinctions of poetry from prose and poetry from science.

Coleridge seeks in the *Biographia* to show how false the antithesis between poetry and prose is, the true opposition being between poetry and science. The distinction between poetry and prose he shows to involve primarily metre and a higher intensity of passion.[64] One of the most crucial reasons for re-establishing the relation of poetry and prose, and for showing that the real antithesis is between poetry and science (though even here this is, from a higher perspective, only a relative antithesis), is to show how poetry and philosophy are integrally involved in each other, a thesis explored more fully in chapter seven. By demonstrating that the language of poetry and prose, and specifically philosophy, are not essentially different, Coleridge will have dismantled one of the most persistent obstacles to a reconciliation between poetry and philosophy, and can then begin to clarify why the best poet is also a profound philosopher, Plato, Shakespeare, and others (not to mention Coleridge himself) being obvious instances. Once this reconciliation commences, other relationships are immediately established. The relations between art and knowledge, pleasure and truth, thought and feeling, religion, or the spiritual, and the rational, the meta-phorical and literal, and discursive and intuitive become oppositions not in the usual exclusive or 'contrary' sense of opposition, but in the sense which the polar philosophy gives to the word. Only homogeneous elements can be opposed to each other (see below chapters two and three).

In 1809 early traces are evident of Coleridge's initial gropings toward the true distinction between poetry and prose, which he was eventually to formalize in 1815 and make the core of the relation between philosophy and poetry (and between volumes one and two of the *Biographia*):

that a poet ever uses a word as *poetical*, i.e. formally – which he – in the same mood & thought – would not use, in prose or conversation, Milton's Prose Works will assist me in disproving – But as soon as literature becomes common, & critics numerous in any Country, and a large body of men seek to express themselves habitually in the most precise, sensuous, & impassioned words, the differences as to mere *words* ceases – as ex. gr. the German Prose writers. Produce to me *one* word out of Klopstock, Wieland, Schiller, Goethe, Voss, &c, which I will not find as frequently used in their most energetic prose writers. The sole difference, *in style*, is that poetry demands a *severer keeping* – it admits nothing that Prose may not often admit; but it *oftener* rejects. In other words, it presupposes a more continuous state of Passion.[65]

This is of course the precise position which Coleridge takes up in the *Biographia*, particularly when he seeks to show the fallacy of Wordsworth's claims. For by this means poetry is not crudely lowered to the level of 'mere' prose; poetry is shown to use the same words as prose, but the essential difference between the two is the greater degree of 'Passion' involved in poetry. The rustic's uneducated speech is inadequate for either. His thought lacks that which is common to both, namely method and the association of ideas by something more than the mere conditions of time and space contiguity. This quotation from the notebooks does not precisely correspond to a particular paragraph in *Biographia*, as most of the others quoted above do. The several points here are expanded by Coleridge into an entire chapter on the nature of the distinction between poetry and prose, the language of poetry, and especially the role of metre and passion in poetry, as distinct from prose or mere non-poetic metrical composition.[66]

Only a few notebook entries later, Coleridge raises the issue which follows from the distinction between poetry and prose. He seeks to discover what the peculiar quality of poetry is which makes it different from prose, since language is not the source of that difference, and since in style the major distinction is one of degree only, that is, 'a more continuous state of Passion':

Poetry is

The species of composition, which represents external nature, or the human mind, – both in relation to human affections – so as to produce immediate pleasure – and the greatest quantity of immediate pleasure in each part, that is compatible with the largest possible <sum> of Pleasure in the whole. –
    Poetry is – simple, sensuous, passionate. – [67]

The idea that the essential quality of poetry is pleasure is expanded some months later in an entry in May 1810, where Coleridge takes up new terms such as 'excitability of the human mind' and 'excitement by sympathy'. Most importantly in this entry a new idea is expressed which is to become incorporated into further developments on poetry. Coleridge defines poetry as:

– A mode of composition that calls into action & gratifies the largest number of the human Faculties in Harmony with each other, & in just proportions – at least, it would furnish a scale of merit if not a definition of *genus* – Frame a numeration table of the primary faculties of Man, as Reason, *unified per Ideas*, Mater Legum <Arbitrement, Legibilitatis mater> Judgment, the discriminative, Fancy, the aggregative, Imagination, the modifying & fusive, the Senses & Sensations – and from these the different Derivatives of the Agreeable from the Senses, the Beautiful, the Sublime/the Like and the Different – the spontaneous and the receptive – the Free and the Necessary – And whatever calls into consciousness the greatest number of these in due proportion & perfect harmony with each other, is the noblest Poem. – [68]

Compare a passage from *Biographia* II:

The poet, described in *ideal* perfection, brings the whole soul of man into activity, with the subordination of its faculties to each other, according to their relative worth and dignity. He diffuses a tone and spirit of unity, that blends and (as it were) *fuses*, each into each, by that synthetic and magical power, to which we have exclusively appropriated the name of imagination. This power [is] first put into action by the will and understanding, and [is] retained under their irremissive, though gentle and unnoticed, controul.[69]

The view that the poet must use all of his faculties in a highly integrated way, including those associated with philosophy and science, such as reason and judgment, suggests again that the poet and philosopher are not engaged in wholly different intellectual activities; at most the preponderance of one faculty over another is different. The insistence on the integration of the faculties, along with the new distinction between poetry and prose, the distinction between pleasure and truth, and various other points, is taken up again in the autumn of 1811 in a notebook entry which clearly anticipates and even forms the literal basis for passages in the *Biographia*. In this entry Coleridge proceeds one step further, and evi-

dences a genuine progression of thought throughout these succeeding
entries which is taking place in the years immediately preceding the
composition of the *Biographia*. Such a clear gradual development of
Coleridge's views on poetry, which culminates in the analysis in the
Biographia, should wholly dispel any notion that the work was over-
hastily put together. For this notion is itself false, and yet it is then used as
if it were indisputably true to justify the sensation of disunity in the
Biographia.

The further step which Coleridge takes in this 1811 entry is to try to be
more specific about how poetry differs from prose, since the definitions he
has proposed 'would include Novels & other works of Fiction which yet
we do not call Poems'. Coleridge explains that 'there must be some
additional character by which Poetry is. . .not only divided from opposites,
but likewise distinguished from disparate tho similar modes of composition'. He formulates more precisely this 'additional character':

It is th†e†at pleasureable emotion, that peculiar state o†f†r degree of Excitement, which arises in the Poet†'s mind† himself, in the act of composition – &
in order to understand this we must combine a more than ordinary Sympathy
with the Objects, Emotions, or Incidents contemplated by the Poet in consequence of a more than common sensibility, with a more than ordinary Activity
of †Mind† the †fancy† Mind as far as respects the Fancy & Imagination –
Hence a more vivid reflection of the Truths of Nature & the Human Heart
united with that constant exertion of Activity which †uni† modifies & corrects
these truths by that sort of pleasurable Emotion, which the exertion of all our
faculties give in a certain degree, but which the full play of those Powers of
Mind, which are spontaneous rather than voluntary, in which the Effort
required bears no proportion to the activity enjoyed – [70]

Again, this passage provides germs which are expanded into a more
detailed account in chapter seventeen of the *Biographia*,[71] as is the next
notebook entry.

The next notebook entry is a rewriting and a rephrasing of these and
all the other points discussed above, with the addition of the poem on the
immortality of the soul by Sir John Davies which Coleridge also included
in the final version of the *Biographia*.[72] This entry seems to be a sign of an
effort to polish and finalize, with poetic examples, the formulation of the
ideas which Coleridge had been developing explicitly since 1809 and
probably for many years more. The next three entries bring up a number
of points regarding poetry and specifically Shakespeare which were also
incorporated into the *Biographia*.[73] These points, coupled with a careful
and thorough examination of the copious notebook entries from which
they were taken, are substantial evidence that the ideas, particularly on

poetry, underwent a long process of germination, both in thought (Coleridge had been concerning himself with precisely these points for twenty years, as is clear from hints in the letters and notebooks) and in writing, as these successive entries with their additions and refinements of core issues show. Several other miscellaneous correspondences with the *Biographia* occur in the notebooks, two of the most interesting being pages of notes and comments on Fichte and Schelling.[74] The Schelling notes were turned into parts of the ten theses in chapter twelve.

A comparison has been made in the foregoing pages of early 'germs', or passages in the notebooks and letters, with the full 'blossoms' in the *Biographia*, in order to suggest that the composition, in distinction from the actual writing down of the work, was underway for many years. The specific project in Coleridge's mind was to write a *Life* illustrating the intimate connection of thought and feeling, and of philosophy and poetry, by means of the distinction between imagination and fancy, and the intuitive and discursive. Coleridge also hoped to show the *application* of the distinction to philosophy, poetry, and religion specifically, though ultimately to the most basic experiences of perception and thought. The passages discussed above are not exhaustive of the early sources of the *Biographia*, as anyone familiar with the letters and notebooks must notice.[75] They have been selected, however, in lieu of others, because of the particular importance which they play in the content (poetry and its relation to the polar philosophy and the rejected associationism) and in the design of the *Biographia* as 'metaphorical situations' which constitute the method of the *Biographia*'s development, and hence its unity. They illustrate the 'prevailing intellectual point of view' of the author which Friedrich Schlegel insisted was the only genuine way of unifying and organizing a work of art.

COLERIDGE ON THE 'BIOGRAPHIA'

Coleridge has often been turned to as the final authority on the worth of the *Biographia*, and the general assumption is that his own words condemn it as a miscellany of digressions. A closer look at precisely what he did say may put his criticisms of it into perspective. The *Biographia* was finally published in 1817. Shortly thereafter Coleridge was already able to offer a judicial assessment which showed no signs of defensiveness, and which proved with only one exception to be his continued view to the end of his life. He says:

In my 'literary life', the publication of which has been delay'd two years, there are a few opinions which better information and more reflection would now annul. But even these will, I trust, be found only in the lesser branches, as knotts & scars that may exist without implying either canker at the root, or malignant quality in the general sap of the tree.[76]

During the two year delay Coleridge had been assiduously studying with J. H. Green the works of Schelling, and had come to believe that the foundation was erroneous.[77] He then 'rejected' certain parts of the *Biographia* which he believed had too closely followed Schelling's hidden dualism and, ultimately, pantheism.[78] It is clear from this statement however that Coleridge did conceive of the *Biographia* as a whole, a 'tree' the 'general sap' of which was not polluted by these few opinions.[79] It seems in fact that he took its unity for granted, since he found it necessary to say that the errors were confined to the lesser branches, in order to maintain that they could not infect the whole. If the parts were unrelated there would have been no need to be concerned about any resulting 'systemic' disease.

Over a year later he explains more precisely his reservations about this section of chapter twelve of the *Biographia*:

This however the Zoroastrian & Schellingian Oracles have in common – that Polarity is asserted of the Absolute, of the Monad: (= Oken's + o). The inconsistency Schelling has contrived to hide from himself by the artifice of making all knowledge bi-polar, Transcendental Idealism as one Pole and Nature as the other – and from the tendency of my mind to confidence in others I was myself *taken in* by it, retrograding from my own prior and better Lights, and adopted it in the metaphysical chapters of my Literary Life – not aware, that this was putting the Candle horizontally and burning it at both ends.[80]

This criticism is confined to the formulation of the relation of polarity to the absolute, and as a result says nothing detrimental either about the method of the *Biographia* as a whole or about its unity.

Some months later a more pessimistic note is sounded, however, which is out of tone with the other comments about the *Biographia*. Coleridge writes: 'At least, were it in my power, my works should be confined to the second volume of my "Literary Life", the Essays of the third volume of the "Friend", from page 67 to page 265, with about fifty or sixty pages from the two former volumes, and some half-dozen of my poems.'[81] How seriously we take this 'choice' should depend upon how characteristic is. There are several other comments besides the two above which show this criticism to be out of keeping with a more frequently stated assessment, such as is found close to the end of Coleridge's life:

The metaphysical disquisition at the end of the first volume of the 'Biographia Literaria' is unformed and immature; – it contains fragments of the truth, but it is not fully thought out. It is wonderful to myself to think how infinitely more profound my views now are, and yet how much clearer they are withal.

The circle is completing; the idea is coming round to, and to be, the common sense.[82]

This statement comes closest to expressing the position which will be set out below on this section of the *Biographia*, namely that the errors were not errors in the strict sense because they were not contrary to truth, but rather errors because they were only fragments of the truth. In so far as they were fragments pointing beyond or outside the *Biographia*, the direction of development was not given and they were apt as a result to lead to misconceptions.[83] In this passage Coleridge certainly seems to be saying that these fragments of truth nevertheless belonged to the circle of truths which he devoted his life to completing; they were not stray tangents to be cut away.

One final comment must be considered before proceeding to the philosophical sources of the *Biographia*. On the back fly-leaves of a copy of the *Statesman's Manual* Coleridge scribbled a note from which we excerpt the following comments applied to that work:

the Common Heading of these Essays...[is] an attempt to fix the true meaning of the Terms, Reason, Understanding, Sense, Imagination, Conscience & Ideas, with reflections on the theoretical & practical Consequences of their perversion from the Revolution (1688) to the present day, 1816 – the moral of the whole being that the Man who gives to the Understanding the primacy due to the Reason, ...loses the one and spoils the other –...Now surely a series of Essays, ...where all the points treated of tend [to] a common result, cannot justly be regarded as a motley...Patchwork, or Farrago of Heterogeneous Effusions! even tho' the form and sequence were more aphorismic...[and disconnected] than is really the case.

He then insists that he could apply the same test of unity and progression to many other works, and, in particular, 'to two distinct Treatises in the Literary Life, besides the Essay on Authorship as a Trade'.[84] Here Coleridge certainly does not seem to regard the *Biographia* or any of his other works as an 'immethodical miscellany'. The form and sequence seems disconnected only according to conventional narrative development of biographies, or of the format of systematic treatises of philosophy, neither of which characterize adequately the genre of the *Biographia*. That neither of these was Coleridge's purpose is a point which will be more fully elaborated below.[85]

It is unnecessary to indicate more than (in passing) that because Coleridge speaks of 'two distinct Treatises . . . besides the Essay . . .' it need not be assumed that the *Biographia* falls into disunity: the fact that one can distinguish distinct parts does not preclude a well-formed whole. We speak of the stems, leaves, and flowers of a plant and never suppose that this prevents us from seeing that they can be actual parts only if there is a whole.

2

❦◆❦

Philosophical sources of the *Biographia Literaria*

THE UNITY OF PLATONISM AND EMPIRICISM

A fundamental issue in philosophy at least since Kant can be expressed by the question 'What is experience?' Coleridge brings clarity to the purport of such a question in a marginal note to Kant's *Critique of Pure Reason*:

> The perpetual and unmoving Cloud of Darkness that hangs over this Work to my 'mind's eye', is the absence of any clear account of – Was ist Erfahrung? What do you mean by *fact*, an empiric Reality, which alone can give solidity (inhalt) to our Conceptions? – It seems from many passages, that this indispensible Test is itself previously manufactured by this very conceptive Power – and that the whole not of our own making is the mere Sensation of a mere Manifold – in short, mere influx of motion, to use a physical metaphor. – I apply the Categoric forms to a Tree – well! but first *what* is this tree? How do I come by this Tree? – Fichte I understand very well – only I cannot believe his System.[1]

The subsidiary question which we are led to ask is whether the experience of a thing is one and the same with that which is the occasion of it. Coleridge maintains in the *Philosophical Lectures* that philosophy has its origins in this distinction between the subjective and objective: 'the whole progress from that time to this present moment is nothing more than an attempt to reconcile the same'.[2] Two fundamental principles formed the basis of the reconciliation of subject and object, and are as ancient as the followers of the school of Thales. The first is the law of homogeneity: 'action and reaction can only take place between things similar in essence'.[3] Put another way, 'no substances or beings essentially dissimilar could possibly be made sensible of each other's existence or in any way act thereon'.[4] Thus the perceiver and perceived are maintained to be similar and perhaps essentially the same, for as Coleridge says in his description of the Pythagorean view: 'the very powers which in men reflect and contemplate, are in their essence the same as those powers which in nature produce the objects contemplated'.[5]

The second principle which formed the basis of the philosophy of reconciliation states that: 'the final solution of phenomena cannot itself be a phenomenon'.[6] The solution must rather be in 'the connexion of the visible thing, the phenomenon, with the invisible thing, under a cause common to both and above both'.[7] Otherwise, we are troubled by an infinite regress which, Coleridge insists, the materialist can bring to a halt only by assuming that for which it is necessary to account.[8]

There are these three main alternatives to a philosophy of reconciliation,[9] first, that which places the solution in the object, materialism; second, that which places the solution in mind, subjective idealism; and third, that which denies a solution and maintains an absolute duality. Throughout the *Philosophical Lectures* the first is rejected as a non-philosophy, or 'psilosophy'.[10] A succinct and scathing criticism of this first position Coleridge had formulated as early as 1796 in a letter to John Thelwall:

Dr Beddoes, & Dr Darwin think that *Life* is utterly inexplicable, writing as Materialists – You, I understand, have adopted the idea that it is the result of organized matter acted on by external Stimuli. – As likely as any other system; but you *assume* the thing to be proved – the '*capability* of being stimulated into sensation' *as* a *property of* organized matter – now 'the Capab.' &c is *my* definition of *animal Life* – .[11]

Many years later Coleridge was to make the same criticism of Locke in an equally brief but forceful image: Locke's error was 'the fallacy, that the Soil, Rain, Air, and Sunshine, *make* the wheat-stalk & it's Ear of Corn, because they are the conditions under which alone the seed can develope itself'.[12] Not only was the materialist guilty of assuming that which needed to be accounted for; the state of mind which allowed such an approach was that of taking for granted all the mysteries which need to be explained:

Time, Space, Duration, Action, Active, Passion, Passive, Activeness, Passiveness, Reaction, Causation, Affinity – here assemble all the Mysteries – known, all is known – unknown, say rather, merely known, all is unintelligible/and yet Locke & the stupid adorers of †this† that *Fetisch* Earth-clod, take all these for granted – .[13]

Coleridge explained the popularity of materialism by the priority which the developing mind must at first give to the senses and to outward phenomena:

We have been accustomed by all our affections, by all our wants, to seek after outward images; and by the love of association, therefore, to whole truth we attach that particular condition of truth which belongs to sensible bodies or to bodies which can be touched. The first education which we receive, that from our mothers, is given to us by touch; the whole of its process is nothing more than, to express myself boldly, an extended touch by promise. The sense itself, the sense of vision itself, is only acquired by a continued recollection of touch. No wonder therefore, that beginning in the animal state, we should carry this onward through the whole of our being however remote it may be from the true purposes of it.[14]

Coleridge claims that the result of this first experience and education is a continuing obsession with outward presences, whereas the faculties ought to be progressively leading toward a concern with thoughts and mind as the objects of attention. We are ruled by the 'habit of attaching all our conceptions and feelings, and of applying all the words and phrases expressing reality, to the objects of the Senses: more accurately speaking, to the images and sensations by which their presence is made known to us'.[15] This stagnant slavery to the senses is the cause of the materialist philosophy,

demanding for every mode and act of existence real or possible *visibility*, knowing only of distance and nearness, composition (or rather juxtaposition)[16] and decomposition, in short the relations of unproductive particles to each other;[17] so that in every instance the result is the exact sum of the component quantities as in arithmetical addition. This is the philosophy of death, and only of a dead nature can it hold good.[18]

The materialist arbitrarily excludes 'all modes of existence which the theorist cannot in imagination, at least, *finger* and *peep* at'.[19] The limitation of such an attitude Coleridge captures in his image of the materialists as 'Snails of Intellect, who see only with their Feelers. – '[20] This apparent contradiction of *see*ing with organs of mere touch itself suggests the inadequacy of sensual experience to account for all experience or for a reality.

Another result of this tyranny of the senses was that the materialist seemed to Coleridge to lack the faculty of contemplating one-ness except as an abstraction, and Coleridge contrasts this with his own habits:

– my mind had been habituated *to the Vast* – & I never regarded *my senses* in any way as the criteria of my belief. I regulated all my creeds by my conceptions not by my *sight*...Those who have been led to the same truths step by step thro' the constant testimony of their senses, seem to me to want a sense which I possess – They contemplate nothing but *parts* – and all *parts* are necessarily little – and the Universe to them is but a mass of *little things*.[21]

One of Coleridge's primary concerns in the first volume of the *Biographia* is to expose the inadequacy of the materialist for providing an account of experience by analysing the errors involved in Aristotelian, Hartleian, and other atomistic theories of association. The rejection of materialism and the adoption of a Kantian critical posture is most evident in the *Biographia* in Coleridge's treatment of the nature of association. His most important formulation of the errors of Hartleian associationism as a materialist epistemology is expressed in terms of the role which the faculties play in constituting experience. Materialism, by placing reality outside the mind and by making it independent, forces the mind to see its own characteristics as those of a blank tablet which is impressed and acted upon by the 'real'. Experience is the result of a passive, receptive mind being imposed upon by the material world. Coleridge criticizes Hartley for characterizing mental activity as constrained by the sole law of time and space – the two conditions of *externality*, and thus far imposing the nature of matter upon mind. Mind is conceived only in terms of its objects:

Again, from this results inevitably, that the will, the reason, the judgement, and the understanding, instead of being the determining causes of association, must needs be represented as its creatures, and among its mechanical *effects* . . . If therefore we suppose the absence of all interference of the will, reason, and judgement, one or other of two consequences must result. Either the ideas, (or relics of such impression,) will exactly imitate the order of the impression itself, which would be absolute *delirium*: or any one part of that impression might recall any other part, and (as from the law of continuity, there must exist in every total impression, some one or more parts, which are components of some other following total impression, and so on ad infinitum) *any* part of *any* impression might recall *any* part of any *other*, without a cause present to determine *what* it should be. For to bring in the will, or reason, as causes of their own cause, that is, as at once causes and effects, can satisfy those only who, in their pretended evidences of a God, having first demanded organization, as the sole cause and ground of intellect, will then coolly demand the pre-existence of intellect, as the cause and ground-work of organization.[22]

Coleridge makes the same point when he points out in chapter seven of the *Biographia* the consequences of the Hartleian theory which assumes 'that the will and, with the will, all acts of thought and attention are parts and products of this blind mechanism, instead of being distinct powers, whose function it is to control, determine, and modify the phantasmal chaos of association'.[23] Consciousness is conceived of as a result of the interaction of 'the breeze and the harp' without any of the advantages of dualism and with all the difficulties of the interaction between different substances. Of this produced tune Coleridge asks, 'what is harmony but a mode of relation, the very *esse* of which is *percipi*? An ens rationale, which pre-supposes the power, that by perceiving creates it?'[24]

Coleridge analyses in the *Biographia* the irresistible prejudice that objects outside ourselves constitute the real as a prejudice of 'outness' which is *unconsciously* involved in the equally immediate sense of a subject, an I. He explains that the philosopher is forced to assume this 'outness' to be a prejudice since it is otherwise inconceivable how objects absolutely separate from ourselves could become a part of our consciousness or a modification of our being.[25] From this position we might erroneously be led to conclude a subjective idealism such as Berkeley, and before him the Eleatic school, adopted.[26] Hence we can understand Coleridge's early enthusiasm for Berkeley. This alternative to materialism places reality in the subject, or mind, and denies existence to the world except as a subjective modification of mind. In Coleridge's later view, however, the subjective idealist rejected 'all that was objective as real, and affirmed that the whole existed only in the mind and for the mind, that all the multitude of objects that appear to us are founded in delusion and that in mind itself was to be found the sole reality of things'.[27] The crucial difference, for example, between the memory of a table and a present table or the distinction between sensation and object sensed is blurred.[28] The denial of existence in space and time is almost too absurd for the mind to accept. It would be difficult to construct an account of our experience or the external world on the basis of a denial of it. Experience would be reduced to a dream, as Coleridge explains in a marginal note to the *Critique of Pure Reason*:

But Kant I do not understand – i.e. I have not discovered what he proposes for my Belief. – Is it Dogmatism? – Why then, make the opposition between Phaenomena and Things in themselves – τα οντως οντα? Is it Idealism? What Test then can I find in the different modifications of my Being to verify and substantiate each other? What other distinction between Schein and Erscheinung, Illusion and Appearance more than the old one of – in one I dream to myself, and in the other I dream in common: The man in a fever is only outvoted by his Attendants – He does not see their Dream, and they do not see his.[29]

The position to which we are at last brought is an undeniable dualism of mind and matter:[30] 'Notwithstanding the arguments of Spinoza, and Descartes, and other advocates of the *Material system* (or, in more appropriate language, the *Atheistical system!*), it is admitted by all men, not prejudiced, not biased by sceptical prepossessions that *mind* is distinct from *matter*. The mind of man, however, is involved in inscrutable darkness (as the profoundest metaphysicians well know), and is to be estimated (if at all) alone by an inductive process; that is, by its *effects*.'[31] Coleridge cites Anaxagoras as the earliest known dualist, who tried to resolve the problem of interaction by a *Nous* which, however, in his case, was a mere hypothesis: 'As long as ever mechanical causes could explain the thing, so long the *Nous* was not heard of; when a miracle was to be worked, then only, when he had no further reason to give, this *Nous* was introduced'.[32] Dualism, whatever form it takes, cannot explain experience; it can only *state* the problem of the interaction of two assumedly heterogeneous existents and admit its ignorance of the solution.

To Descartes Coleridge gave the honour of being 'the first man who made nature utterly lifeless and godless, consider[ing] it as the subject of merely mechanical laws'.[33] He reiterates in the *Biographia* that 'to the best of my knowledge Des Cartes was the first philosopher, who introduced the absolute and essential heterogeneity of the soul as intelligence, and the body as matter'.[34] Coleridge criticized Descartes's use of the word 'idea', in introducing 'material ideas' to explain the interaction of vital mind and his lifeless matter. The extreme conclusion drawn from the Cartesian mechanism of nature which especially offended Coleridge's mind was the subjection of man to mechanical laws and the subsequent denial of free will.[35] The barrenness of the dualist system is drawn out in a marginal note to Kant's *Metaphysische Anfangsgründe der Naturwissenschaft*:

So vain is the attempt to find in a *Science* the ultimate ground of any other Science. Even Schelling who (with the help of F. Baader) had seen the inadequacy of Kant's *two* Powers as constituting Matter, and had supplied a third as the copula and realization of the two, has yet succeeded no better *in fact*: tho' by *stealing-in* the Law of Polarity he has counterfeited a more successful appearance.[36]

Dualism can, and indeed must, be taken as a starting point since the distinction between mind and nature is a fact of experience.[37] But Coleridge insists repeatedly that to distinguish it is not necessary to divide absolutely: 'It is a dull and obtuse mind, that must divide in order to distinguish; but it is a still worse, that distinguishes in order to divide.'[38] For Coleridge this great problem of the interaction of the two distinct existences could only be solved by progressing to some position which neither denies one or the other, nor maintains their absolute difference. The impossibility and unintelligibility of an unresolved dualism is clearly argued in the *Biographia* when Coleridge shows that a dualistic theory of perception or association is no real philosophical advance on a materialist system such as Hartley's, the fallacies of which he had shown in the preceding chapter. Coleridge criticizes the dualist's postulation of a soul as thinking substance and a body as a space-filling substance:

the apparent action of each on the other pressed heavy on the philosopher on the one hand; and no less heavily on the other hand pressed the evident truth, that the law of causality holds only between homogeneous things, i.e. things having some common property; and cannot extend from one world into another, its opposite.[39]

Another way of stating this problem of interaction Coleridge formulates in terms of the relation between the *esse* and the *scire*: if *esse* and *scire* are assumed to have been originally distinct, how can they ever unite with each other?

how *being* can transform itself into a *knowing*, becomes conceivable on one only condition; namely, if it can be shown that the *vis representativa*, or the Sentient, is itself a species of being; i.e. either as a property or attribute, or as an hypostasis or self subsistence. The former is, indeed, the assumption of materialism; a system which could not but be patronized by the philosopher, if only it actually performed what it promises. But how any affection from without can metamorphose itself into perception or will, the materialist has hitherto left, not only as incomprehensible as he found it, but has aggravated it into a comprehensible absurdity.[40]

If an object from without were to act upon the conscious self, it might be supposed that it would only produce something homogeneous to itself. Moreover, it is not the object itself that we 'know' from this model, but only its action or impression upon us. Hence materialism explains neither the fact of mental experiences nor the fact that we experience not effects of objects but the object itself as immediately present. Instead of assuming that being and knowing were originally distinct, Coleridge maintained that 'Truth is the correlative of Being' and is conceivable only by assuming that both were originally identical and 'coinherent'; 'that intelligence and being are reciprocally other's substrate'.[41]

Some of the first efforts to account for the interaction of mind and nature resulted from the problem that objects can appear differently in different circumstances, due for example to a variation in the subject from the 'normal' state, as in disease. Coleridge would have known this argument well from Berkeley.[42] From this subjectivity of perception, it was concluded that the mind is in part responsible for the nature of the objects outside it.[43] From almost the earliest beginnings of philosophy the solutions offered involved a recognition that we do not entirely experience objects in themselves, as Coleridge discusses in the *Philosophical Lectures*.[44] In some cases a division was drawn up between qualities that did belong to objects and those which were superimposed by the mind, that is, between 'primary' and 'secondary' qualities.[45] When it was asked how these primary qualities which were not deducible from secondary sense perception were known, another position was advanced. Primary qualities must be innate ideas which inhered in the mind and structured our sense experience of secondary qualities.[46] A clear conception of the nature of the relation of these two distinctions was lacking, however, and their inadequacies became apparent,[47] as Coleridge describes in the Locke–Descartes letters to Josiah Wedgwood in 1801.[48]

The difficulty which these doctrines tried to formulate seems inherent in our linguistic expression: there is a perceiver, a thing perceived, and the experience or perception which is the product of this interaction, a subject, object, and a verb.[49] For Coleridge the complication arises when we take a critical view of perception, and see that as perceivers we experience the object by means of sense organs. One is forced to the conclusion that the product of the interaction is a function of the nature not only of the object perceived, but of the instrument used to perceive it, the sense organ. Coleridge then asks, what is the extent of the involvement of our senses in perceptions?

All Sensations and their correspondent Objects have doubtless something in common; but it is impossible to abstract it, ...Equally impossible is it...to distinguish by determinate boundaries, what part proceeds from the sensitive faculty itself, and what from the outward Causes or the Things acting on the faculty...The cause of this impossibility is that we become conscious both of the one and of the other...in...one & the same way;...namely, as modifications of our own Being. What precedes the modification as its cause, we can never know; because our consciousness originates in the modification.[50]

Coleridge argues that the mind has still other faculties in addition to the senses which go into the making up of our world picture, such as memory, understanding, judgment, etc. If he is to be consistent he must conclude that since mind stands behind all experience (i.e., that all experience occurs by means of the mind), knowledge of the world in general is tainted by the medium mind. We are thrown into a radical subjectivity as the known object is shown necessarily to be not the 'thing-in-itself' but only the 'thing-as-perceived'. The world that we know is the 'world-known-through-mind', not the 'world-in-itself'. No part of experience can escape this subjectivity, hence the fundamental error of the distinction between primary and secondary qualities.[51] As Leibnitz thus completes the maxim of the Peripatetics: 'Nihil in intellectu quod non prius in sensu', except the mind itself.[52]

Coleridge insists that if nothing can be known of the thing-in-itself because mind intervenes between the perceiver and the world, any absolutely dualistic distinction between mind and world seems to be destroyed, for one would no longer experience anything of the world except in so far as it is a modification of his own being *qua* subject.[53] Coleridge was thus driven to *subjective* idealism by this experience of objects as no longer absolutely independent of the perceptions of them. There are, however, two points which eventually turned him from the shoals of this dogma. The first is the conclusion which must be drawn from the inability to know things as they are. Coleridge believed that if the world as thing-in-itself was unknowable, so was the agent or perceiver of that world.[54] As soon as we turn our attention to the experiences we have of ourselves, we are forced to use our mind and faculties as instruments of perception, and the same taint from the medium of perception results in relation to the 'agent-in-itself'.[55] Coleridge, with Kant, maintained that the 'inner' world of experiences may not be subject to the distortion of the senses, but it is certainly subject to the distortions of memory, judgment, feeling, etc. There is moreover an absurdity in the proposition that a perceiver can be known of which there is no known thing perceived.[56] If we insist that our thoughts are not known indirectly, but immediately, all the questions concerning personal identity must arise. Coleridge asks whether our identity is just a sum total of all our thoughts and impressions, or whether 'the clusters of ideas, which constitute our identity, . . . ever connect & unite into a greater Whole.'[57] He asks if there is no 'I' to be known except the succession of sensations: 'How opposite to nature & the fact to talk of the one *moment* of *Hume*; of our whole being an aggregate of successive single sensations. Who ever *felt* a *single* sensation? Is not every one at the same moment conscious that there co-exist a thousand others in a darker shade, or less light.'[58]

If there is no I separate from this experiencing, to Coleridge it would hardly make sense to talk of a world separate from experience, for then we have a perception of a world without a perceiver. The body cannot answer to this I, since it clearly is known through the senses and is a complex product just as external objects are. Although our knowledge of body may seem more extensive, it is no different in experience from that of objects in general. We can only formulate our experience as some sort of synthesis of perceiver and perceived, since apparently neither the I nor the world can be known.[59]

In the *Biographia*, Coleridge criticizes Hartley's theory of association for failing to account for the sense of self and personal identity. As he explains, both the concepts of personal identity and of 'an infinite spirit, of an intelligent and holy will' become unintelligible on a materialist theory of association. All activity is explained as the mechanical interaction of physical forces external to the mind, the mind in no sense causing them, but at most being able to look on and watch itself being acted upon and stimulated. Moreover, 'the sum total of my moral and intellectual inter-course, dissolved into its elements, is reduced to *extension, motion, degrees of velocity*, and those diminished *copies* of configurative motion, which form what we call notions, and notions of notions'.[60] Coleridge further explains that if the understanding functions only to combine the material of association which comes from the primary sensations, the latter of which derive all reality from externally caused impressions, then concepts of God, will and reason must either be fictions, or innate. If innate, they overthrow the system.[61]

Coleridge was fascinated with the question of the oneness of consciousness, 'That deep intuition of our *oneness*', which is not merely in our 'recollective consciousness'.[62] He describes the intuition in a notebook entry:

By deep feeling we make our *Ideas dim* – & this is what we mean by our Life – ourselves. I think of the Wall – it is before me, a distinct Image – here. I necessarily think of the *Idea* & the Thinking I as two distinct & opposite Things. Now <let me> think of *myself* – of the thinking Being – the Idea becomes dim whatever it be – so dim that I know not what it is – but the Feeling is deep & steady – and this I call *I* – †the† identifying the Percipient & the Perceived – .[63]

Coleridge played with this feeling of personal identity, insisting that 'the thought is indeed rather to be *felt* than thought, but it is not the less valuable on that account'.[64] This feeling he elsewhere describes as the consciousness of continuousness: He distinguishes three states of being of creatures:

1. those who exist to themselves only in *moments*, and whose continuousness exists in higher minds.
2. those who are conscious of *a* continuousness, but not only not of their whole continuousness, but who do not make that consciousness of a continuousness an object of a secondary consciousness – i.e. who are not endued with reflex Faculties.
3. those who tho' not conscious of the whole of their continuousness, are yet both conscious of *a* continuousness, & make that the object of a reflex consciousness – And of this third Class the Species are infinite; and the first or lowest, as far as we know, is Man, or the human Soul.[65]

If Coleridge is protected from subjective idealism by the absurdity of a perceiver without a perceived, and vice versa, he further protects himself by another clarification of the situation of the perceiver. Subjective solipsism gains most of its force from a sophism which involves taking the perceiver as individual, and *only* as individual. Hence each perceiver is left with a world of his own, and this solipsism is one of the most objectionable features to Coleridge of subjectivism.[66] Its corollary, the denial of the independent reality of objects, is also somewhat odious to the facts of ordinary experience.[67] As long as the perceiver is conceived of as within the bounds of the individual alone, the chasm between minds and beings is unbridgeable. But Coleridge believed this conception to be arbitrary and utterly without grounds. If it is said that 'man is the measure of all things' one may choose to mean 'each man', but one may also signify by 'man' the species, of which every individual is a representative. Men share prominent structural features with each other which are in part responsible for the world perceived, and it is reasonably deducible that men perceive to a large degree a common world. Certain perceptions are undoubtedly individualistic, since man is bounded to some extent by his individuality; being not merely individuals but also men, humans share a great number of experiences. However much the 'world' may be a product of interaction of a subject and object, Coleridge is by no means saddled with solipsism as a result of idealism.[68]

It is the failure to recognize this distinction between man as individual and man as species which leads to a denial of an important distinction which Coleridge makes between subjective idealism and an idealism that is not prone to subjectivism. For Coleridge as for Kant, the world can be appearance without destroying the independence of objects and the commonness of our experiences. Coleridge showed moreover through his 'One life' theme that the boundaries may be further extended to encompass the idea that man is also an animal, and more extensively, a member of the class of living creatures, as well as simply a being. Though his experienced world is undoubtedly to some extent anthropomorphically conceived, it is also equally undoubtedly shared in some measure with every other being. For Coleridge, the point at which we choose to call this world objective is a matter of preference and in no way suggests that at any point the 'world-in-itself' is experienced. As Coleridge indicates in 'On the Philosophic Import of the Words OBJECT and SUBJECT', the meaning of the distinction between objective and subjective becomes blurred, without some context or relative referent.[69] By 'objective' we must come to mean 'shared by other percipients', not 'absolutely independent of perception'. The latter formulation is an erroneous conclusion drawn from the perspective of a naive realism which fails to take into account the medium of the mind's faculties functioning between itself and the noumenon. Coleridge no longer needs to postulate a Berkeleian Supreme Mind to sustain the parts of the world which are not being perceived at a given time, and the first hints of the Coleridgean 'One life' theme are emerging.[70]

A similar though more formal protection from subjective idealism we may designate as 'relative dualism'. Coleridge's analysis of the possibility of experience shows him that the perceived should be understood to be a product of the mind-in-itself and the thing-in-itself interacting, though of these two 'entities' we can know nothing. We cannot even know that they exist, and must set them up merely as logical entities demanded by a language of subject and object differentiation. This differentiation must be taken not strictly, but as a convenience of expression. Coleridge is still left with a dualism within the continuity of appearance: the inner appearances (thoughts, sensations, memories, judgments, etc.) distinguished from the spatial objects outside us – the outer appearances. Coleridge characterizes this distinction as between 'Thought and Thing':

First, then what is the difference or distinction between THING and THOUGHT? ... In other words, what do we mean by REALITY? – I answer – that there exist a class of notices which have all a ratio of vividness each with the other, so that tho' the one may be more vivid than the other, yet in the sane and ordinary course of nature, they are all alike contra-distinguishable to another class of notices, which are felt and conceived as dependent on the former, and to be to them in some sort as a stamp on paper is to a seal sharp-cut in hard Stone. The first class we call *Things & Realities*; and find in them – not indeed absolutely, but in a sense which we all *understand* – ... a *permanency*, and *expectability* so great, as to be capable of being contra-distinguished both by these, and by their *vividness* to the second class, that is our Thoughts, which therefore as appearing posterior & faint we deem the Images & imperfect Shadows of the former.[71]

Coleridge further explains that ideas, in the strict Platonic sense, are thoughts of a transcendent mind, from which proceed all things in a way analogous to that by which *our* thoughts proceed from things, his ideas being however incomparably more actual than things.

In insisting that all knowledge is of experience, Coleridge need not deny the existence and distinctness of external objects, as subjective idealists are said to do. He must simply deny that external objects are objects in themselves, that is, that externality is a quality of objects absolutely independent of perception. It was to explain the possibility of experience of external objects that Kant formulated his doctrine that space and time are *a priori* conditions of sensuous intuition. If spatiality cannot be a property of objects in themselves (since if it were we could not experience it), it must be a *condition* of experience (or sensuous intuition) in general.[72] Such a view would make it possible to account for the certainty of geometry and mathematics, or, as Kant called it, their *a priori* synthetic character.[73] And it would also explain how, knowledge being necessarily of appearance and not of absolutes, we still have experience of objects as external or separate from ourselves. Kant further explained that the concepts which were not derived from experience, such as necessity and causality, were categorizing functions of the mind, but experienced only when coupled with sensuous content.[74]

This relative duality Kant formulates according to the conditions of sensuous intuition: objects of externality are conditioned by the forms both of space and time, while objects of inner determination are regulated by the intuition of time only. Neither is an experience of absolutes, for the very meaning of experience and knowing implies a medium which precludes the possibility of anything except appearance.[75] To Coleridge this conception of space and time had as its most 'negative' or 'critical' effect (in the Kantian sense of these words)[76] the consequence of reducing the notion of reality as 'behind' appearance, or 'outside' us, to non-sense.[77] That cold, lifeless, colourless, odourless substance supposed to be the unperceivable ground of the world when stripped of all its accidental qualities is exposed by Coleridge as the fiction of an *abstracting* mind, for space is subjective, i.e., a condition of the perceiver, not the perceived.[78] Nor, Coleridge insists, is the noumenon, the real, 'in' our minds, for it has nothing to do with spatial conceptions. The same considerations apply to time. Hence the here and the now are phenomenal characteristics, not noumenal ones.[79] The 'real', Coleridge sees as being free of such properties, since they belong entirely to appearance. The empirical world is real, then, relative to the senses and understanding, to those faculties, as Kant says, which can give us constitutive knowledge. But that world is not the real as absolutely independent of the faculties of sense. Though it may be the only real that can be known, it is a relative functional real, an appearance, and, as Coleridge and Kant insist, not the noumenon which the mind in its metaphysical flights of speculation seeks to encompass.

It must have been this distinction between appearance and noumenon, and the corresponding analysis of space and time as the conditions of sensuous intuition and experience, which helped Coleridge to formulate his objection to Hartleian associationism. Hartley's error according to Coleridge was his mistaking the conditions of a thing for its causes and essence:

Contemporaneity is the *limit and condition* of the laws of mind, itself being rather a law of matter, at least of phenomena considered as material. At the utmost, it is to thought the same, as the law of gravitation is to loco-motion.[80]

Contemporaneity as the common condition of association is present in all association, and the naive conclusion is that this constant presence is the essence. Coleridge restates the general law of association to say that

whatever makes certain parts of a total impression more vivid or distinct than the rest, will determine the mind to recall these in preference to others equally linked together by the common condition of contemporaneity, or (what I deem a more appropriate and philosophical term) of *continuity*. But the will itself by confining and intensifying the attention may arbitrarily give vividness or distinctness to any object whatsoever.[81]

To recapitulate, in seeking the cause of experience, the noumenon of phenomena, the real of the appearance, Coleridge rejected the cause as material, and rejected the priority given to nature – that it was more real than mind.[82] We have traced his reasons for rejecting the *finite* mind as the reality prior to nature: the inner world of impressions is as much appearance as the outer world of external objects, or things. The chasmic dichotomy between the two is bridged by a relative distinction, with the continuity unbroken, and mind and nature are tentatively reunited.[83] In order to strengthen the unity Coleridge presumes that a long process of familiarization with the new view must occur. The continual onslaughts of habitual 'outness prejudice' must be met with a repetition of the thinking which led to its logical rejection, until that rejection becomes itself familiar, and the *sensation* as well as the sense is experienced.[84] Since mind and nature mutually include everything that we conceive to exist, and represent the totality of being, Coleridge seeks the real in something that is neither the one nor the other, but that which is common to both as the ground.[85] A modern and adequate formulation of this position of reconciliation, which expressed the scientific developments in magnetism and electricity, was found in the law of polarity.

After exposing the inadequacies of materialism, empiricism and the mechanistic and atomistic 'psilosophies', and after rejecting the alternatives of dualism and solipsistic idealism, the *Biographia* leads up through chapter twelve to the statement in chapter thirteen of polarity and the 'two forces of one power'. It is in these two chapters that the sources from Schelling are most evident. Coleridge prefers in the *Biographia* to refer to the philosophy of polarity not by means of the polarity metaphor, but by means of the ancient phrase 'coincidence of opposites', or 'two forces of one power'. It was in these terms that he claimed to rediscover the 'polar' philosophy 'first promulgated by Heraclitus, 2000 years afterwards republished, and made the foundation both of Logic, of Physics, and of Metaphysics by Giordano Bruno'.[86]

SCHELLING

Coleridge's use of Schelling in *Biographia* chapters twelve and thirteen is well known. His adoption of the idea of polarity is the aspect of these borrowings which will concern us here. In this discussion we will be moving away from the analysis of sources toward an emphasis on Coleridge's *use* of sources (as method) or their function (as processes). Coleridge's use of his sources, especially the near verbatim borrowings and the quotations, is one example of a method, the character of which is to be indicated more fully in the three chapters below on the *Biographia's* structure. The occurrence of quotations and the borrowings are a particular feature of the *Biographia* which give it the surface appearance of a collage or mosaic of passages from the most diverse philosophies and which give it its 'syncretic' character. But it should be stressed that there is for Coleridge a vital distinction between syncretism and synthesis.[87] This distinction is also vital to a method which cannot be adequately formulated by a metaphor of a mosaic. For 'mosaic' is an instance of mere juxtaposition, in contrast to transformation and true interpenetration of parts to form a whole. It is an adoption of the syncretic over the synthetic, and is diametrically opposed to the central Coleridgean conception of the vital relation of part to whole, a relation which is the basis of the connection between organicism and the philosophy of essential dualism, which is expressed in the one life theme.

In the *Biographia* we find that Coleridge thought it the highest perfection of philosophy that it should be at the same time poetry. It was important for Coleridge to hold the two forms, philosophy and poetry, in a balance of reconciliation (as we shall try to show fully in chapter seven below). It may then be possible to understand the Schelling borrowings not merely as expressions of philosophic dogma, but also as valuable for their 'poetic' significance as method: they have been borrowed because they are examples of metaphoric situations which Coleridge used throughout the *Biographia* as his method of engaging the reader in dialectic (see below chapter five). They function precisely as the various borrowings of poetry in *Biographia* ii function, as *instances* (in Coleridge's pregnant sense[88]), as 'living parts' of the *Biographia* because they express through their own miniature design the structure of the work. In each case the fancy/imagination distinction is realized only by the identification process which calls into play the true mode of dialectic, the move from subject–object separation up to a unified transcendent level of apprehension, by means of metaphor which finds identity in difference, and expresses the 'unknown' in terms of the known, the 'other' in terms of the self.

The following passage from Schelling is an example of a metaphor characterizing the movement of the mind in the throes of dialectic which Coleridge has described for us several times in the metaphor of the snake, of the progress of the water insect, and of the act of leaping.[89] We also cannot fail to notice that the passage is metaphoric of the mind's activity in striving to apprehend, and that it can only be fully appreciated if the experience, or *feeling* as Coleridge would say, of the mind striving to expand infinitely (unify, synthesize, and reconcile the object with itself) while contracting (diversifying, distinguishing, objectifying) accompanies the linguistic formulation of it. Metaphor encourges this synthesis:

grant me a nature having two contrary forces, the one of which tends to expand infinitely, while the other strives to apprehend or *find* itself in this infinity, and I will cause the world of intelligences with the whole system of their representations to rise up before you. Every other science presupposes intelligence as already existing and complete: the philosopher contemplates it in its growth, and as it were represents its history to the mind from its birth to its maturity.[90]

Just as we will suggest in chapter six that with respect to the method of the *Biographia*, the full value of the poetic borrowings in volume two lay not in their beauty as poems in themselves, but in a larger context, as symbolic parts of the *Biographia*, we also want to suggest here that the same 'expansion' of context, and hence significance, is operative in these borrowed passages of philosophy. An entirely new level of perception and of self-consciousness is required to see that this expansion/contraction metaphor is not applicable merely to the forces of external nature, but that more importantly this is the description of the forces of intelligence in the human mind, struggling, for example, to apprehend this metaphor, forces which operate to organize the world of external nature, including the text of the *Biographia* as an instance of that external world. Moreover, the object of the *Biographia* is also to contemplate the growth of intelligence of the mind from its birth to its maturity.[91] Hence the Schelling passage has been chosen for its appropriateness, not only as descriptive of the purposes or material of the *Biographia*, but also as an instance of its structural design of employing at crucial moments extended metaphors to 'cap' the preceding discursive material. It is noteworthy that the Schelling passage follows three other passages, mixing poetry and philosophy, all expressive of the counteracting forces and their progression toward reconciliation.

Coleridge came to criticize Schelling harshly for what he believed to be a lack of a true trinary character in a system which ultimately reduced itself to a pantheistic philosophy. The borrowed passages in the *Biographia* I, are often assumed to be somehow at odds with that later rejection. J. H. Green found it puzzling that Coleridge used Schelling in the *Biographia*, for he believed that Coleridge had already seen this crucial defect in the German.[92] The consistency of Coleridge's position becomes clear once the notion is given up that he was using Schelling in a doctrinaire way, and once it is seen that it was the integrity of the metaphors for his *own* purposes and method of composition which fascinated Coleridge. Indeed, we might maintain that it was the metaphor in Schelling, the intuitive, not the discursive, which Coleridge was trying to capture in these passages. This view is borne out if we notice that immediately following the Schelling passage a short section occurs which constitutes the *completion* of it, raising this passage from its inherent pantheism to a statement of the trinary system. Coleridge was clearly already aware that something was lacking in Schelling's system, though he may not have seen as yet how far the 'disease' went. The Schelling passage appropriately serves merely as a base from which to appeal to Kant's negative quantities and the crucial distinction between contraries and opposites. Thus Coleridge brings Kant into the discussion and thereby introduces the element missing in Schelling, the tertium aliquid which should not be a convenience imposed from without (as Coleridge felt Schelling's was), but which should have its spring and necessity *within* the system. Kant is being used in these pages (*BL*, i, 196–8) as a *corrective* to and *completion* of Schelling. Coleridge carries the scheme even further than Kant, before the chapter breaks off with this dizzying final sentence:

The counteraction then of the two assumed forces does not depend on their meeting from opposite directions; the power which acts in them is indestructible; it is therefore inexhaustibly re-ebullient; and as something must be the result of these two forces, both alike infinite, and both alike indestructible; and as rest or neutralization cannot be this result; no other conception is possible, but that the product must be a tertium aliquid, or finite generation. Consequently this conception is necessary. Now this tertium aliquid can be no other than an inter-penetration of the counteracting powers, partaking of both.[93]

The defect of Schelling is indirectly pointed to in another long passage in chapter twelve which once again immediately follows a borrowing from Schelling. After developing the ten theses, much of which stems from Schelling (*BL*, i, 184–7, theses vii–x), Coleridge has this Heraclitean completion of the two opposite forces still to develop:

It will hereafter be my business to construct by a series of intuitions the progressive schemes, that must follow from such a power with such forces, till I arrive at the fulness of the *human* intelligence. For my present purpose I *assume* such a power as my principle, in order to deduce from it a faculty, the generation, agency, and application of which forms the contents of the ensuing chapter.[94]

Kant is then appealed to once again immediately following a Schelling borrowing, to complete and correct Schelling, and once again Coleridge expands the use of 'intuition' (which is at the root of his difference with Kant on the nature of ideas as merely regulative or also constitutive)[95] and carries metaphysics into divinity.[96] Throughout these several theses we can point to a broader context of self-consciousness in which both the synthesis of subject and object, and the insistence that self-consciousness is nature and our ultimate object of attention, express the relation of the reader to a text. We will emphasize below that the reader's own mind and intellectual processes are one important subject-matter of the *Biographia,* just as is suggested by the Schelling theses on self-consciousness. It is also clear that the process of self-consciousness involves reunification of the subject–object dualism, which is expressive of the romantic aesthetic of art, the unification of the text and the reading mind discussed in chapter four below. To realize this further context is to see the subject–object distinction as a metaphor for the relation of the reader to the text (hence the relevance of the metaphor of polarity for art), just as it is also a metaphor for mind and nature. A perception of 'identity in difference' is once again required for an understanding of the significance which is imposed upon these borrowings as metaphoric situations within the context of a composition such as the *Biographia,* which has for its primary purpose the awakening of the faculty of imagination.

An adequate description of the *Biographia* as a unity is also found in the quotation immediately above. This description suggests that the 'whole' of the *Biographia* is in a metaphorical sense, that 'ensuing chapter', or is at least a rewriting of it. The second volume is written in a less philosophical language. But this fact by no means suggests that it is a less adequate or systematic rendition than the one promised as a future work. That power of imagination is necessarily assumed, since it cannot be in any way proved except by being experienced. It is applied in the exercises in practical criticism in *Biographia* ii and it is generated and becomes an agency in the metaphorical situations which occur at critical moments in the discussion and which form the structure and method of the *Biographia* in its functioning as a unity, as we shall try to elaborate more fully in chapter five.

3

Early sources of polarity in Coleridge's thought

It is clear that when Coleridge discovered the metaphor of polarity in Schelling's *System des transcendentalen Idealismus* sometime after 1810, he was enthralled by it. It seems to have focused issues for him and caused a crystallization of ideas. The nature of this crystallizing and unifying process must be precisely determined in order to appreciate the role of polarity in Coleridge's thought.

Coleridge says in the 1817 *Friend*, that:

EVERY POWER IN NATURE AND IN SPIRIT *must evolve an opposite, as the sole means and conditions of its manifestation*: AND ALL OPPOSITION IS A TENDENCY TO RE-UNION. This is the universal Law of Polarity or essential Dualism, first promulgated by Heraclitus, 2000 years afterwards republished, and made the foundation both of Logic, of Physics, and of Metaphysics by Giordano Bruno.[1]

From this short definition three major formulations can be derived. First, opposition with a tendency to reunion, second, essential dualism, and third, polarity, all of which seem to express a single IDEA of unity-in-distinctity. At about the same time Coleridge wrote a letter to C. A. Tulk explaining the dynamic philosophy and concluded:

Accept this very rude sketch of the very rudiments of '*Heraclitus redivivus*' – One little presumption of their truth is, that as Wordsworth, Southey, and indeed all my intelligent Friends well know and attest, I had formed it during the study of Plato, and the Scholars of Ammonius, and in later times of Scotus (Joan. Erigena), Giordano Bruno, Behmen, and the much calumniated Spinoza . . . long beore Schelling had published his first and imperfect view – . If I had met a friend and a Brother in the Desert of Arabia, I could scarcely have been more delighted than I was in finding a fellow-laborer.[2]

The attribution to Heraclitus is not usually taken altogether seriously,[3] for it is tacitly assumed that Coleridge was trying to minimize his debts to Schelling. It is necessary to explore the background of Coleridge's later thought to discover in what sense he might have formed an 'essential dualism' or a philosophy of opposition in coincidence. One fact which seems to cloud the issue is that, according to the *OED* the word 'polarity' was first used only in 1649 by Sir Thomas Browne.[4] How could Heraclitus possibly have promulgated the 'Law of Polarity' if the idea had not even existed? Coleridge also insisted above that Giordano Bruno used it as the foundation of 'Logic, of Physics, and of Metaphysics', and Coleridge couples Bruno with polarity in other writings.[5]

Owen Barfield, in his appendix to *What Coleridge Thought*, has thoroughly explored the question of Bruno's polarity and concludes:

Two questions arise: first, did Bruno in fact ever use the expression, 'Law of Polarity'? and secondly, apart from labels, is there in fact to be found in Bruno anything that is fairly recognisable as the law of polarity as Coleridge propounded it? The first and less important question must almost certainly be answered in the negative. We suggest, though with slightly less confidence, that the second must be answered in the same way. But this raises the whole issue of the difference between Coleridge's law of polarity and the so-called 'coincidence of opposites'.[6]

Bruno was also writing prior to the first recorded use of the word in Latin. Our focus must legitimately shift to a search for an essential dualism in the form of a coincidence of opposites, for as Barfield explains:

the essence of polarity is a *dynamic* conflict between coinciding opposites. Coleridge, as we have seen, cites Heraclitus as the first promulgator of the law of polarity; and the element of conflict, the quality of psychic oppugnancy, between opposites is evident there in a way it hardly is in Bruno...this quality of oppugnancy, considered as the fundamental energy in the life of nature, is far more express in Böhme than in Bruno.[7]

Barfield feels a lack of the *dynamic* in the dualism of Bruno, as well as his immediate precursors, Cusa and Lull. But Coleridge remarks of Bruno:

By Quality Behmen intends that act of each elementary Power, by which it energizes in its particular kind. But in the Deity is an *absolute synthesis of opposites*. Plato in Parmenide and Giordano Bruno passim have spoken many things well on this awful Mystery – the latter more clearly. (My italics.)[8]

It is difficult to be convinced by Barfield's conclusion that Lull, Cusa, and Bruno's coincidence of opposites 'is that of a static relation between finity and infinity rather than that of an energising relation between infinitely expanding and infinitely contracting forces',[9] which Coleridge was left to amplify. Not only is the evidence from these three sources lacking; it is also not clear that a 'coincidence of opposites' can be anything other than dynamic. The conception itself defies a static sense, and is precisely significant in the rejection of a barren dualism for a transcending or coinciding power.

We find further evidence for a non-static interpretation of Lull, Cusa, and Bruno in a summary which Mr Barfield gives of their coincidences with Coleridge:

we are tentatively disposed to detect the following predominant historical correspondences with different aspects of the thought of Coleridge as we have tried to present it. With Lull (the absolute and the relative Principles), the relation between understanding and reason; with Cusa, that relation between the whole and the part, by virtue of which the whole is present in each part, and ultimately the infinite is present in the finite (this is really the sense of Cusa's coincidentia oppositorum); with Bruno himself, the individual creative imagination and, together with that, a more dynamic, 'centro-peripheric' coincidence of opposites, which it remained for Coleridge himself to interpret or develop as a polarity of forces.[10]

The relation of reason to understanding, whole to part in the organic sense, and Coleridge's conception of the creative imagination can all be seen as variant metaphors for polarity. For all are informed by the same IDEA of relation as interpenetration.[11] These *particular* correspondences with Coleridge are most important evidence for the 'essentiality' of the dualism of all three men, and of the dynamic nature of their opposition philosophy.

Although Barfield is somewhat over-cautious here in exploring the connection of polarity with Bruno's logic he later comes to a more assured position. Bruno was an avowed and adamant anti-Aristotelian in logic because Aristotelian logic led only to a metaphysics of quantity. Coleridge clearly understood that to take such a position meant to reject a logic of dichotomy for a trichotomy.[12] It was for him the foundation of all other truths:

The Reasoning on this page might be cited as an apt example of the inconvenience of the Dichotomic Logic ... Two terms in manifest correspondence to each other are yet opposed as contraries, without any middle term; the consequence of which is that one of the 2 becomes a mere negation of the other, ex. gr. Real – Unreal = o ...

Compare *the Logic of* dichotomy with that of Trichotomy, or what is the same, Pythagorean Tetractys. In this we seek first for the Unity, as the only source of Reality, and then for the two opposite yet correspondent forms, by which it manifests itself. For it is an axiom of universal application, that 'Manifestatio non datur, nisi per alterum' ... Thus the finite and infinite are the 2 necessary forms of Being manifested, which can never be divided – the instances in which either is assumed singly, will be found mere abstractions, or else mere forms of subjective imagination, such as are Atom, or Infinite Space.

And what is Space? A something with the attributes of Nothing. But in *real* Science we must say –
1.   Being
      or identity of Finite and Infinite
2.   The Finite in the Infinite)(the Infinite in the Finite[13]

This marginal note puts a great emphasis upon the duality of finite/ infinite to express essential dualism, and yet Barfield criticizes Bruno's 'essential dualism' as less essential because of this very emphasis on the infinite/finite duality.[14] The importance of Bruno's anti-Aristotelian stance in logic cannot be underestimated as an indication of his understanding of the necessity of a dynamic coincidence of opposites for philosophy in general, since the logic is itself the foundation for the metaphysics. Coleridge explains this anti-Aristotelianism:

Plato's words are preparatory exercises for the mind. He leads you to see that propositions involving in themselves a contradiction in terms are nevertheless true; and which, therefore, must belong to a higher logic – that of ideas. They are self-contradictory only in the Aristotelian logic, which is the instrument of the understanding.[15]

Compare this with a similar statement in *Aids to Reflection*:

This is the test and character of a truth so affirmed [a truth of the reason, an Idea] that in its own proper form it is *inconceivable*. For to *conceive* is a function of the understanding, which can be exercised only on subjects subordinate thereto. And yet to the forms of the understanding all truth must be reduced, that is to be fixed as an object of reflection, and to be rendered *expressible*. And here we have a second test and sign of a truth so affirmed, that it can come forth out of the moulds of the understanding only in the disguise of two contradictory conceptions, each of which is partially true, and the conjunction of both conceptions becomes the representative or *expression* (the *exponent*) of a truth *beyond* conception and inexpressible.[16]

Clearly the distinction between Platonic and Aristotelian logic depends upon the reason/understanding distinction, and as well upon the idea of dynamic opposition by which contradiction is transcended. Meaningful paradox is the mode of expression of this transcendence.

Not only was Coleridge aware of the importance and centrality of a new logic (actually a reanimation of the Platonic and Pythagorean). Bruno also realized that it was the basis for opening up the greatest secrets of nature, and says critically of Aristotle: 'remaining with his foot in the *genus* of opposition, he was so fettered that he could not descend to the *species* of contrariety...but wandered at every step, as when he said that contraries could not exist in the same subject'.[17]

It was with logic as the focal point that Coleridge early began his

investigation of the 'Coincidentia oppositorum', the idea of the reconciliation of opposites. By 1803 he had formulated a detailed prospectus of his
'great work' which was to examine the differences between the Aristotelian logic of dichotomy based upon the understanding alone, and the
Platonic, Brunonian, or Baxterian logic of trichotomy based upon the
reason.[18] It was at this time that he mentioned in notebooks and letters
Bruno, Baxter, Boehme and Cusa.[19] In this realization of the necessity of a
logic of trichotomy can be traced Coleridge's first serious investigations of
the metaphysics which were eventually to be restated in terms of the
metaphor so powerfully and innovatively expressive of the dynamic coincidence of opposites, polarity. Well aware as we now are of the implications of rejecting Aristotle for Plato, the description of his great work
takes on the importance in the development of Coleridge's thought
which it has not previously been allowed. In the years of its preparation,
from 1800 through 1803 and 1804, Coleridge sowed the seeds of the
reflection and thought which he was to put into publishable form only
many years later.[20] The long account of his plans he explains:

I entitle [the work] Organum verè Organum, or an Instrument of practical
Reasoning in the business of real life: to which will be prefixed 1. a familiar
INTRODUCTION to the common System of Logic, namely, that of Aristotle and
the Schools. 2. a concise and simple, yet full, Statement of the Aristotelean
Logic, with references annexed to the Authors, and the name and page of the
work, to which each part may be tra[ced], so that it may be at once seen, what
is Aristotle's, what Porphyry, wh[at] the addition of the Greek Commentators,
and what of the Schoolmen. – 3. Outline of the History of Logic in general.
1. Chapt. – The origin of Philosophy in general, and of Logic speciatim.
2. Chapt. Of the Eleatic and Megaric Logic. 3. of the Platonic Logic.
4. of Aristotle, containing a fair account [of] the Ὄργανον of which Dr Reid
in Kaimes' Sketches of man has given a most false, and not only erroneous, but
calumnious Statement – as far as this account had not been anticipated in the
second Part of my work – namely, the concise and simple, yet full, &c. &c. –
5. a philosophical Examination of the Truth, and of the Value, of the Aristotelean System of Logic, including all the after additions to it. 6. on the
characteristic Merits and Demerits of Aristotle and Plato, as Philosophers in
general, and an attempt to explain the fact of the vast influence of the former
during so many ages; and of the influence of Plato's works on the restoration
of the Belles Lettres, and on the reformation. – 7. Raymond Lully. 8. Peter
Ramus. 9. Lord Bacon – or the Verulamian Logic. 10. Examination of the
same, and comparison of it with the Logic of Plato (in which I attempt to make
it probable, that tho' considered by Bacon himself as the antithesis and Antidote
of Plato, it is bona fide the same, and that Plato has been grossly misunderstood.) 10 [sic]. – Des Cartes/11. Condillac – and a philosophical examination
of *his* Logic, i.e. the Logic, which he basely purloined from Hartley. – Then

follows my own Organum verè Organum – which consists of a $\Sigma \acute{\upsilon} \sigma \tau \eta \mu \alpha$ of all *possible* modes of true, probable, and false reasoning, arranged philosophically, i.e., on a strict analysis of those operations and passions of the mind, in which they originate, and by which they act, with one or more striking instances annexed to each from authors of high Estimation – and to each instance of false reasoning, the manner in which the Sophistry is to be detected, and the words, in which it may be exposed...I have thus amply detailed the contents of my work, which has not been the labour of one year or of two/ but the result of many years' meditations, and of very various Reading. – [21]

It is impossible to realize the significance of such a passage unless one is thoroughly acquainted with the centrality of an exchange of a logic of dichotomy for one of trichotomy. The logic of trichotomy, the Platonic, or Verulamian logic, contains the principles of 'essential dualism' and 'opposition with a tendency to reunion' through its requirement of a transcendence of the understanding's law of contradiction. Contraries become *logical* only, and can exist as real only in the form of opposition. These are the issues implicit in this passage, and they become explicit on numerous occasions in addition to those cited above.

In a notebook entry during the Malta trip, Coleridge turns again to the issue of contraries and opposites:

Negative Quantities/=opposed forces. Logical by Contradiction ends in absolute nothing, nihil *negativum*, quod est etiam irrepresentabile – a ball in motion and at the same time not in motion, motion in each sentence having been used in the same sense, is a contradiction in terms/ in Nature it is *not*, or rather say, it *isn't* so as not to give a moments reality by the use of the word per se, is – but there are oppositions without contradiction, and *real* – nihil privativum cogitabile – two tendencies to motion in the same body, one to the N. other to S., being equipollent, the Body remains *in rest*. – the second assumed Tendency is a real negative Quantity – better therefore called, a *privative* Quantity. $-4 \ -5 = -9$ is mere pedantry – there is no real *sub-traction*/ it is true *addition*. – and + have no meaning but as symbols of opposition.[22]

The importance of such an entry as this cannot be ignored, for it is here as early as 1805, in relation to a *Kant* article that Coleridge first discusses opposition in terms of North and South *Poles*, and he uses the word 'equi*pollent*'. We can now easily translate this entry to focus upon the concepts suggested, by dispensing with the N–S Poles or directionals. What is crucial is the idea of two *counteracting* forces, not differentiated from one another merely by direction, but by nature. What is clearly miss-ing is the relation of the two, the possibility of interaction which is not adequately accounted for by the idea of 'rest'.[23] Not many months had passed before Coleridge *had* completed the picture, though, and had hit upon the idea which expressed that mysteriously sublime relation:

The quiet circle in which Change and Permanence *co-exist*, not by combination or juxtaposition, but by an *absolute annihilation of difference* . . . Change without loss – change by a perpetual growth, that <once constitutes & annihilates change> the past, & the future included in the Present// oh! it is aweful. (My italics.)[24]

Here we find the clue to interaction which he was later to develop as *in*difference, interpenetration, copula, synthesis, identity, etc. We find in this passage the production and dynamism that polarity must express in the image of growth, the image of the circle, and the transcendence of *Time*.[25]

Putting these two passages together, both of which were prior to mid-1806, we discover a striking similarity with a passage in the *Biographia*. This passage has a pivotal position, leading up to the analysis of imagination in chapter thirteen which is then broken off. Only the short statement on imagination as primary and as secondary, as distinguished from fancy, remains. In speaking of Kant, Coleridge says:

Opposites, he well observes, are of two kinds, either logical, that is, such as are absolutely incompatible; or real, without being contradictory. The former he denominates Nihil negativum irrepresentabile, the connection of which produces nonsense. A body in motion is something – A liquid cogitabile; but a body, at one and the same time in motion and not in motion, is nothing, or, at most, air articulated into nonsense. But a motory force of a body in one direction, and an equal force of the same body in an opposite direction is not incompatible, and the result, namely, rest, is real and representable . . . Now the transcendental philosophy demands; first that two forces should be conceived which counteract each other by their essential nature; . . . secondly, that these forces should be assumed to be both alike infinite, both alike indestructible . . . the results or generations to which their interpenetration gives existence, in the living principle and in the process of our own self-consciousness.[26]

Coleridge speaks on several occasions in the *Biographia* about the interaction of forces. Some of those remarks have a definitely Schellingian flavour.[27] Another passage besides the Kantian one above suggests the connection of the fancy/imagination distinction with the idea of opposite forces, and ultimately with polarity:

There are evidently two powers at work, which relatively to each other are active and passive; and this is not possible without an intermediate faculty, which is at once both active and passive. (In philosophical language, we must denominate this intermediate faculty in all its degrees and determinations, the IMAGINATION. But, in common language, and especially on the subject of poetry, we appropriate the name to a superior degree of the faculty, joined to a superior voluntary control over it.)[28]

This statement is prophetic of the eventual distinction in chapter thirteen between primary and secondary imagination: *relative* to secondary imagination, primary imagination seems to be passive – it provides the materials which imagination (in its ordinary sense) transforms into new representations and new unities. But *essentially*, primary imagination, perception, is also active and one in *kind* with secondary imagination. The very act of perception requires at once a relatively passive faculty which becomes the object, and a relatively active faculty which as subject perceives the object. The two forces, primary and secondary, are, at ground, of the same kind. Perception appears to be passive because its activity occurs at levels below the consciousness. Hence its objects seem 'given', external, and independent of perception.

This relatively passive faculty can maintain its integrity only as long as the secondary faculty of action supervenes. When it fails, the perception stagnates into a proxy of its former essential activity. It produces a scenario of images and memories without any potential for transformation or for integral unity. Fancy, the mode of memory freed from time and space, sets in. In this passage we can see how a formulation or a *metaphor* of interpenetration via a *mediatory* power contains not only the distinction between the power and its relative forces, but also the distinction between the forces as opposition. It also contains the distinction between the forces with the power supervening, and the forces stagnating in division from the power. At the time that Coleridge was first formulating his fancy/imagination distinction, he was deeply immersed in the distinction between contraries and opposites and the logic of the understanding or dichotomy as opposed to the logic of reason, trichotomy.[29] The relation of fancy to imagination is one more form of the relation expressed by these formulations and by polarity. Imagination interpenetrates the fancy, working with it to embody universals in images to produce those vehicles of intuitive knowledge which Coleridge designated by symbol, and which Shelley called metaphors. Though the concept of two forces is mentioned explicitly only two or three times in *Biographia* i, the idea occurs implicitly on several significant occasions, as for example in Coleridge's description of what we do when we leap, what we do in remembering, in his metaphor of the water insect, and, in volume two, in the snake metaphor, all examples of the metaphoric situations, to be discussed below.[30]

An entry in a notebook of 1817 is evidence of Coleridge's continuing experimentation with the 'Coincidentia oppositorum', even after he had become familiar with the metaphor of polarity. We can see from this entry that the former is still an effective device for relating:

The best pledge of Impartial Intentions is given by him who begins by proposing one or more fundamental Principles – and afterwards judges of the Particulars that fall under his notice by their greater or less co-incidence with these Principles or with the Rules plainly deduced therefrom. And this will be strengthened into strong presumption of Impartiality in the Judgements themselves, if in these Principles he should have discovered the common ground which containing the positive truth which exists partially in each of two contending Opinions suggests the source and explanation of the error in both... For we have it in evidence as fact, that the most influencive Errors have ever been...partial Truths mistaken for the whole Truth, Truths divorced from their correspondent and supporting opposites, and converted into contrary Falsehoods by being reciprocally unbalanced and disintegrated...he alone deserves the name of a Philosopher, who has attained to see and learnt to supply the difference between Contraries that preclude, and Opposites that reciprocally suppose and require, each the other.[31]

Coleridge goes on to apply this concept to *Church and State*, but breaks off in mid-sentence. A look in *Church and State* shows that he took it up again many years later in relation to the two forces of permanence and of progression:

Permit me to draw your attention to the essential difference between *opposite* and *contrary*. Opposite powers are always of the same kind, and tend to union, either by equipoise or by a common product. Thus the + and − poles of the magnet, thus positive and negative electricity are opposites. Sweet and sour are opposites; sweet and bitter are contraries. The feminine character is *opposed* to the masculine; but the effeminate is its *contrary*. Even so in the present instance, the interest of permanence is opposed to that of progressiveness; but so far from being contrary interests, they, like the magnetic forces, suppose and require each other. Even the most mobile of creatures, the serpent, makes a *rest* of its own body, and drawing up its voluminous train from behind on this fulcrum, propels itself onward. On the other hand, it is a proverb in all languages, that (relatively to man at least) what would stand still must retrograde.[32]

We see in this passage that Coleridge has combined the opposition/contrary distinction with a metaphor of the serpent's movement and the need for a fulcrum and rest, which is for Coleridge 'no unapt emblem of the mind's self-experience in the act of thinking', that is, the emblem for imaginative awareness.[33] The 'rest' as fulcrum is interpenetrated by the forward force of propulsion, which suggests the metaphor of relation expressed by polarity and the principle of opposition.

In the notebook entry quoted above Coleridge has drawn a close parallel between mistaking a part for the whole or divorcing truths from 'their correspondent and supporting opposites, and being converted into contrary Falsehoods by being reciprocally unbalanced and disintegrated...' This immediately gives us the clue that the relation of part to whole in the true and organic sense is one more way of formulating the nature of opposition as simultaneously a tendency to reunion, i.e., the law of polarity. The whole is analogous to the power, the part to the forces. The former interpenetrates, informs, and is the *being* of the parts, whose existence is evolved in relation to each other. They are distinct, yet each part tends toward reunion through the grounding power of the whole. This is best characterized in Coleridge's definition of the symbol: 'It always partakes of the Reality which it renders intelligible; and while it enunciates the whole, abides itself as a living part in that Unity, of which it is the representative.'[34] The symbol is the educt of imagination, and the symbol of the part/whole expresses once again the relation which constitutes imaginative, intuitive knowledge.

We have tried to show that polarity is a term which acts as a focal point around which a number of relations revolve, such as the distinctions between imagination/fancy, part/whole, symbol/allegory, organic/mechanical, and opposition/contrariety. The relation which was most central to Coleridge we have not yet dealt with explicitly in relation to polarity, but it was implicit throughout and is the reason/understanding distinction. Coleridge talks about the understanding enlightened by reason, or of the reason as like an expression pervading the different features of an intelligent countenance, or like the mind which, containing its thoughts, is present in and through them all.[35] He speaks of the impregnation of the understanding by the reason and of the reason as a power 'supervening': 'Perhaps the safer use of the term, understanding, for general purposes, is, to take it as the mind, or rather as the man himself considered as a concipient as well as a percipient being, and reason as a power supervening.'[36] Thus the reason/understanding becomes another expression of the power/force relation, or the idea of opposition in union. Whether the metaphor of polarity actually supersedes the metaphor of the coincidence of opposites in any other sense than that it is a restatement in modern terms of an old idea is questionable.

Coleridge's interest in the essential idea of opposition which informs all of the above stated relations goes back to his earliest studies in metaphysics. One more of his favourite expressions corroborates this view. It is the proverb which he found so delightful and at times so gripping, one which we tend to take rather too sanguinely and without an insight into the principle which it expresses. The proverb, 'Extremes Meet', can be seen as important in being another metaphor for the reconciliation of opposites. As early as 1802 Coleridge was captivated by the power of this succinct little phrase: 'It is an old proverb that Extremes meet, and I have often regretted that I had not noted down as they occurred the interesting

Instances, in which the Proverb is verified.'[37] A year later he had become even more convinced of the pregnancy of the proverb:

I have repeatedly said, that I could have made a Volume, if only I had noted down, as they occurred to my Recollection of observations, the instances of the Proverb, Extremes Meet/ – This Night, Sunday, Dec. 11, 1803, ½ past 11, I have determined to devote the last 9 pages of my Pocket book to the collection of the same.

EXTREMES MEET . . .[38]

A few years later in September 1807 we find a notation which is still more pertinent to our interest in the relation of the proverb to the idea of two opposite forces. Coleridge connects it here directly with the forces which he used again and again in the *Biographia* as a metaphor of self-consciousness, rest and motion:

Rest, Motion – O ye strange Locks of intricate Simplicity, who shall find the Key? He shall throw wide open the Portals of the Palace of Sensuous or Symbolical Truth; and the Holy of Holies will he find in the Adyta. Rest = Enjoyment, and Death! Motion = Enjoyment and Life! O the depth of the Proverb, Extremes meet![39]

By 1809, in the fifth number of *The Friend*, the significance of the proverb took on the proportion of a central focus which polarity eventually had: 'Extremes meet – a proverb, by the bye, to collect and explain all the instances and exemplifications of which, would constitute and exhaust all philosophy.'[40] This claim may be no exaggeration, for the proverb can act as the expression of the idea of relation *par excellence*. The proverb occurs later in the second *Lay Sermon*, and in *Aids to Reflection*, and is kept in the rifacimento of *The Friend* in 1817.[41] Coleridge's interest in it never abated.

The law of polarity is a formulation which also expresses the nature of relation *par excellence*; it does so effectively by being at once a definition and an example of that relation which constitutes a knowledge construct, as opposed to the factum, or datum, or atom of the mechanist. Coleridge calls the various distinctions discussed above 'Relations or polarities, . . . so many organs of thought, . . . so many intellectual *Senses*'.[42] He explains:

An IDEA therefore contemplates the Alpha and the Omega (One – all; Finite – Infinite; Subject – Object; Mind – Matter; Substance – Form; Time – Space; Motion – Rest; Futuration – Presence; (or vice versa, Being – Becoming; &c &c – and it is indifferent which of the Pairs you take, *for they all are Symbols of the same Truth produced by different Positions*) as One – in other words, it contemplates them in the Copula of their Identity, and so far it belongs to the Eternal *Relations* of Things. . . Thus it is evident, that the same Truths may be taught in a great variety of Symbols. (My italics.)[43]

The distinctions discussed above are examples of these 'Pairs' or 'Symbols of the same Truth'. Polarity too is one of these, more central only because it is *less* 'position-specific' than some. Even it must still be a position and not an absolute, and in this sense it is in no way transcendent to the pairs. It is certainly no less involved in a position (that is, is no more a universal metaphor) than the 'Coincidentia oppositorum' of Heraclitus and Bruno, Cusa, and Lull, and of Plato's highest logic. As a fresh metaphor it can awaken us to a greater sensitivity to the importance of the relation which all the old metaphors express. They have become familiar, and may have lost the power of truth for stimulating the mind to grasp the idea expressed. But Coleridge seems correct in thinking that the idea expressed by polarity is as old as thought itself.

His enthusiasm for Schelling can in part be explained by the excitement he must have felt in discovering in the *System des Transcendentalen Idealismus* a modern reformulation of this ancient and compelling wisdom. Similarly, his disenchantment with Schelling focused on this same central point, for he accuses Schelling of 'burning [the Candle] at both ends'.[44] He says that 'by stealing-in the empirical Law of Polarity he has counterfeited a more successful appearance [than Kant]'.[45] According to Coleridge, Schelling's error was in postulating polarity of the absolute, while the concept of the reconciliation of opposites explicitly denies such an absolute duality. In this sense, it may be a more effective formulation, for while polarity need not be so interpreted, it is arguably vulnerable to such an erroneous interpretation.

4

⫸⫷

Irony and indirectness: the German philosophy of art

In the following chapters we will suggest that a method of metaphor and a process of irony act as structural unities in the *Biographia* to give coherence to the surface fragmentation of the work. In view of the centrality of imagination and symbol in Coleridge's thought, the method of metaphor seems to be a plausible account, in spite of the problematic aspects of imagination (the faculty which evolves metaphors) discussed in a subsequent chapter. Irony is a structural principle less easily acceptable to an English (or American) public, even when it is proposed as a process (such as the reading process), which is less under the conscious control of an artist than 'method' implies. In this chapter we will suggest that the reluctance to accept irony as a significant aspect of Coleridge's works stems primarily from a misunderstanding of the present use of the term, and from a lack of familiarity with the philosophic/aesthetic tradition of Karl Solger, Friedrich Schlegel, and Ludwig Tieck, with which Coleridge had much in common. In the tradition of German aesthetics (and in the Socratic–Platonic basis of the German tradition), the concept of irony takes on a more profound sense than the usual English usage, even when irony is discussed as 'dramatic'. The Socratic–Germanic tradition used the concept of irony to suggest a *principle* of art which encompassed aesthetic/ creative experience often without the awareness or willingness of the author or spectator. How the artist (and spectator) could remain unaware of irony while it was operating at critical levels of his works we will try to show by examining the German aesthetic concept of irony, its influences upon Coleridge (influences developed both theoretically and practically), and Coleridge's close thematic connections with Karl Solger. The concept of irony explored in this chapter will be seen to be an outgrowth of the metaphysics discussed in chapters two and three. Ideas of polarity and opposition, self-consciousness, and the mind as creative in perception, the relation of mind and nature, thought to thing, art to reality, all have their

59

corresponding roles to play in this theory of art as inherently ironic, that is, as involving the critical posture of a spectator–artist within the work of art.

Ironic interpretation of literary works in virtually all periods of English literature has grown immensely over the past forty years, especially in relation to Donne, to Shakespeare, to the first half of the eighteenth century and to the modern period. Even Chaucer, some medieval works, and the latter half of the nineteenth century have not been excluded from ironic interpretation. The period of romanticism in England is notable only for its general exclusion from this critical perspective, with the single exception of Byron and a few scattered and infrequent references to Wordsworth and Keats.[1] Any remarks made about the other Romantics, including Blake, are at best sketchy and undeveloped. With regard to Coleridge particularly there seems to be no occasion on which his name is linked with irony, unless it is to deny any connection.

During this upsurge of interest in ironic interpretation a complementary study of the concept of irony has been progressing, and efforts are being made to clarify the term and classify its various manifestations. In any such study one invariably confronts the complex and vast field of material known as German Romantic Irony. This field includes the writings of such Germans as the Schlegels, Solger, Tieck, Jean Paul Richter, Adam Müller, Novalis, and Goethe. Until recently, the vast realm of theoretical writings of these writers on aesthetics and on irony in particular has been generally ignored in England, perhaps because the theory required a degree of familiarity and interest in the metaphysics upon which it was based.[2] In 1960 this deficiency was to some extent rectified with the publication of Ingrid Strohschneider-Kohrs's *Romantische Ironie in Theorie und Gestaltung*.[3] The author not only tries to focus upon the concept of irony, but also seeks in a detailed analysis to show the variations in theory amongst the major German Romantics.

Even now, the results of such a study, based as it was upon a long tradition of interest in Germany in the Romantic theory of aesthetics, have not been assimilated into the *English* critical tradition, as almost any casual examination of recent works on irony will show. Although these recent studies have certainly made some advances upon earlier ones, they have failed to absorb the consequences for a concept of irony which the work of the German Romantic Ironists and subsequent German secondary literature has made available. The effect of this failure to grasp the most profound levels of meaning of this Romantic concept has been to obscure the intimate relation between the English Romantic poets and irony[4] – a relationship which is central to the design of the works of this period. Its misapprehension has led to considerable misunderstanding of Romantic texts, and all too frequently to a disparagement of them based on notions which are antithetical to the way the works are designed to function within experience.[5]

The most important lengthy study of irony to come out recently, Muecke's *The Compass of Irony* (1969), is subject to precisely this criticism.[6] Muecke makes a more sustained effort than usual to come to terms with the concept of Romantic irony developed by the Germans in their theoretical writings on aesthetics and metaphysics. Yet he fails to articulate the aspects of the theory which would lead to the core of the concept of irony and its radical consequences for any theory of art and creativity (and of perception and knowledge). This superficial grasp of irony leads to that misapprehension of its application to the English Romantic poets which we have come to expect. For although Muecke mentions Shelley and Wordsworth, his main example of irony in the Romantic period is Byron,[7] and, as will become clear, this preference for Byron is a sign that the concept of irony is not completely understood. Muecke's conclusion with regard to Coleridge is to exclude him firmly from any ironic appreciation:

Coleridge, his thought dominated by concepts of subordination, reconciliation, and unity, has not fully emerged from the 'closed world', whereas Schlegel with ironies of 'unresolved conflicts' is quite evidently governed by a concept of 'open-mindedness'. For Coleridge, the function of the imagination is, as it were, to enclose the chaotic world in a perfect harmonious sphere: For Schlegel, its function is to present the chaos and transcend it, and then to present the transcendence and transcend that, substituting for Coleridge's circle an upward and forward pointing arrow.[8]

This description misapprehends Coleridge's method. If irony seems out of keeping with the romantic temperament, and Coleridge's in particular, we may recall that for the German Romantic Ironist, and for Socrates, the posture of irony is a posture of the most sincere earnestness, however satirical, sarcastic, or humorous it may appear on the surface.[9]

THE COMMON/HIGH IRONY DISTINCTION

The most fundamental aspect of the concept of irony developed by the Germans is the distinction between common and higher irony. The purpose of the German distinction is to establish from the outset that what is meant by 'irony' is something more significant and philosophically more important than mere satire, buffoonery, or sarcasm. Irony may manifest itself through these 'devices' but it need not. Nor is an apprehension of them a sign that the reader has grasped the irony of the text in its more 'Romantic' sense. This distinction is no doubt quite familiar to the English ironologist, but it is not sufficiently clear to the English literary critic in general, who when he hears the word 'irony' unconsciously assumes that he is about to be confronted by the sarcasm, satire and humour character-istic of 'common' irony. If these are not present, he rejects the possibility of its presence. Friedrich Schlegel makes it clear how inappropriate such a rejection is, when he insists that no things are more unlike than satire, polemic, and irony, since irony in the Romantic sense is *self*-criticism ('Selbstpolemik') transcended.[10]

It is from Tieck that we get the most explicit statements about the distinction between common and higher irony:

In den meisten Definitionen wird die Ironie zu einseitig genommen, ich möchte sagen zu prosaisch, zu materiell. Hegel hat Solger in diesem Punkte missverstanden. Er fasst es so auf, als habe Solger an die gemeine Ironie gedacht, an jene grobe Ironie Swifts. Aber schon aus Plato kann man wissen, dass es noch eine ganz andere höhere gibt.[11]

[In most definitions irony is understood too onesidedly, I might say, too prosaically, too materially. Hegel misunderstood Solger in this respect. He assumes that Solger was thinking of common irony – that crude irony of Swift. Yet one can know from Plato that there exists another far higher irony.]

As Oskar Walzel insists in his article on method and irony in F. Schlegel and Solger, 'Höhere Ironie sei nicht Spott, Hohn, Persiflage und ähnliches, sondern tiefster Ernst, der zugleich mit Scherz und wahrer Heiterkeit verbunden, sei, sei nicht bloss negativ, auch durchaus positiv.'[12] ['High irony is not mockery, derision, persiflage, or anything similar to these; but is rather the most profound earnestness, which at the same time is bound up with joking and true joviality. It is not merely negative, but also through and through positive.'] Tieck connects higher irony with the irony of Shakespeare, Aristophanes, Plato and Socrates:

Wie soll denn die höhere Ironie des Aristophanes oder gar des Shakespear, von so vielen Lesern gefasst werden?...Uber dem Ganzen eines platonischen Dialogs (nehmen wir nur das Gastmahl) schwebt doch wohl eine höhere geistiger Ironie, als sich etwa in Sokrates scheinbarer Unwissenheit verkündigt. Und wie wollen denn Kritiker oder Philosophen jene letzte Vollendung eines poetischen Kunstwerks, die Gewähr und den höchsten Beweis der ächten Begeisterung, jenen Äthergeist, der, so sehr er das Werk bis in seine Tiefen hinab mit Liebe durchdrang, doch befriedigt und unbefangen über dem Ganzen schwebt, und es von dieser Höhe nur (so wie der Geniessende) erschaffen und fassen kann, nennen? Wenn wir die Vorstellung nicht mit Solger, oder mit Friedrich Schlegel – (wie dieser es früher im Athenäum schon andeutete) Ironie nennen sollen, so gebe und erfinde der Einsichtige einen anderen Namen.[13]

[How should the higher irony of Aristophanes or even Shakespeare be understood by so many readers? ... Over the whole of a Platonic dialogue (take just the *Symposium*) hovers a higher intellectual irony than is communicated even in Socrates's apparent ignorance. And how do the critics or philosophers want to name that final completion of a poetic work of art, the guarantee and the highest proof of true inspiration, that aetherspirit, which however much it penetrates into the depths of the work with love, nevertheless hovers satiated and unconstrained over the whole – the whole which can only be created and grasped from this height alone. If we should not name the concept irony, with Solger and Friedrich Schlegel (as this latter earlier meant it in the Athenäum), then some prudent man can give and invent another name.]

We might meet this challenge that if we do not mean by 'irony' what is commonly meant, then we should find another word, by admitting that its meaning has been obscured. But the history of the word in its connection with Socrates is so important for the Romantic concept of irony that we would prefer to keep the term and risk some initial resistance rather than to lose its connotations. When the connection between this 'common' irony and the higher irony of the Romantics is understood, the reasons for retaining the term will seem more legitimate. Kierkegaard suggests an alternative and indirectly hints at the distinction between common and higher irony in the following passage:

Throughout this discussion I use the expressions: *irony* and the *ironist*, but I could as easily say: *romanticism* and the *romanticist*. Both expressions designate the same thing. The one suggests more the name with which the movement christened itself, the other the name with which Hegel christened it.[14]

Yet Kierkegaard himself constantly insists in *The Concept of Irony*, that 'irony' has constant reference to Socrates, whereas 'romantic' does not.

In view of the above distinction, it may be thought that the familiar distinction between verbal and dramatic irony is the English equivalent of this German formulation. Although the verbal/dramatic dichotomy is a step toward the German distinction, it does not comprehend it. At most it suggests, first, that verbal irony can operate structurally, permeating a work as a whole. Hence dramatic irony suggests a complex interaction of instances of verbal irony. In its second sense, it suggests a 'Weltanschauung', a cosmic irony or irony of fate. But it fails to show the intimate link between this view of reality and any theory of aesthetics, a link which is central to the German conception. Even when an ironologist occasionally touches upon the question of self-consciousness of a character, or of the audience, as when treating a play of Sophocles, he fails to establish the immediate relevance of irony to the artist or to the spectator. It is only through this immediacy that experience of any sort can achieve ultimate validity.

We can gain a more adequate understanding of the distinction between *Romantic* and *dramatic* irony by noticing that the latter never breaks through the boundaries of the artifact itself. It never deals with the dichotomy between subject/spectator and object/work of art. It does not pose questions about the relationship between the artist and his material, but confines itself to the structure, plot, design, etc., of the text within its conventional bounds. The Romantic ironist on the other hand sees the relation of the artist to his material and derivatively, the relation of spectator or audience to the artifact, as of prime importance. He goes beyond the conventional boundaries of the work and sets up a more encompassing context for investigation: his object of attention is the synthesis of subject and object, that is, of artist and product, and the manner in which they interact in experience. It is this 'transcendent' perspective which makes it possible to gain a reconciliation of the oppositions between artist (and spectator) and artifact, and to see how the apparently opposite roles of artist and spectator are analogous.

Romantic irony superimposes a new context upon aesthetic experience and causes a 'perspective flip'.[15] The artist–spectator is no longer looking at the work of art alone as his object of attention. He is focusing attention on his own interaction with the work of art, and is thereby creating for himself a new object and a new, critical perspective or context of investigation. The scientist long ago learned that he could not observe an object 'objectively', since the act of observation creates subjective conditions which vitiate the 'purity' of his observations. He can never see the thing independently of the effects upon it of the observation. The spectator of art must also come to understand this limitation of perspective. Kant has shown the radical extent of this limitation and has indicated the related idea that it is delusion to seek the 'thing in itself' at any level: it is a fiction of a divisive understanding which sees the world only in terms of irreconcilable oppositions.[16] The Romantic ironist reorients himself in relation to his object, and makes his object a synthesis of the conventional subject and the conventional object. From this new perspective he can focus upon the work of art in experience and take into consideration the many possible approaches from a psychological emphasis, an ethical emphasis, a theological emphasis, a marxist emphasis, a political or sociological emphasis, and so on. In his new context he will be able both to relate these approaches through the central perspective or common context of irony, and be able to develop them in freedom from the personal prejudices and social habits of response which tyrannize over the spectator who has not detached himself from his narrow literal individuality.[17]

Dramatic irony is the irony which Strohschneider-Kohrs refers to as the merely 'inhaltlich oder stofflich Perspektive...die allgemeine tragische oder dramatische Ironie' ['content or material Perspective. . . the general tragic or dramatic irony'], in contradistinction to the 'Begriff der Ironie als einem künstlerisch-kompositorischen Prinzip durchaus' ['concept of irony as a principle of artistic composition']. The former is the 'Begriff der Ironie [als] eine stofflich-inhaltliche Einzelheit eines Kunstwerks' ['concept of irony as a material-content detail of a work of art'], the latter 'die Art künstlerischen Verstehens' ['the type of artistic comprehension'].[18]

IRONY AS A PRINCIPLE OF ART

The concept of irony of the German Romantics in its central formulations relates to the issues which Coleridge found himself most fascinated by in his metaphysics and aesthetics, namely the metaphor of polarity and opposition, dialectic, self-consciousness, and the relation of finite to infinite or of appearance to reality. In their efforts to clarify and develop the concept of irony, these Germans diverge from each other more apparently than actually, owing to variations in terminology, emphasis, and approach. For our purposes, it will be sufficient to treat their concept of irony in its general aspects as if they were agreed upon the fundamental issues with which irony grapples.

In the romantic conception, irony was considered to be the principle of artistic creation. As Muecke explains, 'to Karl Solger irony was the very principle of art',[19] or as Strohschneider-Kohrs says, 'mit dem Begriff der Ironie in der Romantik Fragen von spezifisch ästhetisch Bedeutung zur Sprache gebracht werden'[20] ['with the concept of irony in romanticism, questions of a specifically aesthetic meaning were brought out']. Irony was the attempt to reconcile the opposition between classic and Romantic or modern art and the objective-subjective opposition.[21] The concept of irony also contained a level which was an attempt to theorize not just about aesthetic experience but about experience in general. For the Romantics that which was at the root of both aesthetic experience and experience in general was contradiction or opposition:

The metaphysical principle of irony. . . resides in the contradictions within the universe or God. The ironic attitude implies that there is in things a basic contradiction, that is to say, *from the point of view of our reason*, a fundamental and irremediable absurdity. (My italics.)[22]

Friedrich Schlegel made numerous statements about the paradoxical and contradictory nature of existence, saying that paradox is the *conditio sine qua non* of irony. He called Absolute Romanticism a 'tension of opposites'[23] and said that 'Ironie ist die Form des Paradoxen'[24] ['Irony is the form of Paradox']. Opposition and contradiction as a description of experience expressed through the medium of paradox found its way into philosophy as polarity, and had two primary characteristics. First, opposition or the philosophy of polarity implied dialectic as the proper and only adequate conception of progression or productivity. Polarity also expressed the relation between the 'Bedingt und Unbedingt',[25] the conditioned and the unconditioned, the finite and the infinite – in all the various formulations. F. Schlegel points out the essence of irony as dialectic when he says that 'Ironie ist Analyse der These und Antithese') ['Irony is the analysis of thesis and antithesis']. He expresses the positive and productive nature of opposition in the activity of dialectic when he describes the incessant and self-creating alternation of two contradictory thoughts.[26] 'Unaufhörliches Transzendieren und Progressivität' expressed and achieved by the dynamics of dialectic were the goal of the Romantic ironist, 'ewige Werden' and 'unendliche Producieren' through the 'unendlichen Entzweiung entgegengesetzter Thätigkeiten'[27] ['unending dissension of opposing activities'].

An important aspect of this concept of irony was the insistence by all the ironists that the 'Unbedingt' toward which the 'Bedingt' strove could only be grasped in terms of the dialectic, though they admitted that this was an inadequate formulation of it:

Auf die Frage, wohin die dialektische Bewegung der Ironie gehe, zu welchem Zielpunkt und Zustand, zu welchem Inhalt hin sie 'auf-hebe' und führe, antwortet nur der Hinweis auf ein unvollendbares Werden, auf eine sich immer erneuende Bewegung.[28]

[To the question, where does the dialectical movement of irony go, to what goal and state, to what content does it raise itself and lead, the allusion to an uncompleted Becoming and to a perpetually renewing movement, is the only answer.]

They made the distinction between a 'Darstellung des Absoluten' and the 'absolute Darstellung'[29] ['representation of the Absolute', and the 'absolute representation'], and insisted that art should not be mistaken as the former, which was a stagnant notion. Although art might be the highest expression or the closest possible approximation of the finite to the infinite, it could never reach the infinite itself. Walzel describes F. Schlegel's position:

Auch für ihn umschliesst (das Kunstwerk) das 'Unbedingte'. Allein – und da berührt er sich am nächsten mit Solger – er ist sich bewusst, dass es irdisches Werk ist und als solches hinter dem Unbedingten zurückbleiben muss. Am höchsten gilt ihm der Künstler, der diese Grenze seines Könnens kennt. Plotinus lässt sich das ausdrücken: Das echte Kunstwerk ist vom göttlichen 'logos' beseelt; allein das Licht des 'logos' ist am stärksten und ungebrochensten, wo es noch nicht die Erscheinung durchleuchtet, sondern sein Eigendasein wahrt. Der Künstler also schafft Gottnähes, aber Gottnähe ist nicht Gottsein.[30]

[For him also the Unconditioned encompasses the work of art. Finally – and here he comes closest to Solger – he is aware that it is a mortal work and as such must remain below the Unconditioned. The artist who is conscious of this boundary to his abilities is valued the most highly. Plotinus expressed it thusly: 'The true work of art is imbued with the soul of the divine logos'; but the light of the logos is strongest and most continual, where it does not shine through appearance, but rather where it preserves its own inherent being. Hence, the artist creates something close to divine, but that closeness is not the divine itself.]

The limitations of the 'Kunstwerk' are clearly defined in Solger's *Erwin* when at the end of that work he explicitly discusses irony and speaks of the idea in its 'Verkörperung'.[31] Elsewhere he makes it clear that through the symbol the ideal permeates the finite reality, and he distinguishes the symbol from the image, sign or allegory.[32] The symbol is a finite or sensuous representation of the idea, and in that sense it is imperfect. In another sense it is the existence of the idea – it is the idea in its actuality as opposed to its ideality (which can never be 'represented'). Hence a symbol is always true – it is not the mere image of truth.[33] Solger then describes 'Phantasie' as the 'sich entäussernde Kraft der Idee im Bewusstsein; sie ist die seelischgeistige Fähigkeit, die Idee in Wirklichkeit zu verwandeln'[34] ['self-alienating power of the Idea in consciousness; it is the soul-spirit ability to transform the Idea into Reality']. Finally he insists that the symbol is the essential language of art.[35]

In this effort to describe the nature of symbol and the limitation of art, and the imagination as the faculty which transforms the idea into actuality, we see the paradoxical relationship of the finite to the infinite represented again. One of Tieck's favourite ways of formulating the opposition was by the terms 'menschlich und Göttlich'. Irony is 'Das Göttlich-Menschliche in der Poesie'[36] ['the divine-human in poetry']. In order to see the relation of man to God, or more generally speaking, finite to infinite, man must be seen as a symbol of the divine, as a sensuous representation of the idea and of perfection. Kierkegaard chose this formulation of the opposition to express the profound irony of existence and showed the absurdity of taking man's existence literally, as cut off from the life-giving source of the divine.[37] Man's existence and existence generally can never be understood except as permeated by God, and as a symbol of the idea.

To experience and understand this relationship of the finite to the infinite as paradoxical through the symbol, or the work of art as a construct of symbols, the sensuous, finite, and 'Bedingt' must be overcome, but overcome in the only sense in which it can be transcended by a finite being, in the apprehension of the idea permeating that finiteness.[38] The finite is not, nor can it ever be, left behind: it can only be transcended in the sense that it no longer only experiences its finiteness. Rather it grasps the permeation of its finiteness by an infinity.[39] Individuality, particularity, and self must be fused with universality; actuality must be united with ideality.[40] This synthesis or unification exists in experience only as an act of intuition, though in and of itself it may *be* in some other sense.

Annihilation becomes an essential concept in the elucidation of irony. But it is, as one must expect, a paradoxical annihilation: it is an annihilation which is simultaneously destructive and productive. The ego, the finite, and the conditioned, qua ego, finite and conditioned, must be annihilated. The narrow limitations which give these their sensuous existence must be overcome not by extinction but by a transcendence. The finite ego is no longer all that is experienced, though it must still be a means by which the infinite is approached.[41] The 'negative' aspect of annihilation is immediately complemented by a positive, productive achievement:

Annihilation der im Schaffensprozess durchschrittenen Momente und bestimmter Gestaltungszüge des objektivierten Werks bedeutet, da sie nicht aus relativen Beziehungen, sondern aus der freien Selbstbeschränkung, aus dem Wissen um den unauflöslichen Zwiespalt von Bedingtem und Unbedingtem geschiet, *nicht Destruktion*, sondern wirkt *als Aufhebung* von Fixiertem und Bedingtem zu einem durchgehenden künstlerischen Gesamtsinn hin.[42]

[Annihilation of the moments traversed in the creative process and of the specific formal characteristics of the objective work means, that annihilation occurs not out of relative connections, but rather out of free self-limitation, out of the knowledge of an insoluable schism between the conditioned and unconditioned, but *not destruction*; it works rather as a raising up of the fixed and conditioned into a thoroughly artistic sense of wholeness.]

The ego in ordinary consciousness is all-consuming and all absorbing: it swallows the world up in its own image without awareness and then sets itself up against this image. This tendency toward selfhood must be restricted if the self is to be raised above such a blind, unconscious dualism to move into a new relation with the infinite. This is the negative side of irony, 'Selbstbeschränkung'.[43] It is precisely that activity of Socrates of freeing the mind from habitual and unthinking attitudes and prejudices which the mind mistakes for objective knowledge. These are the limits which ultimately establish the ego. By removing these limits, space is created in which the mind is freed to move into new territories of thought. In the effort of the ego to restrict itself, it must become aware of precisely those limits, those habits and customary responses, which it imposes upon the world unconsciously as if they were qualities of the world instead of qualifications of the subject. If these habits, customs, and unconscious responses actually constitute the ego, then becoming conscious of them means ultimately becoming self-conscious. 'Selbstbewusstsein und Reflexion' are the other aspect of irony which make annihilation and transcendence possible.[44]

For Schlegel and Solger the Logos was the principle which made any transcendence of ego and selfhood an actuality, and this requirement of the Logos stands in direct contradiction to the conventional view of Romantic theory as advocating sentimental and uncontrolled outpourings of feeling:

Schlegels Begriff der Ironie nennt den Logos, die Verstandeskraft, die Reflexion als mitwirkende Bedingungskräfte für künstlerische Schaffen. Schlegel kennzeichnet die Ironie als ein Agieren, das in Wechselwirkung mit einem ersten Gegebenen der Poesie einen dialektisch sich fortzeugenden Prozess ergibt. Es sind für diesen Begriff der Ironie also – wie es oben bereits gennant wurde – die Kategorien des Bewusstseins und der Bewegung relevant; genauer: die Ironie ist ein *Bewusstsein*, . . . Schlegel betont in seinem Ironie-Postulat unermüdlich Bedeutung des Logos, der Absichtlichkeit des "philosophischen Vermögens" für die Kunst und fordert für eine dem Prinzip der modernen Bildung gemässe Kunst das Mitwirken der intellektuellen Kräfte. Er wendet sich damit sowohl gegen jede Art sentimentalen und betont expressiven Ausdrucks wie gegen jede Art von Stoff-und Gegenstands horigkeit.[45]

[Schlegel's concept of irony names the Logos, the power of comprehension, the reflection, as a conditioning power operant in creative activity. Schlegel defines irony as an agitation, which produces, in alternation with a first production of Poetry, a dialectical, self-continuing process. For this concept of irony, the categories of consciousness and of movement are relevant – as we mentioned already above. More precisely, irony is a consciousness. . . Schlegel emphasizes tirelessly in his irony postulate the significance of the Logos, the intention, the 'philosophical ability' for Art, and demands, for an art which follows the principle of modern formation, the involvement of the intellectual process. He turns against every type of expression which is sentimental and overly expressive, and against every type of bondage to content and object.]

In the specific application to art of this demand for reflection and self-consciousness in the subject, the formulation is a demand for control by the artist over his material. 'Selbst-beherrschung durch Selbstbeschränkung' is the first reflective act for the artist in relation to his material. This self-consciousness we can relate to the more general conception above of the perceiver or subject in relation to the world. The artist must be in control of his material so that he does not embody his own unconscious limitations, his prejudices, customs, and habitual responses, all the things which constitute his ego, into his 'material' or into the work of art. If he fails to restrict this tendency of the ego to image itself into everything it does and knows, his art will be limited and lacking in universality.[46] But this conscious process is permeated by another process which we might refer to as instinct, or the energy of the infinite and the 'unconscious'. Genius is the interpenetration of the 'Absicht' by the 'Instinkt': 'In jedem guten Gedicht muss alles Absicht, und alles Instinkt seyn'[47] ['In every good poem everything must be intention and instinct']. This interaction of the two poles is expressed in another way when Schlegel says that the artist must not try to 'force' his way into his material; he must wait until the moment is ripe for creative activity. In this sense control is balanced by submission to an energy greater than the artist, which partially controls him:

Man muss mit der Selbstbeschränkung nicht zu eilen, und erst der Selbst-schöpfung, der Erfindung und Begeisterung Raum lassen, bis sie fertig ist. Drittens: man muss die Selbstbeschränkung nicht übertreiben.[48]

[A man should not hurry his self-limitation: he must first leave room for self-creativity, invention and inspiration, until he is ready.
Third: One must not overdo self-limitation.]

However contradictory and problematic this insistence that 'Intention *and* Instinct' operate simultaneously may seem, through it is expressed the relation of the finite to the infinite, which in any formulation must seem paradoxical to the reason. An important handling of the issue of intentionality in art is also suggested. Schlegel's insistence upon the necessity for the unification of a philosophic mind with the poetic in all high art, and his statement that irony is a 'philosophisches Vermögen',[49] might mislead us to suppose that an artist who is truly great understands his art's significance completely. The Romantic poet has been almost universally understood to believe that art is entirely instinct. Both of these positions are extremes which fail to reconcile the paradoxical nature of existence and the relation of the individual to the universal. For the Romantic ironist, genius is neither the one nor the other, but a reconciliation of the two extremes, and the work of art is the product of that dynamic synthesis of the conscious and the unconscious. Thus the artist both controls and is controlled by his creative activity. The annihilation of the limitations of the ego may be seen as the means by which the force of feeling, or of instinct, finds an opening into the realm in which it can become intellectualized and articulated. Hence it is mistaken to see irony as ultimately an intellectual activity, as opposed to an activity of feeling. It is the perfect synthesis of the two, the unity of thought and feeling.[50] How could it not be, when it is based as it is on a philosophy of the reconciliation of opposites?

We may also formulate the opposition between intention and instinct in terms of the self, ego, or selfhood, and the SELF. Ego sets itself up in opposition to the world, but its true relation to the world can only be comprehended when it is understood that opposition implies homogeneity. Moreover, because all of our experience is mediated through the self, the subjective side of the pole swallows the world up into itself, and becomes lost in a solipsistic subjectivism. Release from solipsism can come only in the recognition that the individual is not the literal reality but a symbol of a paradoxical totality. For the imagination the individual cannot exist except in and through the universal; hence the self is only a portion of a universal SELF which accounts for the fragmentary quality of all existence. To describe this state of permeation of the individual by the universal, the Germans used the terms 'objectivity' and 'distance',[51] to emphasize that the artist who is in control of his material heightens his consciousness of the present moment of creation by adopting the perspective of an observer over his own activity. He transcends his narrow ego involvement, and establishes himself on a higher plane of reference. – His attention is focused entirely upon the present moment. Thus the artist adopts the 'contrary' role of spectator, and thereby achieves the necessary synthesis of involvement as maker and of detachment as spectator. The obvious corollary which we find emphasized explicitly by Coleridge is the role reversal of the 'actual' spectator (the reader) with the artist's posture, if the reader is to complete his activity with self-consciousness.

COLERIDGE AND THE GERMAN ROMANTIC CONCEPT OF IRONY

From the preceding chapters it should be apparent that the most important aspect of the concept of irony, that of opposition and reconciliation, was shared by Coleridge and the Germans. Opposition was the foundation and core of the common metaphysics upon which Coleridge's attitude to art and reality was based, as well as that of the German Romantics. Both set themselves firmly upon the transcendental idealism of Kant as 'completed' by Fichte, and they then applied to aesthetics the conclusions of this metaphysic:

Schlegel verwendet das dialektische Denkschema und die logischen Stützen der Fichteschen Philosophie und bezieht sie in seine Gedanken über Bedingung und Möglichkeiten künstlerischen Verfahrens ein.[52]

[Schlegel uses the dialectical thought-schema and the logical supports of the philosophy of Fichte, and includes them in his thoughts about conditions and possibilities of artistic processes.]

Coleridge's constant preoccupation with the mind as the object of attention, and with the necessity to found knowledge upon the act instead of the thing,[53] indicates his emphasis upon the necessity for an analysis of experience arising from self-consciousness and a dynamic, dialectical conception of truth. Two further areas of coincidence with this concept of irony which have not been dealt with above are his comments upon the symbol (the relation of the idea to the image) and his emphasis upon judgment in the literary criticism on Shakespeare.

Though Coleridge may be indebted to A. W. Schlegel in his Shakespeare criticism, he took up the argument as to the nature of Shakespeare's genius and insisted upon the cooperation of judgment with instinct.[54] This characterization of creative activity also informs the German ironist's view of art. He also emphasizes the necessity for the dual action of these two opposite forces of instinct and intention, and thus articulates the nature of genius: a paradox for the understanding but appropriate for the reason. In the fragment 'Shakespeare's Judgment Equal to his Genius', from an 1818 lecture, Coleridge insists that the 'judgment of the great poet is not less deserving of our wonder than his genius...Shakespeare [is] himself a nature humanized, a genial understanding directing self-consciously a power and an implicit wisdom deeper than consciousness'. And additionally: 'In every work of art there is a reconcilement of the external with the internal; the conscious is so impressed on the unconscious as to appear in it...He who combines the two is the man of genius; and for that reason he must partake of both. Hence there is in genius itself an unconscious activity...'[55]

This characterization of genius and the poetic process inevitably leaves the understanding dissatisfied, for the understanding is at rest only when it chooses between alternatives and oppositions. Coleridge describes the imagination as hovering above two polarities, and Keats talks of negative capability. The artistic process remains a mystery, known only in the moment of integration of the faculties of thought (intellection, articulation) and feeling (instinct). Either alone must remain inadequate to account for creativity.[56]

Coleridge's peculiar contribution to this common theory of aesthetics was to add a new (though certainly implicit in the German, and at times almost explicit) context to the aesthetic experience. The Germans had been pre-eminently absorbed in the relation of the artist to his work and the nature of creative acts in so far as they produced works of art. Coleridge was engaged in taking this interest one step further, to a point which is demanded by the theory itself if it is to be complete. He explored and dramatized the relation of the *spectator* to the material and to the artist, which was a logical consequence of the previous contexts, and which it was necessary to establish if art was to become the universally valid product which it was supposed to be. That is, the value of art could not be conceived of as limited to the experience of the artist in making it. Unless this further context were fully drawn out and explored, the way in which art could ever become valid for the spectator would remain misunderstood. How art 'communicates' would be misconstrued, and the most effective art would go unperceived without a reanalysis of the spectator's relation to art on the basis of this ironic perspective.[57]

By making an analogy between artistic activity and the activity of fundamental perception (through the primary/secondary imagination distinction), Coleridge drew out into full view the ramifications of the German Romantic concept of irony. This further level of focus which Coleridge added to his works constitutes the fullest artistic expression of self-consciousness, for it is only when the artist understands his art as an activity analogous to 'world-making', that is to perception in general, that he can put at his disposal the insight and intelligence which art brings into play and apply it to all aspects of experience. This progression of Coleridge's to a more complete and immediately valid context of self-consciousness constitutes the method which in the following chapters we will try to indicate in detail.

A further area of coincidence can be seen in a comparison of Coleridge and Solger. Both men emphasized the interaction of religion, philosophy, and art, and were determined to try to interrelate them. Any adequate account of one of the three must inevitably involve the other two. Solger briefly explains this integrated view of knowledge:

Philosophy, art, and religion are the three necessary parts of a harmonious culture; Philosophy without art is means without purpose; art without philosophy is end without beginning; and both without religion are utterly debased, vile and godless: philosophy becomes insolence and violence, and art arrogant amusement.[58]

Hence we find in Solger's writings, as in Coleridge's, that the metaphors and models of one discipline are constantly being applied to the others to elucidate each more completely.

Solger's main reaction to the philosophy of his times was also very Coleridgean: he rejected the empiricism *and* the rationalism of the day, and espoused a type of 'Perennial Philosophy' which was the union of the two and involved an intense reflection upon immediate experience.

The world fluctuates between rationalism and the deification of empirical reality. The more closely the art of thinking and higher experience are united, the more perfectly truth dwells amongst mankind...The falling apart of the two tendencies produces firstly, superstition, which ignores the laws of thinking; and meaningless unbelief, which uses facts as concrete quantities with which to calculate.[59]

Coleridge has also emphasized the necessity for the reunification of the two poles of philosophy, as we have indicated in the previous chapters. Solger adopts a position with regard to the nature of this synthetic philosophy which he does not hesitate to connect with mysticism. All the German Romantics were following in the tradition of Jacob Böhme in this respect: Schelling's well-known articulation of Böhme in terms of his own day is only the one influence most generally recognized.[60] Solger was importantly influenced by Böhme as well, partly no doubt through the lectures by Schelling which he attended at Jena in 1802.[61] Böhme was the one philosopher whom Tieck read enthusiastically – as early as 1800 he was excitedly reading Böhme to his sister Sophie and criticizing him on exactly the point which Solger and Coleridge were to criticize him, the giving of too great a reality to evil and thus producing an irreconcilable dichotomy.[62] Coleridge's early admiration for Böhme is too well known to need more than mentioning, and he and Solger shared two other great springs of philosophical thought aside from their interest in German idealism. They both immensely admired Spinoza and Plato. Solger also heard Fichte lecture in 1800 and said that he listened with infinite delight and profit: 'The course of lectures with him occupies me continually. I admire his strictly philosophical manner of delivery, and almost regret that I did not become acquainted with him earlier. No one else carries his listeners so powerfully away with him, no one else brings one so unsparingly into the sharpest school of reflection. It is a genuine delight to have become acquainted with and to compare the two greatest men of our time in this field, Fichte and Schelling'.[63]

How similar Solger's and Coleridge's understanding was of what constituted mysticism can be seen from the following passage of Solger's:

Denn im Denken besteht die wahre Mystik darin, dass man in jedem Akte desselben die Offenbarung einer faktisch einwirkenden Macht Wahrnehme, ohne welche er, anstatt der lebendigen Frucht der Ueberzeugung, die mit dem Glauben Eins ist, eine taube Hülse treibt. Die wahre Philosophie muss nicht erklären, sondern einsehen, nicht die Erscheinungen absondern, vielmehr sich ihrer als Offenbarungen bewusst werden.[64]

[In thought the true mystery consists in this, that in each act one perceives the revelation of a real, effective power, without which he chases an empty shell instead of the living fruit of conviction which is one with faith. The true philosophy should not explain, but should see with intuition; it should not separate the appearances, but rather become conscious of them as revelations.]

The 'dead shell' is Coleridge's abstraction, and the 'living fruit' is his idea.

Solger's emphasis on the difference between explaining and comprehending, or 'categorizing' as opposed to seeing in a visionary way,[65] suggests the distinction between reason and understanding which he develops in his own way when he adopts the Platonic hierarchy of knowledge. Contrary to the general notion, he insists that there are two types of knowledge, which differ not only in degree but also in kind.[66] These two types of knowledge apply to our knowledge of the world as well as to our knowledge of the self. Yet the higher knowledge is also a unification of the world-self opposition: self-consciousness must transcend the bounds of empirical ego and merge with the consciousness of objects to resolve the opposition in appearance. 'Anschauung' is the faculty of resolution, and the Idea is the form which it takes. The idea can only be apprehended by the higher faculty of knowledge, not by the common understanding.[67] It is the living unity of the particular and the general, which remain abstractly opposed by the understanding.

For Solger the idea was in essence one, but it partook of varying aspects in its manifestation in the empirical world, all of which were related to this centre. Thus the ideas of truth, beauty, and good were different forms of the idea integrally related the one to the other. Hence Solger was emphatic about the interrelations between philosophy, art and religion.[68] All were perceived by the same faculty of 'Anschauung', and were not, as is usually suggested, essentially different. Solger resisted the pantheistic resolution of self-world dichotomy, as did Coleridge, by insisting that the idea, though immanent, was at the same time transcendent. It maintained a paradoxical and ironical relation to the phenomenal world which could only be adequately expressed by an ironical dialecticism.[69]

Solger's application of this philosophy to a theory of aesthetics reveals further close parallels with Coleridge. Solger, like Coleridge, explained that the idea could never appear to the finite mind in and through itself.[70] In order to illustrate the possibility of the manifestation of the idea in the form of the sensuous – a temporal and imperfect appearance – Solger turned to the symbol as the embodiment of the Idea in the world,[71] a solution which was similar to Coleridge's definition of symbol: 'a Symbol . . . is characterized by a translucence of the Special in the Individual or of the General in the Especial or of the Universal in the General. Above all by the translucence of the Eternal through and in the Temporal. It always partakes of the Reality which it renders intelligible; and while it enunciates the whole, abides itself as a living part in that Unity, of which it is the representative.'[72] Solger also makes the Coleridgean distinction between the symbol and the image, and emphasizes the importance of keeping the two distinct, the one being the object of the common understanding, the other of the imagination (and ultimately of intuition).[73] The symbol is the permeation of empirical reality by the ideal, or, expressed in other terms, the actualization or realization of that ideality.[74] In both formulations we have the synthesis of the opposition between ideal and real in a permeation of the former by the latter.

The above coincidence with Coleridge suggest that the basis of Solger's and Coleridge's unified theory of metaphysics and aesthetics was strikingly similar – in spite of the fact that they both worked out the details in their own terms, and in terms so different that there has not been a single study which has related the two men, nor even a suggestion that such a comparison might yield results. This brief account may serve to indicate that the consequences for an aesthetics based on the metaphysics of transcendental idealism were being worked out by such men as Coleridge and Solger who had no contact with each other at the time of the parallel conclusions. Yet the similar conclusions act to corroborate and verify the results of each.

The most striking similarity emerges from Solger's distinction between 'Phantasie' and 'Einbildungskraft', which is similar to Coleridge's fancy/imagination distinction. 'Einbildungskraft', like the fancy, juggles with the fixities of ordinary cognition: it is the relative of abstraction and deals in allegory by dressing the particular in the form of the general, and vice versa, without synthesizing.[75] The 'Phantasie' is the faculty of apprehending the idea and generating symbols, and is the faculty of creative, artistic activity in all realms of experience, in philosophy, religion, and art.[76] Still more significantly, Solger distinguishes the 'Phantasie der Phantasie' and the 'Sinnlichkeit der Phantasie', by which he hopes to draw the analogy between the process of perception as basically creative (as it must be understood in any idealism) and the process of creative, artistic activity.[77] In this respect it corresponds to Coleridge's, and to Tetens's, distinction between primary and secondary imagination, though Solger goes on into a further more detailed analysis of both, which Coleridge does not do.[78]

Irony comes into play in a polar, and yet also an ultimately identical relationship, with inspiration: the idea reveals itself in reality through artistic activity, but at the same time its manifestation in opposition must be understood as the unfolding of the unity of this Idea.[79] Opposition must not be mistaken for the idea itself. That is, it must not be taken literally. This stage of knowledge Solger calls 'Verstand', which itself has two opposing moments.[80] The first is the moment of 'Betrachtung', in which the idea is broken up into its antitheses; in the second moment, 'Witz', the antitheses are destroyed by being synthesized into a unity. In this second moment the idea is itself dissolved.[81] The perfect reconciliation of these two moments is the germ and focus of art, which Solger calls 'künstlerische Ironie':

Die echte Ironie setzt das höchste Bewusstsein voraus, vermöge dessen der menschliche Geist sich über den Gegensatz und die Einheit der Idee und der Wirklichkeit vollkommen klar ist.[82]

[True irony presupposes the highest consciousness by means of which the human spirit is perfectly clear about the opposition and unity of Idea and Reality.]

Coleridge rarely, if ever, used the word irony in his writings, but this sentence of Solger's is certainly precisely expressed by Coleridge's reference to the philosophic mind informing the best poetry.[83]

Other more methodological comparisons between Coleridge and Solger are evident. In a letter to Raumer in the *Nachgelassene Schriften* Solger explains that his intention in the first dialogue of the *Philosophische Gespräche* was to provoke thought rather than satisfy it with solutions by leaving the conclusions to the judgment of each reader.[84] A few weeks later he writes to Tieck that he has finished a dialogue which is more 'dramatic' than any previous ones;[85] in connection with the remark to Raumer it is possible that by 'dramatic' Solger was referring not only to the conversation of the characters in the dialogue, but also to reader–author drama. The word 'dramatic' suggests that the dialogue should stimulate to reflection and creative activity. Then at a later time in a letter to Solger, Tieck praises him for his views upon system:

Liegt doch immer in jedem klugen Wort ein ganzes System, und zwar oft für den Nachdenkenden vollständiger, als wenn dieser nachher dieses sogenannte System mit seinen Lücken und Widersprüchen kennen lernt. Allenthalben ist der Mittelpunkt der Erkennens, alles setzt ein Vor- und Nach voraus, und wer beim rechten Anfange anfangen wollte, der müsste doch schon den ersten Schöpfungstag in den 3t. Akt legen.

[In every intelligent word there is an entire system, and indeed often a more complete system for the reflective person than if he later becomes acquainted with this so-called system and all its gaps and contradictions. *Everywhere* is the centre of knowledge, everything presupposes a before and an after, and he who wishes to begin at the right beginning, must nevertheless place the first day of creation in the third act.]

This comment about 'the system' and Tieck's final remark about the truth of all viewpoints are singularly Coleridgean:

Es giebt tausend Ansichten der Kunst und Poesie. Alle haben Wahrheit, selbst die einseitigsten.[86]

[There are a thousand views about art and poetry. All are true, even the most biased.]

One further remark of Tieck's on Solger's dialogues suggests an application to Coleridge, particularly the emphasis upon 'das proscribirte *ordentlich*' and 'der fremde Massstab' (alien criterion):

Je mehr ich von ihnen lese, je mehr nehme ich meine älteren Kritiken des Einzelnen zurück, und ich komme auf meinen alten Satz zurück, dass man jeden Autor nur aus sich selber kennen und kommentiren lernt, und dass jeder fremde Massstab daran gehalten, ein falsche ist; ich glaube jetzt einzusehn, dass diese Wendungen und Eigenheiten, die mich wohl früher störten, keine Zufälligkeiten bei Ihnen sind, keine Angewöhnungen der Bequemlichkeit, sondern wahre Bezeichnungen des Gemüths, die sich ihnen passend dargeboten, die Sie gewählt haben, selbst über das proscribirte *ordentlich* denke ich nach mehr[er]em Nachdenken anders.[87]

[The more I read of them, the more I take back my earlier criticisms of the particular one, and return to my old maxim, that one comes to know and to comment upon each author only according to that author himself; that every alien criterion held up to something is a false measure. I think I see now that these turns of expression and peculiarities which previously disturbed me, are not accidents in your writing, not a contracting of habits of convenience, but real marks of your disposition, which have presented themselves appropriately, and which you have chosen; even about the prohibited 'respectability' I now think differently than I did, after more reflection.]

Though there are no doubt different formulations in the working out of Coleridge's and Solger's aesthetics and metaphysics, they vary no more and perhaps even less than the differences to be found amongst Solger, F. Schlegel, Jean Paul, and Tieck,[88] all of whom are recognized as similar enough in outlook to be grouped together in a school of German Romantic Irony. Whether these differences even constitute discrepancies, or whether they should be looked upon simply as variations which are testimonies of the individuality of each of the authors concerned, is a point which we will take up later. A. W. von Schlegel's differences from Solger and the other Romantics are of a more radical nature.[89]

In many respects Coleridge's thought may most closely coincide with Friedrich Schlegel, who like Coleridge, philosophized and extolled the importance of 'creative criticism', and emphasized the value of understanding the relation of criticism to poetry. Indeed Schlegel maintained that the critical or analytical state of mind was a characteristic of the *modern* poet, and resulted in a high level of self-consciousness about one's compositions. Like Coleridge, Schlegel demanded of his readers a re-creative act analogous to the poet's construction,[90] and such an active, participatory response led to a criticism which was also poetry (in a broad sense, as art).[91]

In his novel *Lucinde,* he tries to put into practice these principles, and some of his techniques, such as disconnection of the content at surface level, confusion in the narrative development, comments implicating the reader, and apparent obscurity and paradox as well as much irony and wit, are precisely the techniques which Coleridge uses, though Coleridge's use is 'less harsh and branny' and not so much a 'matter of purpose, and fore-thought – industrious omission not absence by nature and consequence of the some thing instead'.[92] Schlegel also claims that it is the poet with a critical mind who is most able to achieve a higher criticism.[93]

In his most important early prose writing, 'Gespräch über Poesie', Schlegel discusses the modern novel and the various and mixed character of its content. The modern novel, he explains, should include philo-sophical, critical, moral, and social ideas poetized, and its unity will arise not from a surface continuity of narrative development, or plot, or character coherence, but rather from the prevailing intellectual point of view of the author, which focuses these varied but inherently related materials into a unity.[94] For that point of view will act as a central law which emerges from the varied material and gives it a far more profound, organic unity than any obvious, accidental ordering of the parts could have achieved. But Schlegel also insists that this various and miscellaneous content must be firmly grounded in the concrete if it is to be transformed into a work of art, and he cites the autobiographical form as the most thoroughly concrete genre. He then insists that poetry and prose should be mixed in this modern 'novel' (clearly he uses the word in a very broad way), and that the philosophical ideas must be synthesized with a poetic quality.[95]

These theories act almost as a commentary to the *Biographia Literaria,* and help to suggest that the hybrid genre which Coleridge chose may not be an accident of incompetence to organize his material, but a genuine effort at the sort of modern genre which Schlegel was insisting would be the model and ideal of the modern artist. Moreover, Coleridge's use of his sources, such as Schelling, Fichte, Kant, Maass, and others, seems to fit into Schlegel's idea that this new work should draw for a new mythology (or resource of ideas, symbols, and images) upon the idealism of, e.g., Fichte, Spinoza's thought, and Naturphilosophie. Part of the purpose of the free use of sources would be to challenge the conventional and delusory notion of what constitutes originality, and replace it with a dynamic conception of originality as inhering in the style and techniques of design of an author, two aspects which alone can express individuality. Schlegel's evaluation of the critic's role as potentially a creative and enlivening one, his maxim that the critic's work involves the 'understanding of understanding' (compare Coleridge on 'thinking about thinking'), his definition of the modern 'novel' as the new and truly innovative genre, and his view that discourse must operate at depth levels to express true organization and genuine originality are theoretical principles which both coincide with Coleridge's own ideas and are startlingly accurate descriptions by anticipation of that 'immethodical miscellany', the *Biographia Literaria*.

5

Metaphor: process and method in
Biographia I

It is generally conceded that a work of art differs from a philosophical treatise in that the latter makes its points discursively: it tells the reader what it is trying to communicate. The work of art, on the other hand, is that which shows or demonstrates by metaphor, simile, etc. It is 'dramatic' in contrast to the treatise or discursive text in that it constructs a situation in which the reader is required to react imaginatively in order to complete the design of the work. The reader will have crucially different preconceptions and expectations depending upon which of these two approaches he takes to a text, and he will interpret and judge what he has read according to those expectations. It is especially important to keep these two alternative approaches in mind when reading Coleridge, in view of his accomplishments in both poetry and prose. In this chapter Coleridge's *Biographia Literaria* will be examined in order to discover whether Coleridge intended it to be read as a treatise, that is, for what it can communicate to us discursively in a philosophically traditional way, or whether in addition to this, and perhaps even contrarily, there is evidence of a more 'artistic' design, such that a situation is created in which the reader is required to act as a kind of author in order to complete the structure.[1] This involves essentially the search for method.

One of the first problems met with in the *Biographia* is its hybrid nature, its mixing of abstruse philosophical discussions with trivial observations on practical, everyday matters.[2] A perusal of the table of contents reveals the variety of subject matters and the apparent fragmentariness of the work, and it raises the question why Coleridge called it a biography.[3] The plagiarisms from Schelling, Kant perhaps, and Maass introduce additional problems. The reader is left to wonder whether he should not reject the work as a mere collection of anecdotes, digressions, and plagiarisms, which has little to offer in terms of tangible knowledge. Though he may praise many passages as highly poetic and inspired, the reader may still deny that there is a unified structure or purpose in this 'immethodical miscellany'.

In this chapter certain passages from the *Biographia* are discussed which seem particularly refractory to understanding and immediate comprehension. Surprisingly, many of these passages are polished versions of material collected by Coleridge as early as 1799, as was discussed in chapter one above. These passages may be transformed from enigmas into meaningful statements, and will function not as scattered treasures but as important joints in the construction, if they are understood as metaphoric situations which occur at critical moments in the continuing discussion, and which thereby constitute a method of procedure and a clue to the structural unity of the *Biographia*. The theses of chapter twelve will be shown to give additional insight into the way in which Coleridge used his sources in the service of this method.[4] More direct, unproblematic statements in the *Biographia* will then be shown to explicate discursively the technique being used at another level. This other level will be shown to constitute the irony of the work, in so far as it reflects the role of the spectator–artist which involves a consciousness of his procedure of observation, perception, and reading generally. The subject matter of this submerged, analogical level of discourse is imaginative reading and response, which coincides with the surface subject matter of imagination as a faculty of mind and its operations, while focusing upon the perspective most important for the receiver of these communications, namely that perspective of reading imaginatively. The metaphor is clearly the most appropriate mode of engaging the imagination and of turning it toward this self-conscious level of operation.

METAPHORIC SITUATIONS

In discussing the errors of a materialist theory of association, Coleridge brings to bear a number of arguments discussed above in chapter two. At a certain point, he gives up the discursive mode and turns to an extended metaphor to illustrate his objections.

Let us consider what we do when we leap. We first resist the gravitating power by an act purely voluntary, and then by another act, voluntary in part, we yield to it in order to light on the spot, which we had previously proposed to ourselves. Now let a man watch his mind while he is composing; or, to take a still more common case, while he is trying to recollect a name; and he will find the process completely analogous. Most of my readers will have observed a small water-insect on the surface of rivulets, which throws a cinque-spotted shadow fringed with prismatic colours on the sunny bottom of the brook; and will have noticed, how the little animal *wins* its way up against the stream, by alternate pulses of active and passive motion, now resisting the current, and now yielding to it in order to gather strength and a momentary *fulcrum* for a further propulsion. This is no unapt emblem of the mind's self-experience in the act of thinking.[5]

This metaphor is 'no unapt emblem of the mind's self-experience in the act of thinking' only if one is accustomed to experiencing the act of thinking in the conscious way of watching the processes of thought, and not merely of performing them. For most readers, this is a significant difficulty: we are inexperienced and undisciplined in 'self-experiencing'. This passage becomes a paradigm of the difficulty which Coleridge's writings assume for us. In such a passage, the act of apprehension is not only the goal but the subject matter. Reading Coleridge becomes a process of temporarily tolerating one's inability to apprehend his meaning with the expectation that, as one reads again and reflects upon them, these passages will eventually reveal an unexpected mode of signifying. Through concerted effort from the reader coupled with the approaches which Coleridge makes from several directions in the hope of 'sparking a light' or 'hitting a chord', the passage which seemed obscure and uphill may gradually assume a distinctness and comparative ease.

Metaphor expresses often unfamiliar relations and the inner logic of things. The sense and the integrity of the metaphor or the relation captured is understood by an intellectual act which regenerates the integrity of the relation in the reader's mind. A passive, acquiescing attention is insufficient to *grasp* a metaphor. Without such a 'validating' act of comprehension, the metaphor remains dead and the integral relation is not grasped.[6] The phrases are mere formulae or words externally imposed and not arising from the material. From Plato to the present day we find exhortations to discipline and to exercise the faculty that performs these acts through the study of geometry and logic, or by reflecting upon metaphors in our everyday language to try to sense the integrity of their relations. 'Dead' metaphors are comparable to geometrical or logical truths which are memorized but not grasped, the test for apprehension in geometry or logic being whether someone can generate proofs and equivalencies step by step. The test for whether someone comprehends a metaphor is not as obvious. No one can 'explain away' the sense of a metaphor by reducing it to literal language. The relation can be hinted at and talked about but never exhaustively reduced to a discursive formulation. The integrity of the metaphor in the passage quoted above has to be grasped by referring it to one's own 'self-experiencing in the act of thinking'. Intense concentration is required to think about thinking. In order to demonstrate the inadequacy of reductionist statements, let us interpret the second part of the metaphor above in a discursive form – not with the illusion, however, that the 'translation' is in any way substitutive of the original. It acts only as a general clue to the metaphor of reading involved in the passage, which has already been suggested by the line, 'Now let a man watch his mind while he is composing'. For the reading process is correctly conceived of as an analogue of the process of composition, as was pointed out in chapter four on the German philosophy of art as irony.

The movement of the mind in reading along the current of the narration, being carried away by the force of this stream, is to be counteracted by the will, operating in pulses of attending and thinking, or rather, halting in the current of the narration to think. The thinking is the active pulse, while attending is the passive. A passive yielding to the current is analogous to reading sequentially and in a linear way. But this yielding to the narrative current should occur only in order that the mind should gain a fulcrum to propel itself upward against the stream. Such specifically metaphorical passages in the *Biographia* are fulcra: something for the mind to resist in order to propel itself against the current of the more discursive passages of the narration.

Another familiar passage in the *Biographia* demonstrates again Coleridge's use of metaphor as the primary vehicle of knowledge and communication. Here once again the act of comprehension is not only the goal, but also the subject matter.

They and they only can acquire the philosophic imagination, the sacred power of self-intuition, who within themselves can interpret and understand the symbol, that the wings of the air-sylph are forming within the skin of the caterpillar; those only, who feel in their own spirits the same instinct, which impels the chrysalis of the horned fly to leave room in its involucrum for antennae yet to come. They know and feel, that the potential works in them, even as the actual works on them.[7]

The sense of this passage is for many readers not immediately apparent. The sense depends upon its striking a chord of familiarity in a mind attuned to self-conscious reflection. At the same time it inspires crucially that reflection which is necessary for comprehension. It acts as another fulcrum to halt the progression of the reading and force the reader to reflect by failing to gratify the immediate need for sense. It in fact warns him to keep his mind open to, or to leave space for that which as yet he does not fully comprehend, such as this very passage in the *Biographia*. It directs the reader inward to his own process of thought, for its subject matter is self-intuition and the philosophic imagination. This passage is a commentary on the process of trying to interpret it; for it is an identity of process and product or of form and content. Such a metaphorical passage is refractory to the unreflective mind, and can only signify to the beholder who should have made himself 'congenerous and similar to the object beheld'. Two forces are brought into conflict. The habit of reading passively and sequentially, and the need for immediate sense or the hatred of obscurity collide with the method of initiation into knowledge as experience. One or the other must give way. If the former preponderates the passage is ignored or brushed aside as nonsense and 'mere poetry'. The current carries the unresisting insect along with it. If the demand for significance prevails, a new tension arises. It is the necessity to exchange the immediacy of the need for sense and the hatred of obscurity for a willingness to 'descend into the cave', to wait with patience, and in the following lines Coleridge gives us yet another passage full of implications for the reader:

it is not lawful to enquire from whence it sprang, as if it were a thing subject to place and motion, for it neither approached hither, nor again departs from hence to some other place; but it either appears to us or it does not appear. So that we ought not to pursue it with a view of detecting its secret source, but to watch in quiet till it suddenly shines upon us; preparing ourselves for the blessed spectacle as the eye waits patiently for the rising sun.[8]

We must leave room for the potential in the expectation that the antennae or the organ of intuitive perception will develop with exercise. The reader cannot afford to reject everything that is not immediately understood. The desire for meaning and clarity must combine with a genial patience and willingness to suspend gratification in order eventually to gain the result. Analogously, though the *Biographia* remains an enigma in terms of its hybridity, fragmentariness, and general obscurity, we will, according to the method of the philosopher, 'rest satisfied with no imperfect light, as long as the impossibility of attaining a fuller knowledge has not been demonstrated'.[9]

THE THESES OF CHAPTER TWELVE

The theses of chapter twelve have proved a stumbling block to many a reader and if the structure is to be perceived, it is necessary to understand how they function in the work. In thesis I, 'truth is correlative to being', we are challenged by the relation of knowledge to being, while in thesis X, intelligence is defined as self-development. These pages must seem philosophically abstruse and of a different character from the preceding sections of chapter twelve which were richly poetic. Yet the discussion of the two metaphorical passages discussed above will show that it is precisely by means of 'winning our way up the stream' and 'leaving room in the involucrum', that these propositions are elucidated. By saying in thesis I that 'to know is in its very essence a verb active', Coleridge directs the prepared mind to the summit of an intuitional act which is the primary means of grasping relations in knowledge. If truth is correlative to being, the truth is known in the act, and only in the act. Knowledge requires actual instances, events and experiences of knowing, as was suggested above in relation to metaphor. If Coleridge was to communicate the active nature of knowledge, he had to design occasions and situations in which the mind of the reader could react imaginatively and come to know for itself that truth is correlative to being. The two metaphoric situations quoted above are such occasions, many more of which are discussed below. Throughout these theses it is stated that self-consciousness is the ultimate form of knowing. This self-consciousness is not knowledge of an altogether transcendent being; it is to be understood as the limit and boundary of knowledge. Self-consciousness is moreover for Coleridge the source and first principle of knowledge. Without the living spirit infused by the experiencing of their truth the theses and metaphoric situations remain meaningless 'metaphysical whisperings' of things that the reader knows he does not understand.[10]

The avowed purpose of the *Biographia* (and of *The Friend*) is to discover the first principles of things. Thesis v shows us that in discovering these principles the two works must eventually give up discursive, 'objective' attempts to communicate such truth. For thesis v says that truth is found 'neither in the object (the *Biographia*) or the subject (the reader) taken separately' but rather 'in that which is ... the identity of both'. Here emerges for Coleridge a first principle of the fine arts: the world of art (and aesthetic experience, or beauty) exists neither in the subject nor the object but in the moments of their identification.[11] Thesis vi states that the 'I Am' is 'a subject which becomes a subject by the act of constructing itself objectively to itself; but which never is an object except for itself, and only so far as by the very same act it becomes a subject'. Applied to the reading situation, we see that the reader must posit himself as object and leave the book for the moment. Yet this cannot be done unless the *Biographia* refers the reader to his own mind, and causes him to seek in himself away from the page the sense and truth behind the passages of the text, which can act only as hints and directions towards an experiential certainty.

Coleridge's constant preoccupation with his readership justifies us in applying these theses to the reading situation for clarification. A further reason is the success in making sense of these theses which is achieved from such a self-verifying procedure. Thesis vii, for example, suggests further the nature of communication: 'If therefore this be the one only immediate truth, in the certainty of which the reality of our collective knowledge is grounded, it must follow that the spirit in all the objects which it views, views only itself'. The 'spirit' in all objects is grasped and is clear only in acts of intellectual apprehension. Correlatively, the mind viewing the *Biographia* views only itself. The symbolic significance of the work of art as mirror emerges, but is meaningful only if we *experience* it as such as opposed merely to articulating the verbal formula, 'Art is like a mirror.' Depending upon the state of ignorance or knowledge of itself and its faculties and processes, the mind perceives in varying degrees the spirit and inner logic of the *Biographia* and the reasons for its obscurities as well as its genius. Yet as long as one fails to see the reasons and connections, one is in no position to judge their inadequacy or appropriateness.[12] Since the act of intuition as imagination is known *in* the act, imagination can only be known in its two-fold character as both the solution of enigmas and the means to their solution: as means and end.[13] Coleridge feels it his duty, as he states in *The Friend*, to help generate that imagination in his reader, or the wholeness of the work as well as the significance of its parts must remain incomprehensible and dead to the unenlivened mind. The difficulty of making this comprehensible is captured in another metaphor: 'By what instrument this is possible the solution itself will discover at the same time that it will reveal to and for whom it is possible [to contemplate intuitively this one power].'[14] The mind can contemplate its ground of knowing only by activating it and when activated.

FURTHER METAPHORS

By extension to the reading situation (and we have seen this extension to be justified by Coleridge's constant references throughout the *Biographia* and *The Friend* to his readership and reading) these ten theses now give us some reason to suppose that the necessity for reflection and for resistance to the current of sequential, linear reading may extend to more of the *Biographia* than was at first apparent. The two metaphoric situations quoted above indicate that one might look for other passages having a similar effect of an alternating pause and progressive movement away from the page into the mind, where words are transformed into knowledge in intellectual experiences of discovering the 'reasons why'. This effect is ensured by the difficulty of deriving immediate sense from these passages, and of thereby making them objects not of thought, but merely of attention.

Such a passage occurs in the thirteenth chapter of the *Biographia* and is again from Schelling: 'grant me a nature having two contrary forces, the one of which tends to expand infinitely, while the other strives to apprehend or find itself in this infinity, and I will cause the world of intelli-gences with the whole system of their representations to rise up before you'.[15] It is difficult to see how the two contrary forces of one power can cause the world of intelligences to rise up, unless we understand the relation of intelligence for Coleridge to the life force. This metaphor must 'ring true', and we must 're-cognize' contraction and expansion to be a proper description of the mind in the act of self-consciousness. The identity connection of a force to the ground of intelligences by intuitional recog-nition is immediate, when the aptness of the metaphor (of the power infinitely expanding and finding itself in that infinity) to describe this reading process strikes the reader. The mind expands away from the page again, away from the outness of things, into its interior, which opens up before it as an infinite landscape.

'The solution itself discovers the instrument': in the intuition of the integrity of the relations, the faculty (instrument) comes to life. It *is* as it is known. Our reading process must be like 'descending into the dark cave of Trophonius, there to rub [our own] eyes, in order to make the sparks and figured flashes which we are required to see'.[16] In contemplating such a passage (not merely reading *over* it), we see how it becomes a recipe of the necessary approach to the *Biographia*. The levels of the metaphor are psychological and methodological, descriptive both of an anatomy of reading and of the design of the work as integrating into itself reader response. The letter in chapter twelve provides another description of the *Biographia*, and also hints at how we must proceed: 'You have been obliged to omit so many links, from the necessity of compression, that what remains, looks (if I may recur to my former illustration) like the fragments of the winding steps of an old ruined tower.'[17] We supply *ourselves* these links, these missing steps, by 'hard reading and hard thinking'. In the very process of trying to ascend the stairway in the tower we build the missing steps. In 'rubbing our eyes, we make the sparks by which we see'. *The Friend* is instructive on this metaphor:

Were but a hundred men to combine a deep conviction that virtuous habits may be formed by the very means by which knowledge is communicated, that men may be made better, not only in consequence, *but by the mode and in the process*, of instruction; were but an hundred men to combine that clear con-viction of this, which I myself at this moment feel, even as I feel the certainty of my being, with the perseverance of a CLARKSON or a BELL, the promises of ancient prophecy would disclose themselves to our faith, even as when a noble castle hidden from an intervening mist, discovers itself by its reflection in the tranquil lake, on the opposite shore of which we stand gazing.[18]

It is essential to notice that this passage, which deals with the process of coming to know, also ascends to a metaphor. The reader is again required to pause and reflect upon the relation of the castle and mist, the lake and the observer on the shore, etc., as correlative to those relations involved in *The Friend* and its reader, the difficulty of the subject matter, the mist of indirect communication, and the mind which must use *The Friend* as a mirror to reveal the truths indirectly, owing to the impenetrability of the mist. In order for this to be more than mere allegory, a transformation of the dead words into intuited relations and experienced metaphors must occur.

A few pages further in *The Friend* we are met with another analysis of the anatomy of communication and the related feelings.

No object, not even the light of a solitary taper in the distance, tempts the benighted mind from before; but its own restlessness dogs it from behind, as with the iron goad of Destiny. What then is or can be the preventive, the remedy, the counteraction, but the habituation of the intellect to clear, distinct, and adequate conceptions concerning all things that are the possible objects of clear conception, and thus to reserve the deep feelings which belong, as by a natural right to those obscure ideas that are necessary to the moral perfection of the human being, to reserve these feelings, I repeat, for objects, which their very sublimity renders indefinite, no less than their indefiniteness renders them sublime: namely, to the Ideas of Being, Form, Life, the Reason, Law of Conscience, Freedom, Immortality, God! To connect with the objects of our senses the obscure notions and consequent vivid feelings, which are due only to immaterial and permanent things, is profanation relatively to the heart, and superstition in the understanding. It is in this sense, that the philosophic Apostle calls Covetousness Idolatry.[19]

This is a challenge to the reader to test for himself the claims made and to find instances both of philosophic idolatry and of objects whose sublimity renders them indefinite. He must *think* on being for a time. Elsewhere in *The Friend* Coleridge advises his reader to do precisely this. The reader must pause and reflect, for only then does the significance of the words emerge. It requires restraint and will to free the mind from a 'sequential' reading. But in these pauses and interspaces of reflection the missing links lie, above and away from the text itself, as a third dimension of *depth*.

Coleridge maintains that we never perceive depth or inwardness by means of the senses; we supply it just as we supply causal connection to a series of associations. It may be that this inwardness of the *Biographia* and *The Friend* as depth must be supplied by the reader's imagination, as are the connections amongst the individual fragments. Coleridge's comments throughout his writings on depth versus surface and inwardness versus outness, are emblematic of the problem of reading the *Biographia*. The *Biographia* is perceived as a surface only, by those whose imaginations remain inactive. Its inwardness and life are hidden from the inactive minds as the inwardness and depth of the 'material world' remain outness and surface to the unreflective.[20] 'Matter has no *Inward*. We remove one surface but to meet with another.'[21] Intense concentration on something such as the page in front of us, or a table, is the prerequisite for testing such an assertion about depth. Yet what reader actually performs it? Height may be mistaken as an *abstract* solution to depth, but it is not inwardness. A willingness to interrupt the sequential reading for a half hour or an hour to reflect on such assertions leads to a realization of the 'missing links' in the *Biographia*. These 'vacancies' and interspaces of thought between the lines are crucial to revealing the links. Shelley suggests that these interspaces are the actual *conditions* for creative activity:

> The secret strength of things
> Which governs thought, and to the infinite dome
> Of Heaven is as a law, inhabits thee.
> And what were thou, and earth, and stars, and sea,
> If to the human mind's imaginings
> Silence and solitude were vacancy?
>
>   Shelley, *Mont Blanc*[22]

The narrative structure and apparent fragmentariness of the *Biographia* are as surfaces of the book which becomes literally imbued with depth and inwardness as the reader's mind draws the sequential lines and yet subsequently adds the depth. Alternating surface or depth movements occur as the mind attends only or truly thinks. Such a description is only a model or a metaphor employed for its explanatory power, and is a valid construct only as long as it stimulates perception.[23]

A geometrical description of a hypothetical process of reading the *Biographia* and the correspondent structure of the book occurs as the lengthy passage in chapter twelve from Schelling. This passage on the linear, circular, and undetermined line is another metaphor of the process of reading the *Biographia* as described above. The subsequent description of the four types of consciousness is descriptive of four types of readers. Coleridge's continuing remarks suggest still another recipe for reading the *Biographia*:

The connection of the parts and their logical dependencies may be seen and remembered; but the whole is groundless and hollow, unsustained by living contact, unaccompanied with any realizing intuition which exists by and in the act that affirms its existence, which is known, because it is, and is because it is known.[24]

The words of Plotinus follow immediately and apply also to the present account of this passage: 'With me the act of contemplation makes the thing contemplated, as the geometricians contemplating describe lines correspondent; but I not describing lines, but simply contemplating, the representative forms of things rise up into existence.' We are turned directly to the acts of contemplation required in reading the *Biographia* as constituting it. It is no accident that the following paragraph begins with the 'heaven-descended know thyself', *practically* and *speculatively*. The denial of the practical dimensions, in this case the reading analogy, leaves the speculative devoid of confirmation, or flat and ungrounded, as Coleridge shows when he says,

It will then remain for us to elevate the Thesis from notional to actual, by contemplating intuitively this one power with its two inherent indestructible yet counteracting forces, and the results or generations to which their interpenetration gives existence, in the living principle and in the process of our own self-consciousness.[25]

Another illustration of these 'metaphorical situations' in the *Biographia* is Coleridge's treatment in volume two of Wordsworth's poem 'The White Doe'.[26] A long section of the poem is quoted in full as exemplary of the imaginative power, but, one may ask, exemplary of whose imaginative power? To recognize it as Wordsworth's genius, we must make our mind 'congenerous' with the object beheld. The poem should not be hypostasized as absolutely independent of any reader's response.[27] Because the relevant portion of the reproduced poem was in the *Biographia*, the reader has another opportunity to wake himself from the stupor of a narrative, sequential reading to the experience of his imagination. One might characterize how this happens as follows: The white doe steals into the view of the poem's narrator as the poem 'The White Doe' steals into the view of the reader. As the imagination of the narrator is stimulated to describe the doe in the poetic relationships which he sees in the act of creating them for himself, the reader also responds warmly and imaginatively to the poem. If he raises himself to a consciousness of his situation as reader, the relationships of the poem/doe, reader/narrator, imagination/ sight, and mental landscape/churchyard are transformed into a new setting. The reader makes the imagination, operating before only as instrument, become the object of his attention and his goal in contemplating. But it is simultaneously the light by which he contemplates. That light as power is both 'expanding infinitely and striving to find itself in that infinity'. These remarks must be obscure if they are read as revealing some 'substantial' truth. They must be taken (because of the 'mist before the castle') as hints, stimuli, or models to an active realization of their validity or adequacy, through the individual reconstruction of the relations which they suggest.

SELF-CONSCIOUSNESS AND METAPHOR

The passages quoted above are instances of Coleridge's awakening his readers to a consciousness of the connections which organize thought and language. We must not allow language itself 'as it were to think for us (like the sliding rule which is the mechanic's sole substitute for arithmetic knowledge)'.[28] Language 'thinking for us' is common-sense, but it is only by delving into the hidden common-sense relations and testing their validity that we can elevate common-sense to reason and opinion to knowledge:

> Truths of all others the most awful and mysterious, yet being at the same time of universal interest, are too often considered as so true, that they lose all the life and efficiency of truth, and lie bed-ridden in the dormitory of the soul, side by side with the most despised and exploded errors...In poems, equally as in philosophic disquisitions, genius produces the strongest impressions of novelty, while it rescues the most admitted truths from the impotence caused by the very circumstance of their universal admission.[29]

By such statements the reader is jolted out of his submissiveness to un-examined, unconscious connections. He is further stimulated by the necessity of regenerating truths by means of demands for more thought than readers may be in the habit of having to give. The distinction between thought and attention is another gesture of alerting the reader to this demand.

 The examples in the above sections, requiring reflection and pause from the process of sequential reading to discover the 'missing links', are explicitly metaphorical. We can now consider those that are more direct in referring the reader to his own mind but which nevertheless demand a metaphorical application to the immediate act of reading – to the Hegelian 'Now'. The following illustration is characteristic of the *Biographia*:

> I began then to ask myself, what proof I had of the outward existence of anything? Of this sheet of paper for instance, as a thing in itself, separate from the phenomenon or image in my perception. I saw, that in the nature of things such proof is impossible; and that of all modes of being, that are not objects of the senses, the existence is *assumed* by a logical necessity arising from the con-stitution of the mind itself, by the absence of all motive to doubt it, not from any absolute contradiction in the supposition of the contrary.[30]

To see how this passage can function, we may focus our attention on the phrase 'of this sheet of paper'. Coleridge may be understood as referring to the paper upon which his words are being written at that moment; the analogy for the reader is pellucid. The paradox drawn to our attention in this case is that in stopping to muse upon the sheet of paper as outside oneself, and by nature other than oneself and other than one's perception of it, the reader is led to focus upon his sensations and perceptions. As he ponders and tries thoroughly to feel and grasp the sheet of paper which he was reading in its being separate from himself, that once tacitly assumed and certain separateness becomes confused and doubted. If he moves on to attend to this very process of thought, the reader realizes then that this procedure has brought into consciousness the prejudice of outwardness, a prejudice of which he was previously hardly aware, because outness is entirely common-sensical. This is the process which can either transform common-sense into reason, or prove it to be only prejudiced and notional. One achieves a vivid awareness of the basic assumptions and connections amongst thoughts to which one had never before been moved to attend because they were so widely accepted. The mind is referred again to itself for confirmation. The particularity of *this* passage is most significant to our approach. As Coleridge chooses the piece of paper upon which *he* is writing to focus his attention, our attention is invariably focused upon that 'same' paper ('same' in a peculiar sense), but the relation of the paper to the beholder is this time of the reader to the printed page, rather than author to page being written. The roles of reader and author become somewhat blurred together and are even in a sense identical.

A passage complementary to the one quoted immediately above should cause the reader to move initially not to serious contemplation of the outness of things, but to contemplation upon himself. Nevertheless, the eventual outcome of the resulting musings and associations will be the same. The boundary between outer and inner becomes critically blurred:

The other position, . . . , I AM, cannot so properly be intitled [*sic*] a prejudice. It is groundless indeed; but then in the very idea it precludes all ground, and separated from the immediate consciousness loses its whole and import. It is groundless; but only because it is itself the ground of all other certainty . . . the former is unconsciously involved in the latter; that it is not only coherent but identical, and one and the same thing with our own immediate self-consciousness. To demonstrate this identity is the office and object of his [the transcendental philosopher's] philosophy.[31]

'Demonstrate' is the key word. The certainty of the above proposition can be talked about endlessly but it can only be *known* in an act of 'recognition'. This is perhaps why the accusation of mysticism is directed against the philosophies grounded in the most thorough-going empiricism and why the empirical and intuitional are so often confounded. Intuitional insight for Coleridge is the only solid and universally valid experience upon which certainty can be grounded. The empirical/transcendental distinction is widely confounded with the transcendent/transcendental distinction and with disastrous consequences. We must look to the latter to define the boundaries of knowledge. The distinction is based ultimately on that same intuition which is the result of the critical philosophy, that the world we know is not that of things in themselves but of appearances, and the mind itself supplies the connections amongst those appearances.

It is in the demonstration of the relation of the 'I AM' prejudice to the prejudice of the existence of things outside us, the 'outness' of Berkeley, that the practical and the speculative unite. The bridging of the two proves to be one of the greatest difficulties of communication, for it involves generating the intuitive in order to prove the discursive. This process brings about the elevation of opinion to knowledge. The speculative will remain only opinion until the life of the practical is breathed into it:

KNOW THYSELF!...And this at once practically and speculatively. For as philosophy is neither a science of the reason or understanding only, nor merely a science of morals, but the science of BEING altogether, its primary ground can be neither merely speculative or merely practical, but both in one. All knowledge rests on the coincidence of an object with a subject...For we can know that only which is true; the truth is universally placed in the coincidence of the thought with the thing, of the representation with the object represented.[32]

Truth in coincidence of the thought with the thing suggests that art is experience, and that the *Biographia* in coincidence with the thinking of the reader is where we must seek the meaning. For the reader it means reading sequentially but then acting immediately upon that reading, during the reading, pausing to make sure he understands, and pausing to seize the truth of the words in his own experiencing of the integrity of their relations: 'The obtruded purpose of *The Friend*...in which the aim of every sentence is to solicit, nay, tease, the reader to ask himself, whether he actually does, or does not understand *distinctly*:- whether he has reflected on the precise meaning of the word, however familiar it may be both to his ear and his mouth.'[33] The author must move the reader to experience actively what passes from the book to his mind.

Throughout the difficult and demanding parts of the work, the passive reader expects, on the other hand, that all will eventually be revealed; when it is not, he is fearful, frustrated, and possibly even outraged. The epithets 'obscure', 'mystical', 'dry', 'ponderous', etc., stream forth occasioned by the impatient need for immediate comprehension: 'pardonably may a writer of the present times anticipate a scanty audience for abstrusest themes, and truths that can neither be communicated or received without effort of thought, as well as patience of attention'.[34] Patience is essential: 'With my best efforts to be as perspicuous as the nature of language will permit on such a subject, I earnestly solicit the good wishes and friendly patience of my readers, while I thus go "sounding on my dim and perilous way".'[35] In these sentences Coleridge suggests how involved geniality is in speculative philosophy, and how irritability and arrogance as well as the tendency to set up an authority other than reason, must be expunged from reading. Coleridge felt the duty to communicate and took it upon himself to tackle the problems of the frame of mind of his reader, in order that his words might be better understood. Traditionally such considerations are thought to be inappropriate to a philosophical undertaking. Coleridge has dared, in the German Romantic fashion, to challenge those notions of propriety and, more importantly, of genre. He crosses the bounds of traditional genres, and consistently with his dynamic and constructive view of knowledge, he synthesizes them to achieve an entirely new mode of philosophical writing. Such a *hybrid* result is at the same time an attack on many of the traditional genres which separate and exclude from their form that which ought only to be distinguished. Coleridge's attempt constituted a refusal to countenance the compartmentalization of knowledge in the complete separateness of science and art or poetry and philosophy. Thus his synthetic philosophy was also a practical method, as is shown in his hybrid genre, his metaphoric style, and his functional use of sources.

Coleridge creates a metaphor to distinguish the transcendent from the transcendental, and the last few lines of this passage demonstrate that which it is designed to signify discursively:

But in all ages there have been a few, who measuring and sounding the rivers of the vale at the feet of their furthest inaccessible falls have learned, that the sources must be far higher and far inward; a few, who even in the level streams have detected elements, which neither the vale itself or the surrounding mountains contained or could supply. How and whence to these thoughts, these strong probabilities, the ascertaining vision, the intuitive knowledge may finally supervene, can be learnt only by the fact.[36]

Coming in the midst of a series of remarks and advices to the reader on reading, this passage can be understood as descriptive, both in the process of comprehending the design and interconnections of the *Biographia's* fragments, and also of a general description of the investigation into the operations of the human mind. It may be accidental that the phrase 'the sources must be far higher and far inward' applies literally to the mind of the reader hunched over his *Biographia Literaria*...*his* literary biography, too, since his understanding of the *Biographia* will be a kind of record of his evolving insights into the general problems of reading and responding to art. That the way in which such passages mirror their own subject matter 'can be learnt only by the fact' explains why any interpretation or explication remains obscure to many readers. Coleridge's efforts to tease the reader into thought are designed to resist stock response and jargon, which remain uninformed by the experience that grounds the words: 'whatever may enable men to talk of what they do not understand'.[37] The danger of metaphor (and the significance) degenerating into the literal, or 'mere jargon', Coleridge treats again elsewhere: 'there is nothing against it, but its own sublimity. It could not be intellectually more evident without becoming morally less effective; without counteracting its own end by sacrificing the life of faith to the cold mechanism of a worthless because compulsory assent.' The danger of the degeneration of metaphor into literal-mindedness cannot be overemphasized, lying as it does at the centre of Coleridge's synthetic philosophy and the romantic movement as a whole. It is the starting point of Shelley's 'Defence of Poetry' and his theory of imaginative activity as the paradigm of human mental activity.

READERSHIP AND COMMUNICATION

In the foregoing pages it has been suggested that the method of the *Biographia* can be described as a stimulation of self-contemplation by the construction of dramatic moments which are dependent upon acts of relational apprehension by the reader for their sense. These acts can often occur only through earnest and time-consuming reflection. Without intense reflection such passages remain enigmatic and paradoxical, but are nevertheless guarded by their paradoxical nature against degenerating into 'cold mechanism' and 'literal-mindedness'.[38] Such a method can be contrasted with the discursive treatise which is the traditional garb and genre of philosophy. The latter seeks to explain literally as much as possible, supposedly avoiding the 'mistake' of missing links. Its style is a 'close reasoning' which the *attentive* reader is expected to follow. The phrase 'poetic method' (as opposed to discursive method) is convenient as a description of Coleridge's style in the *Biographia* because of his reliance upon metaphor as the crucial means of communicating truth. Metaphor is the model of synthetic acts of mind, and the stimulation in another mind of metaphorical apprehension is the most important truth or knowledge that can be 'communicated'. Because of the 'poetical' method of the *Biographia*, Coleridge was able to achieve his own form of a *Prelude*, and there is much evidence for the belief that he considered it as such: it was his growth of a poet's mind.[39] Once the reader accepts the role of co-creator which the Romantic poets demanded of him, along with the shedding of external false authority for the freedom of reason (in Coleridge's sense of the word; but imagination for Shelley and Blake), the *Biographia* becomes the growth of the reader's mind as well. The reader too must act as poet or 'fellow-worker', as Coleridge says in *The Friend*.[40]

Besides the elusive, open-ended, and indeterminate metaphoric situations, and besides the 'recipes' for reading, there are numerous relevant discursive statements in the *Biographia*. These discursive comments are methodological observations, not dogmatic propositions with ordinary philosophical 'content'. They are comments on readership and its state of awareness, explicit directions for how to read properly, and comments about the difficulties of writing and communication.

The issue of obscurity which has arisen several times in the foregoing pages has a special application to readership in an analysis of method. In addition to the passages on obscurity quoted above, Coleridge explains in the following how central an issue it is:

A system, the first principle of which is to render the mind intuitive of the spiritual in man (i.e. of that which lies on the other side of our natural consciousness) must needs have a greater obscurity for those, who have never disciplined and strengthened this ulterior consciousness...On the IMMEDIATE, which dwells in every man, and on the original intuition, or absolute affirmation of it, (which is likewise in every man, but does not in every man rise into consciousness) all the certainty of our knowledge depends; and this becomes intelligible to no man by the ministry of mere words from without.[41]

We have also suggested in the foregoing sections that the *Biographia* is replete with 'self-referring' passages, that is sections which, though they literally have application to a specific topic, also at the same time act as clues for reading the *Biographia* because they are, indirectly, accurate descriptions of its method and mode of interaction with the reader. One such instance of this self-reference we find in the following comment on Leibnitz and synthesis:

Leibnitz himself, in a most instructive passage, describes as the criterion of a true philosophy; namely, that it would at once explain and correct the fragments of truth scattered through systems apparently the most incongruous. The truth, says he, is diffused more widely than is commonly believed; but it is often tainted, yet oftener masked, and is sometimes mutilated and sometimes, alas! in close alliance with mischievous errors. The deeper, however, we penetrate into the ground of things, the more truth we discover in the doctrines of the greater number of the philosophical sects...all these we shall find united in one perspective central point, which shows regularity and a coincidence of all the parts in the very object, which every other point of view must appear confused and distorted. The spirit of sectarianism has been hitherto our fault, and the cause of our failures. We have imprisoned our own conceptions by the lines, which we have drawn, in order to exclude the conceptions of others.[42]

This passage is inserted between borrowings from Schelling and ends with a sentence from Leibnitz. Thus Coleridge has immediately put into practice the style of composition he finds Leibnitz indirectly advocating in the comments on philosophizing.

Coleridge is constantly giving his reader advice on how best to read in order to achieve that identity of subject and object. He also tries to make predictions about the type of responses he is likely to receive from readers, in order that he may anticipate and dispel the difficulties and immediate objections they may feel. The following passage provides the reader with another clue to the way in which the sources and borrowings in the *Biographia* are supposed to function:

and ever and anon coming out full upon pictures and stone-work images of great men, with whose *names* I was familiar, but which looked upon me with countenances and an expression, the most dissimilar to all I had been in the habit of connecting with those names... in short, what I had supposed substances were thinned away into shadows, while everywhere shadows were deepened into substances.[43]

One of our major concerns being the issue of unity and fragmentation of the *Biographia*, the next quotation is pertinent to illustrate this sort of composition:

In lieu of the various requests which the anxiety of authorship addresses to the unknown reader, I advance but this one; that he will either pass over the following chapter altogether, or read the whole connectedly. The fairest part of the most beautiful body will appear deformed and monstrous, if dissevered from its place in the organic Whole. Nay, on delicate subjects, where a seemingly trifling difference of more or less may constitute a difference in *kind*, even a *faithful* display of the main and supporting ideas, if yet they are separated from the forms by which they are at once cloathed and modified, may perchance present a skeleton indeed; but a skeleton to alarm and deter.[44]

We may be rightly puzzled that such a request is ignored by the majority of Coleridge's readers. Others think it an excuse for what they perceive to be disjointedness and a syncretic genre.[45]

THE UNITY OF 'BIOGRAPHIA' I

The apparent fragmentariness of the *Biographia* is a problem which no reader can ignore. Given Coleridge's emphasis on the organic as opposed to the mechanical (expressed in such statements as those on the part/whole relationship), we may justifiably seek to 'read the whole connectedly'. Coleridge describes the *Biographia* in the letter in chapter thirteen as being like 'the fragments of the winding steps of an old ruined tower', fragments because he was 'obliged to omit so many links, from the necessity of compression'. This alone suggests that there are links which the reader must restore or supply in order to reconstruct the winding staircase.[46] There may be interconnections amongst the various fragments and mastercurrents below the surface which need to be recreated in order for the design of the whole to emerge.

It may be possible to anticipate objections that we are seeking order where there may be none, by examining a note in chapter four on the bull. This note seems to be emblematic both of the method of the *Biographia* and of the 'metaphoric situations' encountered above. Here Coleridge makes some very important observations on the most common process of transformation involved in knowing, and the response of the 'learner'. The corresponding passage in the letter is quoted to aid in the communication of the *sense* of the passage.

In opinions of long continuance, and in which we have never before been molested by a single doubt, to be suddenly *convinced* of an *error*, is almost like being *convicted* of a fault. There is a state of mind, which is the direct antithesis of that, which takes place when we *make a bull. The bull* namely consists in the bringing together two incompatible thoughts, with the *sensation*, but without the *sense*, of their connection. The psychological condition, or that which constitutes the possibility of this state, being such disproportionate vividness of two distant thoughts, as extinguishes or obscures the consciousness of the intermediate images or conceptions, or wholly abstracts the attention from them. Thus in the well known bull, '*I was a fine child but they changed me;*' the first conception expressed in the word '*I*' is that of personal identity – *Ego contemplans*: the second expressed in the '*me*', is the visual image or object by which the mind represents to itself its past condition, or rather, its personal identity under the form in which it imagined itself previously to have existed, – *Ego contemplatus*. Now the change of one visual image for another involves in itself no absurdity, and becomes absurd only by its immediate juxtaposition with the first thought, which is rendered possible by the whole attention being successively absorbed in each singly, so as not to notice the interjacent notion, 'changed', which by its incongruity with the first thought, 'I', constitutes the bull. Add only, that this process is facilitated by the circumstance of the words 'I' and 'me', being sometimes equivalent, and sometimes having a distinct meaning; sometimes, namely, signifying the act of self-consciousness, sometimes the external image in and by which the mind represents that act to itself, the result and symbol of its individuality. Now suppose the direct contrary state, and you will have a distinct sense of the connection between two conceptions, without that sensation of such connection which is supplied by habit. The man *feels* as if he were standing on his head, though he cannot but *see*, that he is truly standing on his feet. This, as a painful sensation, will of course have a tendency to associate itself with the person who occasions it; even as persons, who have been by painful means restored from derangement, are known to feel an involuntary dislike towards their physician.[47]

Compare this passage and the letter given in part here:

As to myself, and stating in the first place the effect on my *understanding*, your opinions and method of argument were not only so *new* to me, but so directly the reverse of all I had ever been accustomed to consider as truth, that even if I had comprehended your premises sufficiently to have admitted them, and had seen the necessity of your conclusions, I should still have been in that state of mind, which in your note page 52, 53, you have so ingeniously evolved, as the antithesis to that in which a man is, when he makes a *bull*. In your own words, I should have felt as if I had been standing on my head.[48]

This bull is footnoted to a passage which constitutes an anatomy of criticism with fear and irritability clearly exposed. The anatomy is a picture of that which Coleridge felt he must overcome. The note is an ingenious description of what he was trying to help his readers to accomplish by showing the indispensable participation of the reader. The last four lines of the note explain why Coleridge was the butt of so much criticism, and the passage as a whole illustrates why for many readers the *Biographia* must remain an enigma. The sensation of the connections is a vital part of the understanding, though even the *sense* remains obscure for a large number of readers. It is significant that this cleverly expressed insight is contained in a long, difficult note.[49] The note is certainly a demonstration of its point in the finest way. The note itself is a playing out of the drama which it describes; it too is a bull, which to some extent explains its difficulty and the impossibility of paraphrase. In trying to grasp the sense of the passage, the reader finds many of Coleridge's maxims to be prerequisites or preconditions for comprehension, such as the understanding/ ignorance maxim and the maxims on patience. Geniality is also a primary requirement. Nor is it an accident that in illustrating the bull, Coleridge chose an 'I/me' example as a further effort to 'gain ground' in the reader's mind. Thus he points out the distinct meanings of 'I' and 'me' as sometimes 'signifying the act of self-consciousness, and sometimes the external image in and by which the mind represents that act to itself as the result and symbol of its individuality'.[50] This acute analysis of the process involved in overturning old notions and prejudices (the resulting obscurity initially encountered being due to a lack of conviction and sensation of the new connections), ties this section up closely with the preoccupation in *The Friend* with the problem of obscurity – indeed, the necessity of obscurity in discursive writing. With an apt metaphor, the obscurity lies only in the discursive rendering of the metaphor, or in the mind which has as yet not realized the sensation of the connections or which takes the metaphor literally. It seems appropriate that Coleridge ended his account of the bull with the metaphor of 'standing on one's head', to express graphically the confusion the reader must feel.

We can better sense what Coleridge was resisting, and why the means of dealing with it must at first seem so difficult to comprehend, from a passage closely following the bull: 'genius produces the strongest impressions of novelty, while it rescues the most admitted truths from the impotence caused by the very circumstance of their universal admission'.[51] It is not enough to speak truths, in treatise form; they must be given the 'life and efficiency of truth'. The result of that infusion Coleridge states further on: 'In energetic minds, truth soon changes by domestication into power; and from directing in the discrimination and appraisal of the product, becomes influencive in the production. To admire on principle, is the only way to imitate without loss of originality.'[52] This is a statement instructive both for the reader and for the artist.

While keeping in mind the note on the bull concerning the distinction between the sense and the sensation of connection or relation, and the feelings both of standing on one's head and of irritability toward the 'physician', let us examine more closely the general connections amongst the chapters of the *Biographia*. The first four chapters can be seen as rigorously preparing the reader's mind for the reception of the distinction between imagination and fancy. The importance of such preparation is made evident in *The Friend* in the comments on duty which Coleridge makes repeatedly. It is his duty to see that what he has to say is rightly understood, and that he has made every possible effort to avoid misunderstanding in the process of communication. Since, according to Coleridge, geniality is the condition of the mind's receptivity to unusual thought or ahabitual opinions, he must ensure as far as he can the genial state of mind of his readers. He does this in several ways, first by exposing the fallacies of critics that attend to the wrong objects (persons instead of works) and who have no critical principles. He tries to make his reader's mind receptive to the difficult and unpopular ideas he is trying to communicate by *demonstrating* genial criticism, reasoned out and based on first principles. Coupled with this precaution are constant gentle hints about how not to read and why, backed by a delightful analysis of the mind of the irritable reader/critic. Coleridge has no need to refer to named individuals, since his prime object is the unnamed reader. He refers only to the *principles* that reveal the inner workings of such responses, applicable universally, and this is a practical application of one of his own critical principles.

Following through some of the main topics in these first four chapters, we can watch the interconnections developing as hints of preparation for the rest of the *Biographia*. Since the principle of geniality is of foremost importance, the first chapter is devoted to a genial criticism of Coleridge's own work, with rational examination and precise explanation of the faults of thought and diction and supporting examples. Then Coleridge mentions a type of education that fosters the ungenial mind. Following this he describes the pleasure of being able to attribute a valuable thought to a fellow writer.[53] Further examples of rational criticism tempered by complete good will end the chapter, a model for the reader of genial criticism and self-consciousness.

Chapter two begins with a more precise anatomy of ungenial criticism and the fear and irritability that play an important role in such a state of mind. A note in this chapter on Pope is a further illustration of 'genial' criticism. Coleridge points out a serious error, while still avoiding the least hint of slander or sneer.[54] Nor is this criticism founded on arguments of taste, but rather on discovering first principles and judgments based thereupon. Coleridge's remarks on Milton are further instances, which sound almost prophetic of what J. S. Mill was later to say of Coleridge himself.[55] Coleridge said of Milton that he lived 'among men before whom he strode so far as to *dwarf* himself by the distance; yet still listening to the music of his own thoughts'.[56] The important distinction between the man and the author follows appropriately, and we then come upon the first explicit exhortations about reading itself:

I have attempted to illustrate the present state of our language, in its relation to literature, by a press-room of larger and smaller stereotype pieces, which, in the present Anglo-Gallican fashion of unconnected, epigrammatic periods, it requires but an ordinary portion of ingenuity to vary indefinitely, and yet still produce something, which, if *not* sense, will be so like it as to do as well. Perhaps better; for it spares the reader the trouble of thinking; prevents vacancy, while it indulges indolence; and secures the memory from all danger of an intellectual plethora... Now it is no less remarkable than true, with how little examination works of polite literature are commonly perused, not only by the mass of readers, but by men of first rate ability, till some accident or chance discussion have roused their attention, and put them on their guard.[57]

This is precisely what Coleridge was trying to prevent readers from doing with the *Biographia*. At the same time he was determined not to fall into abstruse philosophical jargon which would exclude the people he was trying to reach, and which would further separate philosophy from literature and poetry. The subsequent observations on genius substantiates Coleridge's insistence that the proper objects of literary criticism are works, not men: 'because his feelings have been habitually associated with thoughts and images, to the number, clearness, and vivacity of which the sensation of *self* is always in an inverse proportion'.[58] Coleridge here seeks to turn the reader's attention away from his own personal interests and tastes, toward thoughts and images and the ideas which the *Biographia* illuminates. It also explains why Coleridge wrote not an autobiography, but a literary biography. His unashamed self-analysis in chapter two has provided many occasions for accusations of sloth, indolence, and self-pity, while the fact that these remarks also reveal the extraordinary expectations and the demands which he made upon himself is ignored.[59]

Chapter two ends with a statement applicable to all critics and readers: 'Indignation at literary wrongs I leave to men born under happier stars. I cannot *afford it*.'[60] In those earlier chapters Coleridge is not, as has frequently been maintained, defending himself. He is trying to trick his reader into a genial frame of mind in order that the reader may gain the most from what is to come, and also in order that the thought which Coleridge is trying to communicate will be understood. It is no small undertaking, nor an unworthy one, to prepare the soil of the reader's mind for the vegetation which an author is to transplant.

Chapter three gives additional notice to the reader not to read the text now before him as a 'pass-time' or 'kill-time'. This comment is placed demurely in a note, for it is characteristic of many readers to skip over notes entirely as unimportant asides. Chapter three contains more discussion of the pitfalls awaiting critics who attack the person rather than the ideas put forward. Then, in a note, we find another description applicable to the *Biographia*:

I have ventured to call it 'unique'; not only because I know no work of the kind in our language...none, which uniting the charms of romance and history, keeps the imagination so constantly on the wing, and yet leaves so much for after reflection; but likewise, and chiefly, because it is a compilation which, in the various excellencies of translation, selection, and arrangement, required and proves greater genius in the compiler, as living in the present state of society, than in the original composers.[61]

This is clearly an apt description of the *Biographia* if we replace 'romance and history' with 'poetry and philosophy'. We have also in this chapter a hint of that which is to be the main concern in the next several chapters, again in a note. After listing an odd assortment of apparently unconnected images, Coleridge says: 'By the bye, this catalogue, strange as it may appear, is not insusceptible of a sound psychological commentary'[62] – perhaps on associationism?

One example of an apparently total digression may help to make the possibility of connections in the *Biographia* more plausible. In chapter three Coleridge discusses his relation with Wordsworth and Southey and the various attacks which were made upon them from time to time. In trying to understand the impetus for these attacks, Coleridge gives, as a possible solution, the fact that 'I was in habits of intimacy with Mr. Wordsworth and Mr. Southey.'[63] And in a preceding note, a similar reason was given: 'but that as to *Coleridge*, he had noticed him merely because the names of Southey and Wordsworth and Coleridge always went together'.[64] This folly is an apt example of the use of the *condition* of association (contiguity in time or space) to account for a causal connection, a serious error and one which led to the materialist doctrine of the condition as the principle or *law* of association. It is to this error that the later chapters of the *Biographia* devote themselves, after the distinction of imagination from fancy, the former being the faculty which makes the distinction between the condition and the law possible. Hence we see that even an anecdote as apparently digressive as the 'spy story' has its function as an instance and illustration of one of the main principles expounded in the *Biographia*.

Chapter four, in which the fancy/imagination distinction is introduced, is a wealth of related topics, including the idea of synthesis (as opposed to mere synartesis), obscurity, reading methods, important statements hidden away in the footnotes, interconnections of the most direct sort with other chapters, and still more remarks and illustrations of genial criticism. In this chapter we find the note about the bull. Then we find Coleridge quoting a section from one of Wordsworth's poems as emblematic of the poem itself, a practice with which we have become very familiar in reading the *Biographia*.[65] This example of Wordsworth's poem should dispel any doubts which we may have had that Coleridge was unfamiliar with the type of mirroring effect of art, operating both for the author or poet and the reader, and which we have been finding throughout the *Biographia*. It is apt that a paragraph on the psyche follows, which connects directly with the passage quoted at the beginning of this chapter. The note at the bottom of the page also contains a poem by 'S.T.C.' in which he incorporates this play on words, just as he had done in the former passage.

Further on in chapter four the first direct statements about synthesis as a mode of composition occur, along with statements that the activity of imagination is the paradigmatic form of knowledge-experience:

the union of deep feeling with profound thought; the fine balance of truth in observing, with the imaginative faculty in modifying the objects observed; and above all the original gift of spreading the tone, the atmosphere, and with it the depth and height of the ideal world around forms, incidents, and situation, of which, for the common view, custom had bedimmed all the lustre, had dried up the sparkle and the dew drops. To find no contradiction in the union of old and new; to contemplate the ANCIENT of days and all his works with feelings as fresh, as if all had then sprang forth at the first creative fiat; characterizes the mind that feels the riddle of the world, and may help to unravel it...it is the prime merit of genius and its most unequivocal mode of manifestation, so to represent familiar objects as to awaken in the minds of others a kindred feeling concerning them and that freshness of sensation which is the constant accompaniment of mental, no less than of bodily, convalescence.[66]

Perhaps we need to 'strip away the veil of familiarity' from the *Biographia* to gain a sense of the several levels upon which it works. We may begin to see *it* as Coleridge describes above. We may see the familiar objects as referring to the piecemeal borrowings which Coleridge takes from various sources and transforms into integral parts of a whole, permeated by a unique tone and atmosphere. He transforms them by a synthesis of apparently contradictory philosophies (as Shelley does in *his* synthesis of Platonism and empiricism).

The dimensions of this fourth chapter are further broadened by pointing to the metaphor in another note which acts again as an occasion for imaginative activity of the kind central to our analysis in the earlier sections of this chapter:

There is a sort of *minim immortal* among the animalcula infusoria which has not naturally either birth, or death, absolute beginning, or absolute end; for at a certain period a small point appears on its back, which deepens and lengthens till the creature divides into two, and the same process recommences in each of the halves now become integral. This may be a fanciful, but it is by no means a bad emblem of the formation of words.[67]

An inverse process to that of synthesis is described and is an instance of the truth of the maxim, 'Distinguish, but do not divide', for at the source there is a common ancestry. This metaphor may also be seen as parallel to the 'two forces of one power' metaphor, though in no sense reducible to such simplification. It is, in any case, another occasion of the need to pause and reflect upon metaphor before passing on to the next idea.

Having dwelt at length upon the section of the *Biographia* which prepares the mind of the reader for the reception of new and unusual thoughts, we can now pass on more quickly through the chapters on association in our search for unity. The introduction of the distinction between imagination and fancy crucially precedes the investigation into associationism. The involvement of this distinction in criticism and geniality is central, imagination being required for love and geniality, while it is the condition of criticism. In the form of reason it is the source of the first principles and connections upon which the work of criticism depends. The role of imagination, as distinguished from fancy, and the long discussion of associationism is central to Coleridge's philosophy as itself a form of associationism. But his is transformed crucially from Hartleian associationism, by synthesizing the truths of various philosophies, the synthesizing power being the imagination. Coleridge dwells upon the history of associationism to indicate the errors and the essential differences from his own form of associationism. Associationism without a dynamic theory of perception, involving imagination as the agent and metaphor as the form, is analogous to the tree with 'rattling twigs and sprays in winter into which a sap was yet to be propelled from some root to which I had not yet penetrated'.[68] Presumably one of the aspects of Berkeley which captured Coleridge's imagination was the notion that to view objects and the 'outness' of the world of nature as separate and other from the perceiver, was merely a convention produced by the degeneration of metaphors into literal objects.[69] That which Berkeley lacked and which Coleridge supplied was a theory of apocalyptic perception, in which the perceived and the percipient are distinguishable but not divisible. The perceiver's experience is a constant, active process of synthesizing and unifying by laws which relate phenomena according to the way in which the mind decides that they are to be related. Thus the inherent connection between the laws of nature and the principles of association and organization, i.e. the ideas, of reason itself. Whatever debt Coleridge may have owed to Kant or to Schelling for the metaphysical formulations of these ideas, he certainly transformed them in *Biographia* I into a philosophy of the phenomenology of perception, working at the immediate practical level of engaging the reader in a project of self-criticism and knowledge.

6

❧ ❧

Processes and methods in *Biographia* II

In the previous chapter it was suggested that the first volume of the *Biographia* has significantly greater unity and literary/philosophical interest than is generally acknowledged. This assessment has been based upon an analysis in chapter two of Coleridge's theory of knowledge and communication and the implications of that theory for a theory of aesthetics. His fundamentally dynamic theory, which is grounded in dialectic,[1] requires a context for the reading of a text which hinges upon a specific relation of reader and text: the two must be distinguished but not divided absolutely. The reader of the *Biographia* must at all times be aware that his intellectual activity is a primary subject of the text,[2] and that the separateness and 'outness' of the text is propaedeutic only and delusive if seen as an ultimate separation. The process of 'understanding' the text is one of discovering the nature of mind, whereby we see the necessity for a continuing effort by the reading mind to hold the text in a state of union with itself. At the same time the mind must recognize its distinctity in order that the dialectic of interaction may occur at all.[3] In German idealist terms, the subject must posit itself as object in order to become aware or have any knowledge of itself. If it forgets that the object is itself, it falls into a state of division. This division is impossible to reunify (for example, in the dichotomy between mind and nature) until the perception of the underlying homogeneity is reawakened, and until subject and object are synthesized once again. In the state of division the mind forgets that all the knowledge which it acquires about the 'other' is finally knowledge about itself. The knowledge of the 'other', whose real value lay in its being a means toward self-knowledge, becomes an end in itself. The cycle is not completed, values become perverted, and stagnation sets in as the process halts and the dialectic is suppressed. If the activity is to be renewed something more than the perception of division and separateness must occur, something more than 'reflex acts of the understanding'.[4] A force of intellectual energy which unifies and synthesizes, which perceives the sameness in difference and unity in the disparate is required.[5]

I have already tried to suggest the ways in which the first volume of the *Biographia* presents, in terms both of content and method, a unified structure behind the apparent fragments and diversions, but a more important critical task is yet to be approached. It involves not only the perception of the unity of volume two, but also the reunification of the two volumes into a single artistic whole. By examining the 'method' of volume two in the light of the analysis of volume one, the first suggestions of a continuity will emerge which can then be developed to explore the relation of philosophy to poetry, knowledge to art, and discursive thought to intuitive thought. In these relations we may hope to discover the unity of the *Biographia* as a whole. Our initial formulation takes the form of a hypothesis that the *Biographia* ii can be seen as a continuing fulfilment of the promise in chapter twelve to 'proceed to the nature and genesis of the imagination'. This 'original chapter' on the imagination discussed in chapter thirteen and rejected as too esoteric in method we may understand to be 'rewritten' and conceived in a less immediately esoteric style in the form of *Biographia* ii. The difference is not in purpose but merely in approach, for although the method and mode of communication are changed, the plan to explore the nature of the imagination is fulfilled. However extraordinary such a hypothesis may appear to be initially, it is necessary to require temporarily that same 'experimentative faith' which Coleridge requested:

sufficient to procure for these shadows of imagination that willing suspension of disbelief for the moment, which constitutes poetic faith...by awakening the mind's attention from the lethargy of custom [the usual way of regarding the *Biographia* as two unrelated works] and directing it to the loveliness and wonders of the world before us; an inexhaustible treasure [is revealed] but for which, in consequence of the film of familiarity and selfish solicitude we have eyes, yet see not, ears that hear not, and hearts that neither feel nor understand.[6]

THE READER AS FELLOW LABOURER

The primary difficulty which Coleridge knew he must face lay in the tendency of the mind to rest and passivity. In the *Biographia*, as in all his works, he emphasizes the importance of not allowing words to degenerate into mere arbitrary signs. He speaks of this degeneration as Plato did in the *Meno*: 'Words used as the *arbitrary marks* of thought, our smooth market-coin of intercourse, with the image and superscription worn out by currency.'[7] The poet or philosopher must remove this film of familiarity by creating new metaphors and images in order to draw our attention to that which out of habit we come to ignore. The following passage is such a 'new metaphor', whose subject matter also happens to be about the necessity of new metaphors.

Like the moisture or the polish on a pebble, genius neither distorts nor false-colours its objects; but on the contrary brings out many a vein, and many a tint, which escapes the eye of common observation, thus raising to the rank of gems what had been often kicked away by the hurrying foot of the traveller on the dusty high road of custom.[8]

Coleridge thus both shows and explains the need for fresh metaphors. The poet is engaged in an activity which revitalizes language, and Coleridge required from the reader the 'perpetual activity of attention': 'The reader is forced into too much action to sympathize with the merely passive of our nature.'[9] 'The traveller on the dusty high road of custom' is a metaphor for the passive reader who fails to notice this passage as a metaphor for the reading process.

The difficulty of communicating the 'nature and genesis of the imagination' goes far beyond this passive tendency of the mind however, and resides in the nature of communication and imagination itself. Overcoming this difficulty is, as we have seen, one of the major objects of Coleridge's works: 'This is the seeming *argumentum in circulo*, incident to all spiritual truths, to every subject not representable under the forms of Time and Space, as long as we attempt to master by the reflex acts of the Understanding what we can only know by the act of *becoming*.'[10] Coleridge makes it clear that it would be vain to write a merely discursive treatise on his own experiences of imagination. But he had a strong sense of the duty to communicate, that is, to write so as to be understood by others.[11] The only means of achieving this was that mode of composition which is most difficult – indirect communication, or the poetic representation of moments or situations in which the imagination of the reader is stimulated to act beyond the mere 'reflex acts of the understanding':

it is the Intuition, the direct Beholding, the immediate Knowledge, which is the *substance* and true *significance* of all – But to *give* or to *convey* to another the *Immediate* is a contradiction in terms – all that a Teacher can do is, 1. to demonstrate the hollowness and falsehood of...every...scheme of Philosophy which commences with matter as a jam datum... But the *Truth* of the Contrary must be *seen* – we must *be* it in order to *know* it. – 2. to excite the mind to the effort, and to encourage it by sympathy – .[12]

Coleridge draws a characterization of the type of reader for whom Wordsworth's poetry was written and this description applies to his own reader as well:

But the ode was intended for such readers only as had been accustomed to watch the flux and reflux of their inmost nature, to venture at times into the twilight realms of consciousness, and to feel a deep interest in modes of inmost being, to which they know that the attributes of time and space are inapplicable and alien, but which yet can not be conveyed except in symbols of time and space. For such readers the sense is sufficiently plain, and they will be as little disposed to charge Mr. Wordsworth with believing the Platonic pre-existence in the ordinary interpretation of the words, as I am to believe, that Plato himself ever meant or taught it.[13]

An esotericism is at work in Coleridge's writings, the fullest and deepest levels of structure being available to those initiated into the activity of imaginative thought:[14]

The best part of human language, properly so-called, is derived from reflection on the acts of the mind itself. It is formed by a voluntary appropriation of fixed symbols to internal acts, to processes and results of imagination, the greater part of which have no place in the consciousness of uneducated man; though in civilized society, by imitation and passive remembrance of what they hear from their religious instructors and other superiors, the most uneducated share in the harvest which they neither sowed nor reaped.[15]

The share is a small one for those who are unable to regenerate in their minds the truths which they hear from without. They are unable to grasp the connections amongst those truths, nor can they use them as preparatory in exercising the intellect for further insights.[16] For them, 'the mind contracts and hardens...'[17] That 'meditative mood'[18] which it is the object of the *Biographia* to stimulate is the counteracting force which expands the intellect and maintains its flexibility. The truths thus discovered must not be allowed to degenerate into mere signs for past experiences; hence the necessity for constant repetition: 'Truth narrative and past is the idol of the historians (who worship a dead thing), and truth operative, and by effects continually alive, is the mistress of poets, who hath not her existence in matter, but in reason.'[19]

Coleridge's characterization of the ultimate end of criticism as the establishing of principles of writing, not '*rules* how to pass judgment on what has been written by others',[20] gives us another glimpse into the problem of a treatise on imagination. In chapter eighteen the questions raised about how a poet knows what to write and the solutions Coleridge offers apply as well to the process of critical reading:

Could a rule be given from *without*, poetry would cease to be poetry, and sink into a mechanical art. It would be μόρφωσις, not ποίησις. The *rules* of the IMAGINATION are themselves the very powers of growth and production. The *words*, to which they are reducible, present only the outlines and external appearance of the fruit. A deceptive counterfeit of the superficial form and colors may be elaborated; but the marble peach feels cold and heavy, and *children* only put it to their mouths.[21]

A treatise on the imagination which was purely discursive and merely words, not at once both instance *and* illustration,[22] would be such a counterfeit fruit.

In trying to establish the ways in which *Biographia* II is a continuing fulfilment of the description of a treatise of imagination *on* imagination, we cannot ignore the striking similarity of the surface structure of volumes one and two with the description of the missing chapter in the letter in chapter thirteen. Coleridge is constantly citing passages and poems from the most diverse writers to illustrate and illuminate the points he is trying to make. The *Biographia* can be described at surface level as a mosaic of borrowed passages. With this obvious mode of composition in mind let us remind ourselves of the relevant remarks in that letter, ostensibly a description of the missing chapter, but which are also a description of the *Biographia* as a whole:

The effect on my feelings, on the other hand, I cannot better represent, than by supposing myself to have known only our light airy modern chapels of ease, and then for the first time to have been placed, and left alone, in one of our largest Gothic cathedrals in a gusty moonlight night of autumn. 'Now in glimmer, and now in gloom'; often in palpable darkness not without a chilly sensation of terror; then suddenly emerging into broad yet visionary lights with coloured shadows of fantastic shapes, yet all decked with holy insignia and mystic symbols; and ever and anon coming out full upon pictures and stone-work images of great men, with whose names I was familiar, but which looked upon me with countenances and an expression, the most dissimilar to all I had been in the habit of connecting with those names. Those whom I had been taught to venerate as almost superhuman in magnitude of intellect, I found perched in little fret-work niches, as grotesque dwarfs; while the grotesques, in my hitherto belief, stood guarding the high altar with all the characters of Apotheosis. In short, what I had supposed substances were thinned away into shadows, while everywhere shadows were deepened into substances.[23]

The 'light airy modern chapels of ease' we may assume to be the novels and other popular reading material of the reading public designed to amuse and gratify without making any demands on the intellect.[24] The darkness encountered in a work of greater scope would be those passages which require intellectual energy for understanding and provide gratification of a non-sensual sort. Those modern poets and novelists whose reputations had been raised by reviews in such journals as the *Edinburgh Review* are replaced in the *Biographia* by the names of men much older and more venerated, but who are names *only* to the vast majority of the reading public. The substances thinned away into shadow are sensual and material gratifications, the shadows turned substance are the intellectual, moral, and spiritual delight resulting from labour of thought and imagination.

In volume two we have further explicit evidence that this volume is an alternative treatise on the imagination. Coleridge says of Wordsworth:

but if I should ever be fortunate enough to render my analysis of imagination, its origin and characters, thoroughly intelligible to the reader, he will scarcely open a page of this poet's works without recognizing, more or less, the presence and influences of this faculty.[25]

It is volume two which is concerned with making Wordsworth's poetry more intelligible to the reader. In it, Coleridge has selected for quotation passages of Wordsworth's poetry which are peculiarly infused with imaginative power,[26] and has tried to direct the reader's attention to the particular ways in which imagination functions in each. These quotations act as 'fulcra' for thought or situations in which the reader is left to a 'meditative mood', out of which the imagination is free to emerge and recognize itself in action.

It is no accident that in dealing with Coleridge's works the essential difficulty should be to grasp the whole and the essential interrelationship of the parts, i.e., the organization: the reader must exercise his own 'power of reducing multitude into unity of effect, and modifying a series of thoughts by some one predominant thought or feeling.'[27] That the *Biographia* seems disjointed, fragmented and unconnected is not surprising so long as the understanding is exclusively employed. Coleridge's description of imaginative activity explains why it must appear so when the understanding alone is active:

This power, first put in action by the will and understanding, and retained under their irremissive, though gentle and unnoticed, controul...reveals itself in the balance or reconciliation of opposite or discordant qualities: of sameness, with difference; of the general, with the concrete; the idea, with the image; the individual, with the representative; the sense of novelty and freshness, with old and familiar objects...and while it blends and harmonizes the natural and the artificial, still subordinates art to nature; the manner to the matter; and our admiration of the poet to our sympathy with the poetry.[28]

Without the imagination the balance or reconciliation of opposite and discordant qualities is lost; all that remains is opposition, contradiction, division, and a work without unity or singleness of purpose.[29] Sameness is not recognized in difference (the primary criticism of the *Biographia*), the general not seen in the concrete, nor the idea seen in the image. Image, familiarity, difference, and opposition all tyrannize over the intellect ruled without the balancing and fusing activity of imagination.[30]

METAPHOR IN 'BIOGRAPHIA' II

In the light of Coleridge's remarks on readership, imagination, and indirect communication, quoted above, we may now examine the method of *Biographia* ii, which we hope to show to be identical with the method in *Biographia* i – that of 'metaphoric situations', which are parts of an underlying whole. As in *Biographia* i, the context for the response to such situations requires drifting into the 'meditative mood'. The narrative force of progression is temporarily restrained and balanced by a meditation which leads the reader below the surface of narrative to the structure beneath it.[31] This is a characteristic more typical of poetry than prose, and should give the reader an 'image of succession with the feeling of simultaneousness!'[32] The consequence of such a method is a dramatic slowing down of reading, the actual depth of meaning and significance of the words on the page being commensurate with the distance the reading mind is carried to explore the landscape of thought merely indicated by the narrative:

Its admirers feel the disposition to go back and re-peruse some preceding chapter at least ten times for once that they find any eagerness to hurry forwards: or open the book on those parts which they best recollect, even as we visit those friends oftenest whom we love most, and with whose characters and actions we are the most intimately acquainted.[33]

An early example of a metaphoric situation in *Biographia* ii, which describes the movement of the mind struggling to apprehend organization, relates closely to the passage about the insect 'winning its way up the stream' in *Biographia* i. Coleridge explains:

The reader should be carried forward, not merely or chiefly by the mechanical impulse of curiosity, or by a restless desire to arrive at the final solution; but by the pleasureable [*sic*] activity of mind excited by the attractions of the journey itself. Like the motion of a serpent, which the Egyptians made the emblem of intellectual power; or like the path of sound through the air; at every step he pauses and half recedes, and from the retrogressive movement collects the force which again carries him onward.[34]

This image of the serpent's movement as a metaphor for intellectual activity, as descriptive indeed of dialectic itself, springs to life as the movement is reproduced in the reader's mind in the effort to comprehend the sense of the metaphor. The reader engages in a kind of intellectual dance, the movements of which are described by the author; but the reader cannot sit idly by and watch or listen while others perform: he must do the dance himself. For only by *feeling* the moves of his own 'dancing' thoughts as they coincide precisely with the metaphor will he truly *know* the dance by performing it.[35] Otherwise the metaphor is a bare image, a formulation of words unconnected with any verifying experience. The metaphor is then accepted as legitimate only upon the outside authority of the author, without any intuition of the validity of the link expressed. Knowledge must be 'wedded...to [the reader's] habitual feelings'[36] in the most literal sense if it is to be knowledge at all and not a mere parroting of authority.

Many of the most effective metaphoric situations which Coleridge has provided for his reader in volume two are in the poems which he has quoted, in his efforts to 'rescue from oblivion' the works of forgotten genius. The first poem which he cites in volume two he directs us to apply to the imagination, although it is an observation on the soul. It is *this* extension or analogy which reading involves generally, applying to the faculties of mind the notices taken of other things. If we go further and apply what we see of the imagination to the process of reading, we discover a 'recipe' for the correct and necessary procedure of approaching a book:

> Doubtless this could not be, but that she turns
> Bodies to spirit by sublimation strange,
> As fire converts to fire the things it burns,
> As we our food into our nature change.
>
> From their gross matter she abstracts their forms,
> And draws a kind of quintessence from things;
> Which to her proper nature she transforms,
> To bear them light on her celestial wings.
>
> Thus does she, when from individual states
> She doth abstract the universal kinds;
> Which then re-clothed in divers names and fates
> Steal access through our senses to our minds.[37]

Here we have an exact description of subject changing object back into its own nature, and of the synthetic process by which nature is transformed into mind, as a text must be taken up into the mind of the reader to be assimilated into his experience. We may not discursively understand how the body changes food into itself – one of the miracles of nature – or how a plant synthesizes sunlight and water so that living substance is created and grows. Yet we know it occurs because we experience it ourselves, even if we can only inadequately 'explain' it. The activity of intellectual synthesis is equally mysterious but equally real. Any explanation of either bodily or intellectual synthesis would be inadequate for knowledge, since words cannot replace the *experience* but can only suggest or stimulate it. The poem then functions metaphorically at two levels, first in its *context* of the poem, and second as a part within the *Biographia*. As a true part, it reflects an analogy with the reading process.

The first metaphor of the movement of the serpent described the mind in dialectical struggle; the second movement describes the mind in the synthetic transformation of imaginative activity. A somewhat different type of situation inviting a very particular reader response occurs in the quotation of George Herbert's poem 'Love Unknown'. Here we find a further opportunity to understand Coleridge's intentions in reproducing passages and borrowings from a fellow writer. In this case, the poem is ostensibly about the relationship of a man to his God, and the inadequacy of his sacrifices and efforts to commune with the Lord. But a careful reading will also show that the tenor of the poem implies an exact application of the reader's relationship with the author. The fact that the poem begins, 'Dear Friend', is only a minor reminder of the connection of the poem to its context within one of Coleridge's works. Though it is not *The Friend* in this case but the *Biographia*, we still know that Coleridge considers friendship as the basis of his relationship with his self-conscious reader.[38] As we read the last stanza a new dimension is added to the poem by its functioning in the context of the *Biographia*, which advances beyond the religious and moral implications which the poem originally contained. A dimension of self-consciousness is apparent in which the reader becomes aware that his own mental state is at one level the subject under discussion, as well as his own degree of intellectual growth. Still more importantly, by making this the subject matter the reader is given the opportunity to move forward in the progression toward greater intellectual awareness. An occasion for a 'flip of perspective' is offered, in which the reader no longer stands outside looking in on a situation as subject divided from object, but suddenly sees himself within the discussed situation. Identification takes place, and is best characterized as the primary vehicle of self-consciousness.[39] As long as the 'other' remains 'other' and the identity is unrealized, the metaphor remains ungrasped and the ego is trapped within its shell in opposition to the world beyond. The dualism of the understanding paralyses the movement toward assimilation, and no dialectic takes place.

When we see that the respondent in the poem is pointing out to the naive, disappointed friend that which Coleridge time and again emphasizes to his readers (their dull and sleepy state of mind, the lip-movement [eye-movement] without the correspondent *feeling*, the perpetual desire of relaxation), we realize that the respondent in the poem is in precisely the position of the inept reader, a position we have all been in at one time or another, and out of which we must be shaken if we are to make any intellectual progress. Once the reader sees both himself and Coleridge portrayed in this poem, he is already freed on this occasion from the laziness of mind and heart which threatens his self-consciousness. The reader's complaints of obscurity, difficulty, and lack of system are identical with the complaints of the poem's narrator, and the reply ought to be the same as that of the other speaker in the poem:

> Dear, could my heart not break,
> When with my pleasures ev'n my rest was gone?
> Full well I understood who had been there:
> For I had given the key to none but one:
> It must be he. 'Your heart was dull, I fear.'
> Indeed a slack and sleepy state of mind,
> Did oft possess me; so that, when I pray'd,
> Though my lips went, my heart did stay behind.
> But all my scores were by another paid,
> Who took my guilt upon him. 'Truly, friend,
> For aught I hear, your master shews to you
> More favor than you wot of. Mark the end!
> The font did only what was old renew:
> The caldron supplied what was grown too hard:
> The thorns did quicken what was grown too dull:
> All did but strive to mend what you had marr'd.
> Wherefore be cheer'd, and praise him to the full
> Each day, each hour, each moment of the week
> Who fain would have you be new, tender, quick.'[40]

The new dimension added to the poem by the context of the *Biographia*, a meta-critique of the reading situation, is the crucial level for perception. It is only at that level that the complete reversal of perspective is achieved. Coleridge but strives to mend what we had marred, and the thorns, cauldron, and font – the difficult passages of the *Biographia* – only seek to exercise the faculty which we have allowed to grow dull and unresponsive. Just as the speaker is deluded if he really believes that he can bask in a moral laziness 'because all my scores were by another paid/Who took my guilt upon him', so the reader deludes himself if he believes that an author should take upon himself the entire burden of intellectual effort, make all clear and plain for the reader, and absolve the reader of the responsibility for active participation.

We see that Coleridge's purpose in quoting Herbert's poem is not simply to illustrate its merit, but to imbue it with a further level of significance which it is almost more crucial for the reader of the *Biographia* to perceive than the poem's original context. The poem takes on a new colouring, which assures it an integral part in the *Biographia* as a whole. It is not simply a fine piece inserted into a mosaic pattern of sources within a larger structure called the *Biographia*. It is a part of that structure, in the fullest sense of the word 'part', because it is an illustration of the whole: it 'partakes of the Reality which it renders intelligible; and while it enunciates the whole, abides itself as a living part in that Unity, of which it is the representative'.[41] It is this characteristic of the 'elements' of sources and borrowings in the *Biographia* which should be emphasized, in order to show that any account which deals merely with the *Biographia* as arrangement or mechanical 'glueing together' of fragments and pieces from other writers is wholly inadequate. Such an account fails to recognize the way in which those borrowings act as symbols, or 'living parts' and as illustrations of the whole.

There is a historical level to the introduction of Herbert's poem which we have so far ignored. This perspective reveals Coleridge appealing to Wordsworth through this poem to accept the criticism which Coleridge makes of his poetry and theory, in the spirit in which it was intended. Wordsworth's response would have been a measure of his own conquest of egotism. But this level is less important for us philosophically than the one discussed above, though it is an example of the continuing operation of geniality throughout the *Biographia*, in that Coleridge probably did more to strengthen Wordsworth's reputation by his honest assessment of his strengths and weaknesses than any amount of indiscriminate praise could have achieved.[42]

There is one further step to explore before leaving the poem. We left the self-conscious reader at the point where the reader identified himself with the complainant and Coleridge with the 'Friend'. But there is a further perspective reversal which can take place and must occur if the fullness of the context is to be realized. At this stage the reader must come to realize that he himself is ideally *both* complainant and friend. Coleridge can act only temporarily and relatively as the friend, while the final authority for direction, censure, and gentle reminders must come from the reader's own will and conscience. The impetus for thought, for continuing effort to act, and for persistence must come ultimately from an inner determination and dissatisfaction with inactivity. A dialogue between 'reader' and 'author' must not be left off even at the higher stages of reflection. It must eventually come to take place in the reader's own mind, with himself as questioner and respondent. It is only at that point that true and full creativity takes place.[43] Whether at some point even this dialogue with the self becomes an impeding instrument, a mode of communication instead of a state of being, can only be answered by each individual. We may be left at the stage of the swan 'that, having amused himself, for a while, with crushing the weeds on the river's bank, soon returns to his own majestic movements on its reflecting and sustaining surface'.[44]

Coleridge often refers to the human intellect, and particularly to genius, as a tree or plant, a common metaphor amongst the Romantic poets.[45] The plant or organic metaphor is an apt mode of expressing the connection between the imagination and organic growth or organization. The 'rules of IMAGINATION are the very powers of growth and production'.[46] Similarly the spring[47] and the principle of organization of the plant (and of all life) are images of an internal, self-originating principle, also identical with the power of growth and production. The distinction made throughout *Biographia* I and II between fancy and imagination is a restatement of that between the mechanical and the organic.[48] Mechanical association, improperly called organization, is mere arrangement according to externally imposed rules, and under the guidance of the fancy and understanding.[49] Imagination *discovers* the internal principle or organization of an object, thus assimilating it to itself. The next organic example takes on a special importance.

In the lines quoted in the *Biographia* from *Paradise Lost*, on the fig-tree, we find another example of a metaphoric situation – the reader is invited to stop and engage in a play of his imagination which explores the possible associations and metaphors of the fig-tree description with the structure of a work of art, including the poem, as well as with the nature of imagination:

The poet should paint to the imagination, not to the fancy; and I know no happier case to exemplify the distinction between these two faculties. Masterpieces of the former mode of poetic painting abound in the writings of Milton, ex. gr.

> The fig-tree; not that kind for fruit renown'd,
> But such as at this day, to Indians known,
> In Malabor or Decan spreads her arms
> Branching so broad and long, that in the ground
> The bended twigs take root, and daughters grow
> About the mother tree, a pillar'd shade
> High over-arch'd, and ECHOING WALKS BETWEEN:
> There oft the Indian Herdsman, shunning heat,
> Shelters in cool, and tends his pasturing herds
> At loop holes cut through thickest shade.
>
> Milton P.L. 9. 1100.[50]

(Coleridge italicized the lines, from 'and daughters' to the end.)

Without minimizing the inherent *effect* of the poem, let us suppose it to be metaphorically suggestive of the structure of the *Biographia*. The description of the Gothic cathedral with its chambers and antechambers relates to the 'daughter trees', and the 'ECHOING WALKS BETWEEN' are particularly analogous to the metaphoric situations we have been describing. For they suggest the creation from a single image of a spontaneous reverberation of thought which the reader is to explore by a leisurely wandering through the walkways of metaphor. More suggestive still of the structure of the *Biographia* are the lines, 'in the ground/The bended twigs take root, and daughters grow/About the mother tree.' The sections of the text which seem to be branchings from the mainstream and even unimportant twigs lead to the common ground which nourishes or informs the main trunk. They act as seeds for the growth of related thought, which still however revolves around the 'mother tree' of discourse. This fig-tree could also be a metaphor for the way in which the different branches of knowledge are related.[51] And it is a symbol for the proper integration of the faculties of sense, fancy, understanding and reason. It is a general expression of the way in which parts are organized into a whole.[52] But all of these interpretations are subsidiary formulations of the more integral metaphor of the fig-tree as genius or as imagination itself and its rules of growth and production.[53]

In closing our discussion of examples in volume two of Coleridge's metaphoric method, we may mention several other instances of such situations which the reader will find reverberating with possibilities for meditative thought.[54] In the previous chapter, Wordsworth's 'White Doe' was said to be functioning as a paradigm both of imagination and of the structure of the *Biographia*. The description in the last part of volume two, of 'Religion as a Temple' operates in an identical way,[55] but perhaps the richest case is the last paragraph of volume two:

It is Night, sacred Night! the upraised Eye views only the starry Heaven which manifests itself alone: and the outward Beholding is fixed on the sparks twinkling in the awe-ful depth, though Suns of other Worlds, only to preserve the Soul steady and collected in its pure Act of inward adoration to the great I AM, and to the filial WORD that re-affirmeth it from Eternity to Eternity, whose choral Echo is the universe.[56]

Here the reason for objectification and outward directing of the mind is explicitly stated: the mind is an instrument only and a means to another end. The night is a reflection of the depth of the human mind itself. The starry twinkling may be thought of as the sparks of culture, of science and the arts, 'the dome of many-colored glass', the flashes of imagination and intuition which hold the inward eye attentive, *not*, however, attentive only to themselves as sparks and flashes, but attentive to the depths of the mind's consciousness, and the relation to the depths of the universe. The *Biographia* is also a kind of 'starry Heaven', with precisely the same instrumental function: the reader attends to its twinklings not to measure *their* shape or strength or colour or brilliance. He attends to them as signs and shadows of the stars of another world beyond the limits of the individual text. He looks between them and focuses upon the interspaces of night in order there to find ultimately the experience which will close the chasmic gap between mind and nature, and raise the analogy of mind to nature to an intense, living reality.

7

Structural unity in the *Biographia*

THE UNITY OF POETRY AND PHILOSOPHY

In order to clarify the connections of *Biographia* I and II, the identity of subject matter in the two volumes must first be indicated, since a similarity of method has already been shown. That identity becomes clear if we turn to Coleridge's remarks in chapter twelve on Wordsworth's failure to understand the reasons for limiting the use of the word 'association'. Coleridge emphasized his distinction between fancy and imagination because he believed that a fundamental difference was being overlooked in matters of association. The word was being used to signify not only the internal and organic relationship of parts to whole (a relation self-generated from the unity in question) but also the merely externally imposed arrangement of arbitrary parts to arbitrary wholes for purposes of classification, memorization, or any other conveniences which render the whole a mechanical whole only. Thus in the word 'associate' we find both activities of reason and activities of understanding, or of imagination and of fancy, signified, as if they were indistinguishable. Coleridge's distinction acts to point out this 'slip-up' in language, whereby the looseness of the use of a word contributes to looseness of thinking, particularly where the distinction is as critical to thought as this one is. As Coleridge explains, one must not in such instances allow language to operate as a slide-rule, leading one to think that there is no distinction. He also emphasizes that it is only in such cases as these that a philosopher is justified in inventing a new word or in changing or restricting the meaning of a word.[1]

Coleridge criticizes Wordsworth for overlooking the two-fold or ambiguous meaning of 'associate'.[2] Since fancy and understanding are faculties requiring less energy of thought, they tend to tyrannize over the reason and imagination except in persons of great strength of mind who overcome the tendency toward mental inertia and linguistic degeneration by the force of intellect. Because of the predominance of fancy and understanding, Coleridge allowed 'associate' to signify only the activity of fancy, limiting it, contrary to custom, but necessarily in order to prevent the continuing obscurity between organization by external as opposed to internal laws. Wordsworth misunderstood the definition of imagination because he allowed 'associate' to act in its ambiguous signification, ignoring any distinctity in the two faculties. Coleridge usually restricted the use of the word to the fancy, meaning to aggregate or arrange or add on. The process of association which involves assimilation, transformation, growth and synthesis, he indicated by 'imagination' – the 'shaping and modifying power', to refer to the internal, organic organizing power. This restriction he kept within the context of defining and distinguishing.[3] Yet he still himself uses the 'power of association' in the first chapters of the *Biographia* to mean the power informing both imagination and fancy. He does so quite correctly, for there he is not concerned with the distinction, but with the *general* activity of mind of combining elements. He maintains the traditional terminology of philosophy in order to deal with an issue which has fascinated philosophers throughout history. The traditional role of 'association' in philosophy was to signify generally the mind's organizing energy, and the problem was to understand more precisely the nature of the organizing energy. Hence Coleridge's enquiry into the nature of imagination is no other than this age-old philosophical problem renamed to apply more appropriately to poetry. The chapters in the *Biographia* on the failure of certain theories of association such as Hartley's and Aristotle's (materialism and dualism in general) point directly to the fact that those theories were wrong because they accounted for the fancy alone,[4] the aggregating power, while ignoring that higher, more integrative faculty of imagination and true organization by internal principle. Thus they were rejected as inadequate, accounting only for the lower faculty, the less energetic faculty, of fancy, as if it were the whole power. They failed to account for the higher intellectual activities involved in mathematics, scientific discovery, and art, as well as morals and religion.

We can now appreciate that the first volume of the *Biographia*, centering as it does around theories of association, is at the same time step by step explaining the distinction between fancy (Hartleian association) and imagination (Coleridgean association), stated briefly in chapter four and taken up again in chapter twelve, thirteen, and in detail in *Biographia* II. Both volumes have the same primary subject matter, the distinction between imagination and fancy, which substantiates the material continuity of the two volumes. The difference which has tended to obscure this continuity is the changeover from the materials of philosophy to those of poetry. Though these may at first seem to create an equally unbridgeable chasm, a look at Coleridge's analysis of poetry will help to close the gap again.[5]

Coleridge sets out in chapter fourteen of *Biographia* II to establish the way in which philosophy differs from poetry. In his description of the object of philosophy we are not only referred to the way in which fancy and imagination are supposed to work together. We are also aware that the *connection* of philosophy and poetry, as an example of a distinction, *not* a division, is implied:

> The office of philosophical *disquisition* consists in just *distinction*: while it is the privilege of the philosopher to preserve himself constantly aware, that distinction is not division. In order to obtain adequate notions of any truth, we must intellectually separate its distinguishable parts; and this is the technical *process* of philosophy. But having so done, we must then restore them in our conceptions to the unity, in which they actually co-exist; and this is the *result* of philosophy.[6]

Our purpose is to show how philosophy (*Biographia* i) and poetry (*Biographia* ii) must be restored to the unity in which *they* actually co-exist. To succeed we need initially to know Coleridge's definition of a poem:

> A poem is that species of composition, which is opposed to works of science, by proposing for its *immediate* object pleasure, not truth; and from all other species (having *this* object in common with it) it is discriminated by proposing to itself such delight from the *whole*, as is compatible with a distinct gratification from each component *part*...a legitimate poem...must be one, the parts of which mutually support and explain each other; all in their proportion harmonizing with, and supporting the purpose and known influences of metrical arrangement.[7]

A poem is distinguished from the other forms of literature such as prose, since it proposes for its immediate object pleasure. It is also distinguished from the metrical arrangements which are commonly called poems, but which have other objects such as facilitating recollection ('Thirty days hath September . . .').

We may now believe that poetry and philosophy have been firmly separated by means of this distinction between their immediate objects, that of philosophy being truth and that of poetry being pleasure. Yet here the work of distinguishing begins to be balanced by a tendency toward reunion.[8] Coleridge reminds us that he has not defined poetry, but a poem. The definition of poetry which follows goes some way towards reconciling not only poetry and philosophy, but also a poem and a prose work in general: 'poetry of the highest kind may exist without metre, and even without the contra-distinguishing objects of a poem' Coleridge cites Plato, Bishop Taylor, Burnet, and Isaiah 1, as examples of the genre of 'poetic prose'. He goes on to say that not even a legitimate poem 'can be, or ought to be, all poetry':

In short, whatever *specific* import we attach to the word, poetry, there will be found involved in it, as a necessary consequence, that a poem of any length neither can be, or ought to be, all poetry. Yet if an harmonious whole is to be produced, the remaining parts must be preserved *in keeping* with the poetry; and this can be no otherwise effected than by such a studied selection and artificial arrangement, as will partake of *one*, though not a *peculiar* property of poetry. And this again can be no other than the property of exciting a more continuous and equal attention than the language of prose aims at, whether colloquial or written.[9]

A poem contains much that is prose, properly speaking, and the poetry that it does contain is not a style peculiar only to a poem, since philosophy may also be poetry. Nor does metre operate as an identifying mark.

We are still confronted however with the difference in immediate objects. Even this difference begins to lose its absoluteness when we find Coleridge frequently making the judgment that 'no man was ever yet a great poet, without being at the same time a profound philosopher.[10] For poetry is the blossom and the fragrancy of all human knowledge, human thoughts, human passions, emotions, language. In Shakespeare's *poems* the creative power and the intellectual energy wrestle as in a war embrace.'[11] Philosophy becomes poetry when the genius of expression, musicality, and feeling are wedded to intellectual genius. In this way poetry is said to contain and supersede philosophy. But how can pleasure be said to supersede truth? Clearly the precise relation of truth to pleasure is the central issue. If the highest philosophy is poetry, and the best poetry is philosophy, then at the most perfect stage of intellectual experience, pleasure and truth must be identical: 'the blessed time shall come, when truth itself shall be pleasure, and both shall be so united, as to be distinguishable in words only, not in feeling.'[12]

We can emphasize the identity of pleasure and truth in several ways, most emphatically by reminding ourselves of the delight that overcomes the mind when it experiences a flash of intellectual insight and knows that it has at last grasped a truth, or when it has unified the sense of truth with the sensation of its validity. Any scientist or mathematician knows this delight in the discovery of a truth or a relation.[13] Coleridge also points out repeatedly the similarity of poetry and geometry, for geometry is seen as one of the paradigmatic forms of 'relational apprehension', which is also the characteristic of metaphor. Further evidence for the connection of philosophy and poetry or truth and pleasure is the fact that metaphor is the prime agency of truth in all its forms of knowledge.[14] On the relation of truth to pleasure Coleridge's distinction between geometry and poetry is instructive:

Paradoxical as it may sound, one of the essential properties of Geometry is not less essential to dramatic excellence; and Aristotle has accordingly required of the poet an involution of the universal in the individual. The chief differences are, that in Geometry it is the universal truth, which is uppermost in the consciousness; in poetry the individual form, in which the truth is clothed.[15]

We could apply this equally well to the distinction between poetry and philosophy so that truth becomes pleasure universalized. Nevertheless, poetry and pleasure are not trapped in the individual and concrete, except in so far as they themselves are representative of the universal and ideal: 'poetry as poetry is essentially *ideal,* that it avoids and excludes all *accident*; that its apparent individualities of rank, character, or occupation must be *representative* of a class; and that the persons of poetry must be clothed with *generic* attributes, with the *common* attributes of the class'.[16] If in philosophy the universal is uppermost while in poetry it is the representative individual, then in the ideal or highest perfection of the two they would cease to be distinguished:

The ideal consists in the happy balance of the generic with the individual. The former makes the character representative and symbolical, therefore instructive; because, *mutatis mutandis*, it is applicable to whole classes of men. The latter gives it *living* interest; for nothing *lives* or is *real*, but as definite and individual.[17]

Philosophy differs from poetry in a privative sense when it lacks this living interest and reality of experience.

The ideal is the union of truth and pleasure, and is best expressed by the GOOD. To see this identity as any other truth is seen (such as a mathematical truth or a scientific discovery) is to have a 'testifying experience'. It is to experience relational apprehension and intuitional insight.[18] There is no discursive proof in the sense that we move from stage to stage without a gap, though that movement may in itself be an illusion. There may always be gaps, but in familiar instances they are bridged by custom and habit, while here they must be bridged by fresh acts of apprehension. In Coleridge's view, the intuition states as firmly that 'x *must* be true because it is' (there is no further *reason* to be given) as the conscience states that 'x *ought* to be'.[19] Both are testifying experiences for the truth of which we rely with *Faith* upon that testimony, from a ground within the human mind, where conscience and imagination are no longer distinguished.[20]

The traditional *division* between knowledge and art is also invalid for Coleridge.[21] A distinction in immediate object only is proper, constantly balanced by the awareness that at root the objects of pleasure and truth are informed by the same principle, namely the Good.[22] This ought to be clear from the role of metaphor as the common vehicle of both.[23] If we look carefully now at the two-volume structure of the *Biographia*, we see that to make a division where there is properly only a distinction is to miss the underlying principle common to both, the perception of which clearly requires imagination.[24] That underlying principle is the imagination as it acts, first in the realm of the Good, where truth, universality, philosophy, or knowledge is uppermost, volume one; and secondly where pleasure, the individual, poetry, or art is uppermost, volume two.[25] To realize the fundamental unity of the two volumes is to understand all the above relationships as ultimately identities in the ideal, which are distinguished only as one *mode* of objectification is emphasized over another. This is not to deny variety in human experience. It is only to assert that while variety exists there is a singleness as well: a contradiction for the understanding, a paradox for language,[26] but a truth for imagination in the only way in which truth can be expressed.[27] Only the understanding sees opposites as contraries.[28] The imagination sees them as the polar forces of a single power. The single text behind the two 'polar' volumes of the *Biographia* which completes the trinary scheme is the text which results from reading, and which contains all the relations and connections which the space-time text seems to lack. This ideal text participates in a reality which is relative to each individual's capacity for relational apprehension. The ideal is, according to Coleridge, simultaneously the most truly real.[29]

It is ironic that the *Biographia* is believed to be an unsystematic disconnected jumble of unrelated elements and an arbitrary whole. It is also ironic that people talk regretfully of Coleridge's metaphysics as interfering with his poetry. For the *Biographia* when properly read and fully understood is poetry in prose according to Coleridge's own idea of the unity of the two disciplines of poetry and philosophy. It is indeed Coleridge's own *Prelude*. It may seem to set out with the immediate object of truth, but it ends in continuous stimulation of delight through metaphoric situations. It is an example of a too rarely used genre, in which the reading process is mirrored in the content of the work. It is the genre, for example, of Plato's dialogues, Berkeley's *Siris*, Blake's prophetic books, and Kierkegaard's *Philosophical Fragments*, to give a few examples. To be serious as opposed to ironic, to be literal as opposed to metaphoric, is to be unselfconscious in important respects. In art, it is a kind of delusion, since irony, in the German and Socratic sense, is the state of human aesthetic existence, and experience is based upon metaphor. We only think we are being literal, for irony lurks behind every serious gesture.[30]

Coleridge believed that the fullest, most valid knowledge could be achieved only when the whole soul of man was brought into play. All the faculties of man must be properly integrated and subordinated to work together to reveal that knowledge:

The poet, described in *ideal* perfection, brings the whole soul of man into activity, with the subordination of its faculties to each other, according to their relative worth and dignity. He diffuses a tone and spirit of unity, that blends, and (as it were) *fuses*, each into each, by that synthetic and magical power, to which we have exclusively appropriated the name of imagination.[31]

Coleridge drew upon philosophy, religion, art, science, education, and politics because he knew that the realm in which all of these branches met, and in which no one faculty and no one branch was uppermost, would be the point at which the fusion he was seeking would occur. One might say that all these branches separated from each other are states or stages of being, but Coleridge was seeking being in its wholeness. The irony of the human condition seems to be that in order to achieve rest it must seek activity, it must divide itself against itself, and make itself object to itself, in order to become one again with itself.

THE PRIMARY/SECONDARY IMAGINATION AS STRUCTURAL PRINCIPLE

The design and content of the *Biographia* are crystallized in the last page of volume one, in the three-fold distinction between primary and secondary imagination, and fancy, which in its role as an ape of and a mode of memory applies to both. The primary/secondary distinction is peculiarly appropriate to the *Biographia* as an expression of the design of the work as a whole.[32] Primary imagination operates below the conscious threshold in that its constructive, active nature remains obscured to the conscious mind.[33] Art is the vehicle for making conscious the process of 'presentation' (perception) which has become through time and habit unconscious.[34] Art 're-presents' the principles of construction and organization which are veiled by custom, familiarity, and repetition, or which have solidified into 'things'. The internal principles and the depth are no longer evident, being hidden by a surface of hardened, crusty perception.[35] Despite the received opinion that the last page of *Biographia* i is inadequate,[36] it seems to be a brilliantly concise account of the design of volume one, which is an analysis of the nature of perception and the mistaken theories of a passive-perceptive process. In this area of perception, fancy – or Hartleian associationism[37] – is contrasted with imagination – or perception as dynamic and fundamentally intuitional. The same page not only looks back to the procedure in volume one, but also looks ahead to the second volume, which turns to a corresponding analysis of secondary imagination and the distinction between imagination and the fancy as it relates to this secondary activity of the artist. Still more importantly, the final page of volume one placed crucially as it is at the centre of the work, is a summary of the integrity of the *Biographia* I and II as a unity, in its stated analogy between perception and art, or derivatively, the tasks of philosophy and poetry.

Imagination becomes the obvious subject matter of the *Biographia* as a whole, first as it operates in perception and secondly through art. In both areas it is distinguished from the passive-mechanical manipulation or fancy which presupposes its material to be fixed, determinate and ready-made for reassembly and arrangement. Primary and secondary imagination, on the other hand, fashion their own material. They reorganize and recreate the substrate, which is not matter but dynamic progressive activity. The genius of this three-fold distinction is that in a brilliantly concise passage Coleridge can simultaneously describe the unity of the structure of the two-volume *Biographia* and also indicate its content.[38]

Through this passage the *Biographia* is set up also as a symbol and an instance of its content: the perception of its unity requires a reading which passes beyond the apparently disparate poles of philosophy and poetry to perceive the underlying unity of the two in their common ground of imagination. The 'polarities' of volume one and volume two are reconciled only by an imaginative apprehension of the relation between perception and artistic creation as at ground identical. Further, this design contains a self-consciousness by the author of his predicament as author. It is in this analysis of the primary activity of mind, perception, that the consciousness comes closest to catching a glimpse of mind. In this sense Socrates advocated 'Know thyself'.[39]

Some of the obvious ironies become apparent once the reader stops indulging his expectations and starts supplying intellectual acts himself. The sub-title of chapter twelve of the *Biographia* strikes him in a new light as he reads 'A Chapter of requests and premonitions concerning the perusal or omission of the chapter that follows'. Coleridge goes on to say, quite outrageously, in the beginning of chapter twelve that

In lieu of the various requests which the anxiety of authorship addresses to the unknown reader, I advance but this one; that he will either pass over the following chapter altogether, or read the whole connectedly.[40]

In view of the fact that prior to publication Coleridge had either removed, or not written, part of the last chapter, this request is peculiarly impossible for the reader to carry out, unless he recognizes the irony, and supplies the imagination himself. Coleridge then discusses the types of readers from whom he cannot expect a favourable 'perusal'.

Coleridge's concern is to try to sweep away the 'mists and clouds from uncultivated swamps', or, analogously, the received opinion about the work which inhibits fresh response. We may remind the reader that his own immediate responses constitute as much a body of 'received opinion' as does any secondary work of criticism.[41] The anecdote about reading Plato, which introduces chapter twelve, the metaphor of the Trans- and Cis-Alpine provinces, the immediately following quotation from Plotinus about the distinction between the discursive and the intuitive, the chrysalis metaphor, the nature of the true philosopher, the 'Anti-Goshen',[42] all refer the reader to the additional level of self-consciousness required in the activity of perception and reading. Finally in these ten pages of preliminary remarks Coleridge prefaces the ensuing philosophical discussion with a description of his own method of composition: True philosophy has this as its criterion:

> that it would at once explain and collect the fragments of truth scattered through systems apparently the most incongruous. The truth...is diffused more widely than is commonly believed; ...The deeper, however, we penetrate into the ground of things, the more truth we discover in the doctrines of the greater number of the philosophical sects...We have imprisoned our own conceptions by the lines, which we have drawn, in order to exclude the conceptions of others.[43]

This passage expresses a principle of composition – the determination not to exclude others to create a system of one's own, but to include and to show the relations of the most apparently disparate philosophies with one's own. The 'mosaic' surface of the *Biographia* is evidence that Coleridge actualized this theory.

This passage might equally act as a principle of critical procedure and reading.[44] Unselfconscious reading is a process of drawing lines; that process must be reversed. The steps of the reversal can be tentatively described as (1) convincing ourselves that our lines are not the only possible ones by means of drawing others or by proliferating meanings and interpretations; (2) making ourselves familiar with the principles or prejudices at the source of the various alternative sets of lines; (3) using them as lines of approach toward the text, not as determinations of it. The criterion for an adequate interpretation will not be the illusory notion that a given interpretation best 'describes' the text freed from interpretations (for the unreachable 'text-in-itself' is the only piece of discursive writing free from interpretation). An interpretation should clear away the clouds and vapours rising out of the uncultivated swamps, while many critical texts act only to increase the mist.

We have suggested the importance of the final page of *Biographia* I as a pattern for the structure of the work as a whole. Here it seems that the crucial tone of irony which operates throughout the *Biographia* is set most obviously. At the top of the page Coleridge says that he is to content himself 'for the present with stating the main result of the chapter, which I have reserved for that future publication, a detailed prospectus of which the reader will find at the close of the second volume'. There is no such detailed prospectus at the end of volume two. Whether or not there is any future work which exactly answers to a treatise on imagination is disputable.[45] The final paragraph of this last page of volume one reads:

Whatever more than this, I shall think it fit to declare concerning the powers and privileges of the imagination in the present work, will be found in the critical essay on the uses of the Supernatural in poetry, and the principles that regulate its introduction: which the reader will find prefixed to the poem *The Ancient Mariner*.[46]

There was no preface to 'The Ancient Mariner' either. The incredulous reader will claim (and always has done) that these three references are merely another example of Coleridge's pathetic unfulfilled plans – but on incredulity we might quote Coleridge himself: 'There would be nothing herein . . . to justify contemptuous disbelief . . . Incredulity is but Credulity seen from behind, bowing and nodding assent to the Habitual and the Fashionable'.[47] He elsewhere makes a statement which is equally relevant to critical procedure:

Having observed to me one day that the †text† opposite errors of Credulity and Incredulity must necessarily meet in the same minds where the Persons have no other grounds for their believing a†ny† thing true, but that they have been accustomed to believe it, he added, that many curious facts and it might be [even] important Discoveries were kept secret by the Persons who had seen them [from] the fear of exciting doubts as to their veracity or judgement.[48]

Critical procedure demands that one should not try to 'explain away' any anomalies in a work until (or perhaps in spite of the fact that) one has exhausted all the means available for discovering a significance within the context of the work. Thus ascribing these 'missing parts' (chapter thirteen, the detailed prospectus, the future work, the essay on 'The Ancient Mariner') to Coleridge's inability to complete his projected works and his need to appear productive, is another example of the clouds and vapours which inhibit a clearer view of the 'range of hills' (themselves hiding a source higher and further inward). These missing parts may be alternatively seen as satirical addresses to the reader who keeps waiting for and expecting to be provided discursively with a knowledge of imagination. Instead Coleridge presents his reader with all that discussion can provide, namely a beautifully designed occasion for imaginative response.[49]

This situation is further delineated by Coleridge in the final sentence of volume one quoted above. Upon close analysis this sentence exhibits an extremely complicated syntax, which acts to disrupt any obvious meaning. Let us analyse the usual perception of it. The 'obvious' sense of the sentence is that more than is contained in the brief statement of the last page on imagination will be found in the 'essay on the Supernatural', which as we know, does not exist. The anomaly occurs when Coleridge adds 'in the present work', by which phrase the meaning of the whole is rendered radically ambiguous, or 'multiguous' or even becomes non-sense. The incredulous reader no doubt assumes that the sentence is carelessly constructed. But the fact that the sense turns on the phrase, 'the present work', fits in rather well with the view that what is crucial throughout the *Biographia* is the *present*, or that which is going on in the Hegelian *Now*: the reading-response process.[50] Additionally, 'the present work', and that which constitutes it, is the object of critical enquiry and of perception. The irony is further enhanced when we realize what is not immediately apparent due to a change in terminology: an 'essay on the Supernatural' would be an essay on imagination, for it is the intuitive which is the supernatural.[51] Moreover, an essay on imagination prefixed to one of the most purely imaginative poems in the English language would seem an absurdity hardly explicable, since the poem itself is the best 'account' of the imaginative process that we could hope to have.[52] Only the reader with absolute and ultimate faith in the discursive alone as capable of rendering an account of the intuitive is taken in by such ironies. The final irony must be that the reader who is most literal-minded fails to take account of the clues embedded in the level of the text. He reads *over* them and misses the import of the whole. Careful reading and real attention to detail are misunderstood in an almost programmed response. The sceptical reader who views himself as most faithful to the text, most literal and most reasonable, is not faithful and literal at all, but simply unperceptive. A preface to 'The Ancient Mariner' would be as ironic as the gloss on the poem. For the function of the gloss is primarily rendered by irony. Moreover, all of the missing parts mentioned on the final page of volume one act as clues that the *Biographia* is indeed incomplete, but not in the sense that it is commonly held to be. It is a fragment in the same sense that 'Kubla Khan' is a fragment, and that all linguistic and poetic experience is fragmentary:[53] it points to experience for its significance but cannot contain and exhaust experience.

The *Biographia* is constructed in twenty-four chapters. Chapter thirteen is literally, as well as essentially, the structural pivotal point or the hinge which holds the two volumes together. It is the centre and the bridge between them. This thirteenth chapter acts as the crowning of the self-consciousness of the reading process, intensely epitomized in metaphoric situations, which has been the method throughout the work, and which reaches its highest dramatic intensity and most forceful irony at the centre. In the analogy of the perceiver and artist we are faced with the basic irony of all consciousness. The most exalted strivings of the reason toward the ideal carry it immediately back to the 'lowest' of its functions, an analysis of perception.[54] The reason and the senses meet, for they are opposites only, not contraries: they are true polarities. Perception of the minute particulars is the 'great mystery' (as Blake describes it) which reason seeks to discover in the noumenon. Coleridge might have observed, 'Extremes Meet! It is wonderful how close Reason and the Senses are, and imagination the union of the two.'[55]

8

Imagination and reason, and the conflict of pantheism and Christianity

In the first few chapters the philosophical foundations upon which the integrity of the *Biographia* depends were indicated, and in the next few chapters certain predominant features of the *Biographia*, such as the use of metaphor, the use of sources, and reader participation, were said to be used as a method and thus indicative of an underlying unity. In this chapter, we will seek to bring Coleridge's practice more explicitly into line with the philosophy discussed above. In the previous chapters Coleridge has been seen as confidently at work on a number of issues and seemingly well in control of them. We shall argue here that his confidence has suffered a significant shock, and that the main issues of imagination and irony are far from being controlled; they remain unresolved not only in the *Biographia* but throughout the rest of Coleridge's published and un-published writings. Irony and imagination we may see as pervading Coleridge's *Biographia* to the extent that he was carried along by their inherent force, unable to direct or control in any usual, conscious way these powerful creative factors.

The uncertainties which later led Coleridge to have to suppress imagination and irony as uncontrollable elements foreign to his Christian philosophy (and to his rejection of pantheism as atheism) will become evident first through an analysis of imagination and its relation to fancy as a polarity, secondly through the peculiar overlapping of this distinction with the reason/understanding distinction, and finally through the sup-pression of the 'imagination' by the 'reason' in subsequent works. The German and Greek sources of Coleridge's aesthetics have been discussed, and most importantly, the concept of irony shown in its German and Coleridgean applications as distinguishable from the more English, empirical concept. This distinction, the origins of which lie not in nineteenth-century German aesthetic thought, but in Plato's Socrates, in Sophocles, in Aristophanes, and in Plato himself, is crucial for appreciating the sense in which irony is used here. Finally, by way of the concept of irony, the *Biographia* will be shown to have significant stylistic connections with 'The Ancient Mariner' and 'Kubla Khan'.

The distinction between imagination and fancy acts as a central pivotal point in the *Biographia*. This pivotal point is also a focal point of controversy, and has been since Coleridge's writing of the work. Wordsworth himself was one of the first to state his uncertainty about the distinction, as Coleridge explains in chapter twelve:

Mr. Wordsworth's 'only objection is that the definition is too general. To aggregate and to associate, to evoke and to combine, belong as well to the imagination as to the fancy'. I reply, that if, by the power of evoking and combining, Mr. Wordsworth means the same as, and no more than, I meant by the aggregative and associative, I continue to deny, that it belongs at all to the imagination; and am disposed to conjecture, that he has mistaken the co-presence of fancy with imagination for the operation of the latter singly.[1]

It is clear from the 'Preface to the *Lyrical Ballads*' that Wordsworth had made no such distinction, using the terms virtually interchangeably. As we will attempt to show below, this indistinct conception led Wordsworth to formulate his erroneous theories about poetry as being best expressed in the language of the rustic.

Other objections were to follow, one of the most notable being Walter Pater's rejection of the distinction in *Appreciations*.[2] He insists that it is a question only of degree, while Coleridge maintains that it is the distinction in *kind* which it is crucial to grasp.[3] T. E. Eliot joins in the censure of the distinction in kind, saying that Coleridge has not proved it, and has 'done no more than to impose it'.[4] He then proposes to show that the apparent differences between Coleridge's theory and that of Dryden on imagination are not as great as they might seem. Apparently this is because Coleridge is mistaken, and not because they can be discovered to be saying similar things. However suspect Eliot's procedure of 'reconciliation', the fact remains that he rejected the distinction.

One of the most sustained resistances to the distinction comes from Livingston Lowes whose enormous undertaking, *The Road to Xanadu*, seems to base its actual method of procedure and practice upon the firm rejection of the distinction as one of kind. Mr Lowes says that imagination is only an intenser power of fancy, that is, the aggregative or assimilative power.[5] The effort to locate Coleridge's sources he describes as a process of discovering the 'hooks and eyes of memory'.[6] At times he seems to claim for his method a high critical importance: 'Without a knowledge of the crass materials, the profoundly significant process is unintelligible.'[7] Elsewhere he says that 'to follow Coleridge through his reading is to retrace the obliterated vestiges of creation'.[8] But the direction of Mr Lowes's enquiry is toward an exploration of the fancy or aggregating power: a map of sources will lead into the workings of the fancy, but as Mr Lowes himself seems to realize by his metaphor of the 'deep well', it tells little about imaginative activity. Mr Lowes's direction of investigation sometimes seems then to encumber the reader with a vast amount of historical source information. This not only cannot help the reader to understand the poem; it may almost stand in the way of a perception of the more important activity of appreciating the 'predominant passion' or the 'shaping and modifying power', which makes all the elements appropriate and which gives them their integrity as a whole. Mr Lowes's emphasis is overstressed when he says that 'without a knowledge of the crass materials, the profoundly significant process is unintelligible'. Such knowledge can be interesting material to the poem, but it cannot be that which makes the imaginative process intelligible – only the poem or work of art in experience can do that, not the accidental and historical sources of the poem's images and metaphors.

Mr Lowes's approach tends toward a Hartleian view of mental activity, in which the fancy is the predominant faculty and is the only faculty which is knowable.[9] In emphasizing source investigations as the primary means of tracing the creative process, he seems to identify creativity with fancy, 'the ape of memory', and seems essentially to adopt the view of the 'dogmatic' empiricist: there is nothing in the mind which was not first in the senses. Coleridge, along with Leibnitz, would answer simply, 'except the mind itself'.[10] The mind is not simply engaged in an activity which can be described as the 'hooks and eyes of memory', which may however be a correct description for a Hartleian or an empiricist. What is important to the reader and critic is that which Coleridge did with those sources, and how he did it; this constitutes the essential quality of the poem, the passion which makes the sources appropriate. The critic will find his field of operation clearly drawn out for him by the boundaries of the work of art, and any external information may be an interesting complement but should never be crucial to the work *as* a work of art and as an imaginative experience.[11]

I. A. Richards, in *Coleridge on Imagination*, also rejects Lowes's view of the imagination/fancy distinction as one only of degree.[12] Coleridge shows us the error to which Lowes's analysis often seems to be tending in his statement about the difference between the methods of Beaumont and Fletcher, and those of Shakespeare. The former two work, as it were, by 'fitting together a quarter of orange, apple, lemon, pomegranate to look like *one* round fruit. But nature who works from within cannot do this. Nor Shakespeare who worked from the germ.'[13] Lowes tends to emphasize the elements, Coleridge the growth into unity. Mr Muirhead makes the distinction clearly: 'In both mathematics and in physics, not to speak of metaphysics, the existence of these sciences depends on the existence of uniting elements. . .which cannot be derived from experience in the sense of being generalizations from it.'[14]

We have discussed briefly the errors involved in appreciating the distinction between imagination and fancy as one only of degree. We now turn to some interpretations of the distinction between imagination as primary and as secondary, and the relation of fancy to both of these. In a well-known and frequently quoted passage, at the end of *Biographia* i, Coleridge says:

The IMAGINATION then, I consider either as primary, or secondary. The primary IMAGINATION I hold to be the living Power and prime Agent of all human Perception, and as a repetition in the finite mind of the eternal act of creation in the infinite I AM. The secondary Imagination I consider as an echo of the former, co-existing with the conscious will, yet still as identical with the primary in the *kind* of its agency, and differing only in *degree*, and in the *mode* of its operation. It dissolves, diffuses, dissipates, in order to recreate or where this process is rendered impossible, yet still at all events it struggles to idealize and to unify. It is essentially *vital*, even as all objects (*as* objects) are essentially fixed and dead.[15]

In his book *The Sacred River*, J. V. Baker carefully examines the eighteenth-century background of the law of association and the use of 'imagination'. He attempts to give an account of this distinction between primary and secondary imagination, correcting what he considers to be I. A. Richards's errors in *Coleridge on Imagination*. Mr Baker has devoted the first one hundred pages of the book to preparing for the 'creativity of perception' as expressed by the primary/secondary imagination distinction, but, in apparent contradiction to this groundwork, he proceeds to merge the two into a blurred relationship, so that primary imagination is subsumed by the secondary, both being involved fundamentally in perceptions of beauty, or in aesthetic response. The secondary imagination differs only in that it acts upon this beauty to create products of art. Mr Baker seems to misconstrue the purpose of the concept of primary imagination, which is to emphasize that the very materials of perception as we can know them are themselves products of the creative primary faculty. He says, for instance: 'Coleridge could not have meant by this the simple act of seeing, by which, for instance, a crowd of tent-like mountains would be assimilated by the eye, the simple drinking-in of the scene. He was always deprecating the despotism of the eye and the tyranny of the senses.'[16] What we may suggest is that Coleridge did indeed mean this 'simple act of seeing' when he talked of primary imagination, while the despotism of the eye referred to the stagnation which invariably set in upon perception through repetition and familiarity.

Mr Baker makes clear his notion of the primary imagination as a sort of primitive aesthetic faculty acting upon materials already 'out there', instead of the 'prime Agent of all human Perception', when he says: 'There is more than one way of looking at a mountain. It would be possible to look at it with a military eye and to see only its contours. It would be possible to look at it aesthetically and emphatically ...'. He says it is this latter way of looking which constitutes Coleridge's active perception.[17] Or again in criticizing Professor Richards's interpretation he says: 'Coleridge talks in terms of the cloud-capped mountain and the great I AM, while Richards can see in perception nothing but busses and beef-steaks.'[18] He again points to primary imagination as a power of aesthetic perception, not of perception *per se* and not of perception of the ordinary world around us, filled with external 'things'.

Mr Baker is offended by Professor Richards's assertion that 'Primary Imagination is *normal* perception that produces the *usual* world of the senses.'[19] Thus while sensing that something is wrong with Richards's characterization, he fails to see exactly what the error is, and slides far deeper into error than Richards himself. Mr Baker fails to see that the primary imagination is actually involved in the production of our everyday perceptions, that is, of the things which constitute experience and the world as external to us. According to Coleridge, primary imagination is the faculty which constitutes this world, and we then unconsciously hypostasize an external world as independent of our perception of it, which becomes a prejudice of 'outness'. Primary imagination builds up the materials and things which we think we perceive passively and receptively. To this extent Coleridge (and Shelley) were in agreement with Kant. Primary imagination *is* involved in the mere act of seeing beefsteaks and busses, and in the simple 'drinking-in of the scene', or in the mountain, observed with only an 'everyday' eye. The plain contours and the simplest 'terrain' perceptions are themselves results of the activity of the primary imagination. They are not, as Mr Baker implies, the 'given' materials or the contours to which we then respond with primary imagination if we are aesthetically sensitive. Coleridge explains that primary imagination is the 'prime Agent of *all* human Perception', not just of aesthetic perception. There is no 'raw' material, there is no given, and there are no atoms, substrate, or *sub*stance which is then responded to by the primary or secondary imagination.

We can explain Mr Baker's error after his preparatory build-up only by the tenacity of the prejudice of outness, which inhibits an understanding of such a dynamic theory of perception.[20] Mr Baker exposes his faith in the 'given' again when he says, 'Certain materials are given in experience' before primary imagination or perception begins to act upon it.[21] The second explanation for his error we may trace to Professor Richards as well. Both must account for Coleridge's conception of perception as creative activity, but they fail to account to their own satisfaction for the mundaneness, the routine, and the ugliness of the everyday world. How can *that* be the result of creative, imaginative activity? Mr Baker adopts as a 'solution' his false conception of primary imagination as subsequent to actual perception of the world in the first instance. Professor Richards simply chooses not to confront the issue, but the result is that he to some extent misleads his readers; Baker's misunderstanding is due to precisely such a gap in Richards's treatment.

Shelley and Coleridge both deal with this problem, Shelley through the phenomenon of the 'dead metaphor', or the degeneration of language. Fresh insight and imaginative response are apt or are even bound to 'run down' by becoming through time and repetition habitual and customary. Products are taken for granted and the idea which they once expressed is forgotten, or taken so literally that its vitality is lost.[22] This same phenomenon occurs in perception: constant repetition leads to the positing of physical objects and patterns or fields of organization, which become disassociated from the processes of perceptive activity which constitute them. Primary imagination sinks below the level of consciousness so that perceptions and constructs seem to be received 'ready-made' to the conscious mind. Secondary imagination can be described as the faculty of bringing to consciousness what would otherwise be lost to human awareness, namely, its own perceptive processes. And for Coleridge there is no given contour or terrain, as Mr Baker mistakenly supposes. Every model which is supposed to be the 'given' inevitably disintegrates upon closer examination from a dynamic, constructive point of view. There is no fixed material substratum external to perception, no mountain, no given. Mr Baker's interpretation of primary imagination, which relies on such a patently materialist foundation, is far from being Coleridge's meaning.

The 'everyday' world of beefsteaks and busses which offends Mr Baker so that he mistakes the role of 'primary imagination', is a result of the process of imaginative perception which has ceased to function actively. It has become a stagnant proxy and a habit through the repetition of what was once a vital act. Once these proxies of acts have become fixed and dead, fancy and memory set upon them, rearranging them according to or perhaps contrary to the order of time and space. Fancy and memory cannot make new materials, they can only juggle existing elements into different positions relative to each other. Imagination is the faculty which rejuvenates these proxies into fresh acts of perception, by 'reapprehending' the principles of organization or relation which through time have dropped below the threshold of conscious awareness. The discovery of a relation is often like that of remembering – the mind recognizes its own previous activity. Coleridge contrasts the mode of operation of fancy:

FANCY, on the contrary, has not other counters to play with, but fixities and definites. The Fancy is indeed no other than a mode of Memory emancipated from the order of time and space; while it is blended with, and modified by that empirical phenomenon of the will, which we express by the word CHOICE. But equally with the ordinary memory the Fancy must receive all its materials ready made from the law of association.[23]

Only by recognizing the central role of imagination in perception is it possible to speak meaningfully of perception as 'a repetition in the finite mind of the eternal act of creation in the infinite I AM'. We can separate three moments in experience and three major distinctions, the points at either extreme being subject to the maxim beloved by Coleridge, 'Extremes Meet': (1) primary imagination, perception, senses, and, loosely, the unconscious realm; (2) fancy, memory, understanding and the realm of everyday ordinary consciousness: (3) secondary imagination, or the realm of poetic-philosophic consciousness.[24] The first and third are both characterized by a quality of 'direct beholding', while the second is distinguished by its deductive, consecutive nature. The second has its proper role only as a mediating power between the two, as a kind of fulcrum, or a resting or assimilative stage. The completing power or stage must follow if stagnancy and encrustation are not to set in. Ordinary consciousness makes possible a higher level of consciousness and a self-consciousness which can manifest itself only in and through the former. But that does not mean that the latter is only an intensification of the former.

Richards correctly characterizes the radically creative function of perception in *Coleridge on Imagination*.[25] In *The Idea of Coleridge's Criticism*, R. H. Fogle also shows that he clearly understands the dynamic nature of this activity of perception: 'The primary imagination performs the creative act of consciousness itself.' The secondary imagination plays with this 'material furnished by the primary imagination'.[26] Coleridge expresses the connection through the metaphor of perception as language, the aptness of which must now be considerably clearer.[27] He explains that the perceiver merely speaks the language of nature by means of the primary imagination. The artist makes the object of his study the language of nature, and seeks not just to speak it fluently, but to discover its laws of generative grammar – hence he becomes a self-conscious speaker through the secondary imagination.[28]

Another area of confusion which arises in any discussion of Coleridge's concept of perception and imagination is the 'law of association'. Association can be understood only by keeping in mind the creativity of perception. Mr Baker explains his view of Coleridge's concept of association: 'Coleridge adhered firmly...to the idea that the associative power... was part of the *vis receptiva*,...part of the passive powers of the mind.'[29] But if this is straightforwardly true, how can we possibly account for Coleridge's rejection of Hartley's associationism? In the *Biographia* Coleridge explicitly rejects Hartley, Aristotle, and all the proponents of the passive view of association. When Coleridge defines the fancy as the associative and aggregative power, he is perhaps using 'associative' in the strict sense of aggregative, or the arranging of parts according to mechanical laws, by juxtaposition, increase by additive processes, or time and space likenesses and contiguities. He is *distinguishing* this from that mental process which in philosophy has been called the 'law of association' and which is inadequately characterized by a theory accounting only for the aggregative process, which is fancy's realm. To equate the law of association with mere fancy is to misunderstand Coleridge's two varying usages of the term which depends upon the context. The 'law of association' in its historical usage is at the foundation of perception: it *is* one aspect of primary imagination in its free operation. Thus in states of reverie, meditation, 'free association', dream, day-dream, fantasy, and drug-induced states, this associative process is revealing of the connections which the imagination is discovering (or creating) amongst its materials, as well as the way in which it creates new and fresh materials for further unifying and idealizing. In such states the mind is liberated from the constrictions which values acting as rules of connection place upon it, values that is which are imposed by a society for external purposes. In ordinary consciousness associations or connections are being made according to external considerations and are not intrinsic or essential connections. They are rather arbitrary and accidental. This is the province of both understanding or fancy, depending upon the materials attended to.

Association freed from these constraints is the fertile soil of new products and fresh materials for the secondary imagination. Thus Baker is again mistaken when he calls association simply the '*vis receptiva*'. 'Association' is historically the term for the mental acts of the mind, but within this general collective term several distinctions must be made. Arbitrary association, modified by choice and guided by considerations extrinsic to the material associated, is fancy. Relative to the distinguished form of association which Coleridge names imagination the former is passive and receptive, that is, it receives 'all its materials ready made from the law of association'. It cannot be that law, if it receives its materials from it. Hence Coleridge is discussing types of association for which Hartley failed entirely to account. Hartley's error is the usual error of philosophers – he analyses a part and thinks he has adequately dealt with the whole. That is, he mistakes a partial function of the faculty of association for its entire powers of organization. To this Coleridge objected. But when Coleridge says that the fancy merely associates, he is now using the term slightly differently, in a more restricted sense, to mean 'aggregate', to distinguish the activity of mechanical association, fancy, from 'organic' association, or imagination. If a *theory* of association (in its fullest and historical sense) is to be adequate, it must account for both mechanical and organic association.

THE.REASON/IMAGINATION DISTINCTION

The distinction between imagination and fancy is never emphasized again in any published works, but is overtaken by the distinction between reason and understanding. The relation between these two distinctions has not yet been made adequately clear, nor is it clear how, exactly, imagination differs from reason. Coleridge's descriptions of the imagination as the power of the 'all in each' the 'one in the Many', as that power which connects and diffuses a tone of unity throughout, etc., are frequent and familiar formulations.[30] But how does this differ from the faculty of reason? The most definite statement about the relation is to be found in the *Statesman's Manual*: imagination is 'that reconciling and mediatory power, which incorporating the Reason in Images of the Sense, and organizing (as it were) the flux of the Senses by the permanence and self-circling energies of the Reason, gives birth to a system of symbols, harmonious in themselves, and consubstantial with the truths, of which they are the *conductors*'.[31] Here the imagination seems to be acting like the intermediate faculty it is said to be in the *Biographia*:

There are evidently two powers at work, which relatively to each other are active and passive; and this is not possible without an intermediate faculty, which is at once both active and passive. (In philosophical language, we must denominate this intermediate faculty in all its degrees and determinations, the IMAGINATION.)[32]

Elsewhere Coleridge again emphasizes the imagination as the power of *embodying* the universality and atemporality of reason's ideas in the sensual: 'imagination is the laboratory in which the thought elaborates essence into existence'.[33] Thus the imagination seems to have a definite connection with the sensuous which distinguishes it from the reason. It creates the 'translucence of the eternal through and in the temporal'.[34] Still more importantly Coleridge writes that 'Fancy and Imagination are Oscillations, *this* connecting Reason and Understanding; *that* connecting Sense and Understanding.'[35] In a long passage in the *Statesman's Manual* Coleridge tries to state the relation of the two:

Of the *discursive* understanding, which forms for itself general notions and terms of classification for the purpose of comparing and arranging phaenomena, the Characteristic is Clearness without Depth. It contemplates the unity of things in their *limits* only, and is consequently a knowledge of superficies without substance. So much so indeed, that it entangles itself in contradictions in the very effort of comprehending the *idea* of substance. The completing power which unites clearness with depth, the plenitude of the sense with the comprehensibility of the understanding, is the IMAGINATION, impregnated with which the understanding itself becomes intuitive and a living power. The REASON, (not the abstract reason, not the reason as the mere *organ* of science, or as the faculty of scientific principles and schemes a priori; but reason) as the integral *spirit* of the regenerated man, reason substantiated and vital, 'one only, yet manifold, overseeing all, and going through all understanding; the breath of the power of God, and a pure influence from the glory of the Almighty; which remaining in itself regenerateth all other powers, and in all ages entering into holy souls maketh them friends of God and prophets'; (Wisdom of Solomon, c. vii.) the REASON without being either the SENSE, the UNDERSTANDING or the IMAGINATION contains all three within itself, even as the mind contains its thoughts, and is present in and through them all; or as the expression pervades the different features of an intelligent countenance. Each individual must bear witness of it to his own mind, even as he describes life and light: and with the silence of light it describes itself, and dwells in *us* only as far as we dwell in *it*. It cannot in strict language be called a faculty, much less a personal property, of any human mind![36]

In the opening sentences of this passage the understanding and imagination seem to be contrasted as the discursive and the intuitive, the implication being that the intuitive interpenetrates the discursive to make it productive and living. Here imagination seems almost to have taken over the function of reason in its usual position, that of the faculty distinguished from understanding. Reason is raised to an even higher sphere, for it is no longer conceived of as a faculty at all, but as the spirit which grounds the other faculties, or as the mind which 'contains' them. A note to this passage may be a further clue to the relation of reason and imagination. Coleridge jots down 'It is wonderful, how closely Reason and Imagination are connected, and Religion the union of the two.'[37] What seems to be suggested from these preceding statements is that imagination is the mediating power between the sensuous and the ideal, in distinction from reason, which is altogether a pre-sensuous faculty. The objects of the reason differ from those of the senses and the understanding by being beyond 'space/time' determinations, and differ from those of the imagination in that they are wholly ideal, and still unembodied, that is, being, but not existing – ideas. The pure contemplation of ideas belongs to the reason alone:

Thus were the very first lessons in the Divine School assigned to the cultivation of the reason and of the will: or rather of both as united in Faith. The common and ultimate object of the will and of the reason was purely *spiritual*, and to be present in the mind of the disciple – . . . in the idea alone, and never as an image or imagination. The *means* too, by which the idea was to be excited, as well as the *symbols* by which it was to be communicated, were to be, as far as possible, *intellectual*.[38]

Thus we have the possibility of putting our minds in a state of contemplation of Ideas, *without* the polluting effects of the expression of them. This state we might call reason, instead of naming it a faculty, since according to Coleridge it is consubstantial with its objects, the ideas.

Imagination, in contradistinction, is the faculty of symbols, symbols acting as the only means by which the idea could be manifested or expressed.[39] Symbols serve the same mediating, expressive role in relation to ideas as the imagination to the reason. Coleridge's distinction between allegory and symbol not only acts to clarify the fancy/imagination distinction, but also emphasizes the relation of symbols to ideas:

An Allegory is but a translation of abstract notions into a picture language which is itself nothing but an abstraction from objects of the senses; the principal being more worthless even than its phantom proxy. . . . a Symbol . . . is characterized by a translucence of the Special in the Individual or of the General in the Especial or of the Universal in the General. Above all by the translucence of the Eternal through and in the Temporal.[40]

Compare this with the later description of the Ideas: 'that which is . . . an educt of the Imagination actuated by the pure Reason, to which there neither is or can be an adequate correspondent in the world of the senses – this and this alone is = AN IDEA'.[41] In connection with the passage cited above on the 'living *educts* of the Imagination' and symbols as the *conductors* of the truths with which they are nevertheless consubstantial, we see how 'wonderfully close' symbol and idea are too.

The most accurate way of coming to terms with the relation of imagination and reason seems to be to suggest that the distinctions between fancy and imagination and understanding and reason overlapped at certain points. Their common ground we can best state as the distinction between the mechanical and organic, the passive and active, or the discursive and intuitive. Other distinctions apply as well, such as that between method and arrangement, symbol and allegory, and so on. Thus when Coleridge was interested in this contrast, the fancy and understanding fell into one category and the imagination and reason fell into another. We can then understand the use of the phrase 'imaginative Reason'. In speaking of products of the 'unenlivened generalizing Understanding', Coleridge contrasts the idea of *product* as a dead, fixed, entity with the *educt*. After altering 'educts' to 'Produce', he says: 'Or perhaps these μορφωματα of the mechanic Understanding as distinguished from the "ποιησεῖς" of the imaginative Reason might be named *Products* in antithesis to *Produce* – or Growths.'[42] When this contrast of the mechanical and the generative was the issue, the reason and the imagination were close indeed, and might even be used interchangeably.

The contrast of mechanical and organic or discursive and intuitive was not the only point of interest in the analysis of the faculties. Another crucial issue was how to infuse the intuitive into the discursive without its losing the vital, living power which protects it from becoming merely discursive. It is in this problem that the imagination becomes distinguishable from the reason, for as we have seen above Coleridge saw the necessity of a mediating faculty. This faculty would keep alive the idea in the expression of it, and could create *conductors* for the truths or ideas of reason. Reason is the source of ideas and the 'faculty' of contemplating them in their spiritual being, while imagination acts to embody those ideas in the sensuous, the result being symbols. Correlatively the degeneration of symbols into allegories suggests the fancy, which mistakes images for ideas and the literal for the metaphorical. The understanding similarly mistakes abstractions for ideas and, in its generalizing function of naming, it assumes that what cannot be *comprehended* cannot be *conceived*; hence ideas are beyond its grasp. Though the fancy and the understanding are different, from the preponderance of the sensuous in the former and the pre-sensuous nature of the latter in its categories of classification, they are importantly similar in that their materials are fixities and determinates which they manipulate and arrange, the one in sensuous images, the other in non-sensuous conceptions, both free from the immediate determinations of time and space contiguity, but still subject to time and space as a condition of the juxtapositioning of their materials.

The *Biographia* is the only major published work in which the primary vehicle for the distinction between the discursive and the intuitive is the fancy/imagination distinction. The imagination is discussed only infreqently in the *Statesman's Manual*, with no mention at all of the distinction between it and the fancy. Nor does the distinction occur in any of the other major works. It is conspicuously missing from *The Friend*, *Aids to Reflection*, *Church and State*, and the *Philosophical Lectures*. What seems to have happened in all these later works was that the reason/under-standing distinction superseded the former distinction. How it could do this without being precisely identical with it we can understand when we consider that it is necessary to recognize a distinction, though definitely not a division, between philosophy and poetry.[43] We may characterize the distinction as one in which the intuitive faculty is operating with a pre-ponderance toward a more intellective emphasis, or on the other hand toward a more practical emphasis. In the one case language is used more conceptually, in the other more sensuously. As Coleridge explains:

the reason...merely considered as the endowment of the human mind, having two definitions accordingly as it is exercised practically or intellectually, – is the ground of theology, or religious belief. Both are good in themselves as far as they go, and productive – the former – of a sensibility to the beautiful in art and nature, or imaginativeness and moral enthusiasm; – the latter – of insight, comprehension, and a philosophic mind.[44]

It is possible to understand that the imagination could be conceived of as reason operating practically, or intuition operating in the spheres of the aesthetic and religious, in the unification of thought and feeling.[45] It is distinguished from reason's primarily intellectual operations. This dis-tinction is a tentative and secondary one only, as Coleridge makes clear when he insists that the best philosophy and the best poetry require the operation of reason both as imaginative (or practical) and as intellective. Coleridge can talk of the 'philosophic imagination, the sacred power of self-intuition',[46] which suggests a fusion of the practical and the intellec-tive.[47] In order to de-emphasize the difference and to impress upon his readers the common ground of reason operating imaginatively or intel-lectively, Coleridge seems to have given up the frequent use of 'imagina-tion', replacing it by 'reason' as operating in relation to the production of symbols or of the connection of thought and feeling. He never again, moreover, made poetry the explicit and exclusive topic of discussion in relation to the operation of the faculties, which may also explain why the understanding/reason distinction gradually replaced that between fancy and imagination. Along with Coleridge's shift away from the writing of poetry toward philosophy came the shift in interest from *embodying* the universal in new and beautiful forms, toward attending to and *contem-plating* the universal *in spite of* the co-presence of the individual: a shift from creating new symbols to a striving toward a fuller participation in the ideas of which those symbols were the conductors.[48]

In the struggle between the two formulations of the discursive/intuitive distinction (between fancy/imagination as one mode and understanding/reason as another) the, for Coleridge, distressing battle between pantheism and Christianity emerges. The claims which pantheism made as a solution to questions of metaphysical import parallel the claims of imagination for autonomy. To regard imagination as the supreme faculty would lead to a pantheistic world view, a view which persistently dogged Coleridge's intellect with its great logical force, but one which he found intolerable in its exclusion of fundamental Christian doctrine and especially of the idea of person.[49] The reason, Coleridge could Christianize (while imagination remained a 'pagan' mystery) by relating it to a central tradition of thought in such powerful Christian figures as the Cambridge Platonists and Kant. The idea of reason in this tradition incorporates within itself the Christian idea of the will, an essential character not present at all in the concept of imagination.

The *Biographia* in this context begins to look as though it is one of the most experimentative of Coleridge's works. In it, he gave to his imagination a free play and scope of activity unhindered by the restraining and conventionalizing forces which the adherence to Christian doctrine imposed upon his thought. There are passages in the *Biographia* which have an imaginative, 'paganistic' originality and individuality which no formulations explicitly Christian could possibly allow. The final paragraph of volume two is one of the most inspiring of the spiritually unfettered yearnings of a mind striving to reveal its innermost individuality in the fullest possible universal expressiveness by discarding the heavy over-lay of religious doctrine:

This has been my Object, and this alone can be my Defence – and O! that with this my personal as well as my LITERARY LIFE might conclude! the unquenched desire I mean, not without the consciousness of having earnestly endeavoured, to kindle young minds, and to guard them against the temptations of Scorners, by showing that the Scheme of Christianity, as taught in the Liturgy and Homilies of our Church, though not discoverable by human Reason, is yet in accordance with it; that link follows link by necessary consequence; that Religion passes out of the ken of Reason only where the eye of Reason has reached its own Horizon; and that Faith is then but its continuation: even as the Day softens away into the sweet Twilight, and Twilight, hushed and breathless, steals into the Darkness. It is Night, sacred Night! the upraised Eye views only the starry Heaven which manifests itself alone: and the outward Beholding is fixed on the sparks twinkling in the aweful depth, though Suns of other Worlds, only to preserve the Soul steady and collected in its pure *Act* of inward adoration to the great I AM, and to the filial WORD that re-affirmeth it from Eternity to Eternity, whose choral Echo is the universe.

$$\Theta E\Omega I \ MON\Omega I \ \Delta O\Xi A$$

FINIS[50]

Even in this passage, we see Coleridge setting out from a vision firmly established within traditional Christian theology. Yet by the time he has reached the heights of inspiration, in the very act of describing the mind as passing out of the ken of reason, he himself soars on imagination beyond the ken of orthodox Christian expression, and uses phrases to express his vision which sound more pantheistic than Christian. Reading this passage one feels a sudden gentle loosening of control at the phrase 'even as the Day softens away into the sweet Twilight...', and we sense the freedom as Coleridge's own inspiration carries him off the ground of Christianity into a wider, airier compass.

These soundings into the unknown of a mind eschewing any contact with a mainland of conventional religious thought and expression, in the effort to reach a living individuality, approach the mysticism and paganism which would lead inevitably to, for Coleridge, a crushing pantheism. In the *Biographia* Coleridge seems to wade further out into the ocean of this 'atheism' than he ever dared to go again. He was haunted by the pantheistic imagination which lured him with the promise of experiencing the 'mystery' in its depths. As we will suggest below, Coleridge ventured into the unknown realms and boundaries of consciousness, spurred on by the 'ancestral voices from afar' to undertake a poetic 'auto-psychoanalysis' only in the poems of his early years. Immediately upon finishing the *Biographia* he retired into the safety of the mainland of ordinary conventional consciousness, and occupied much of his intellectual energy with untangling the issues within the Christian theological tradition. Records of future journeys of this sort, that is, of grappling with the terrifyingly powerful forces which confront the mind and which are recorded in 'The Ancient Mariner' and 'Kubla Khan', are extremely rare and momentary. 'Limbo' may be one such example.

Coleridge's commitment to the imagination can also be stated in terms of his dissatisfaction with Kant. His conservatism and adherence to a Christian ideology may be expressed analogously in his 'correction' of Plato. Kant's philosophy he 'completed' by insisting that ideas (Platonic ideas) were constitutive, and not merely regulative.[51] Although he calls reason the source of these ideas, for Plato they were objects of the intuition, which is closer to Coleridge's imagination than to his Christian concept of reason. But by using 'reason', Coleridge was Christianizing Plato, that is, correcting that philosophy's tendency toward a possible paganistic interpretation. In a sense, then, Coleridge adopts the Platonic constitutive ideas, and when by virtue of that commitment he believes himself to be careening into the abyss of pantheism, he seizes upon a line of Christian terminology, shifts his attention away from the mysteries of the contemplation of this abyss of imagination and toward theological issues. By this line of movement he halts the plunge into mystery. Yet he remains dangling from a line over the chasm which his individual creative mind is nevertheless committed to. Coleridge's use of 'Reason' becomes no longer Kantian in his subsumption of a Platonic faculty of intuition into it. Nor is it purely Platonic, because of the Kantian commitments to will and Christian personeity. In a sense, this new product comes closest to 'reason' as used by the Cambridge Platonists.

In the *Biographia* Coleridge employs the formulation of the discursive/intuitive distinction which is predominantly applicable to art, in terms of imagination and fancy, in spite of the fact that his primary concern throughout the first 'philosophical' volume is apparently strictly philosophic. His major theme is the inadequacy of the passive theory of association in accounting for the activity of mind which is primarily intuitive and which forms the basis of all other mental acts. This inadequacy applies to the Hartleian account (or lack of account) of the intuition, whether it be sensuous or intellectual. In choosing the 'artistic' formulation for the distinction between passive and active (which he had already thoroughly worked out in *The Friend* in 1809–10 in strictly philosophical terms) Coleridge achieves a further structural advantage for unifying the concerns of the *Biographia*. He emphasizes the common faculty which underlies and informs poetry and philosophy, and the common danger of stagnation on both theoretical and practical levels if the interplay of the active/passive mental functions is not discriminated. In describing in the *Biographia* his youthful efforts as poet, and in subsequent 'digressions' on authorship, spies, arrogance, etc., Coleridge, as we have suggested in chapter five, is giving examples of genial or ungenial readers and reading processes and is addressing himself to difficulties created by mistaken notions of the nature of the reader's role, communication, and truth. After this subtle and indirect, Socratic *propaedeutic*, Coleridge launches his readers into the difficulties of associationism, and finally of transcendental idealism and the role of imagination in both. Volume one of the *Biographia* we might conceive of as the ascending side of the pyramid of method, the inductive process, while volume two constitutes the descent through application to specific materials of the principles arrived at in the analysis. In this way Coleridge has constructed a thorough-going Platonic architecture of method as the unity of structure in the *Biographia*, the *procedural* aspect corresponding to the thematic: not only does he develop his content according to the Platonic inductive-deductive systematic. His content is the justification of that two-fold process, for the distinction of an active from a merely passive faculty of mind as the paramount force in the construction of experience implies and indeed presupposes precisely such a methodology, as opposed to the merely deductive 'method'. Without an active faculty of mind there would be no way of proceeding inductively, since the hypotheses and 'leading ideas', which may eventually be transformed into theory, are *never* deducible from the 'data' (contrary to the assumption that hypotheses are derived wholly from, and theories entirely validated by, evidence; evidence can at best disprove theories; it can never wholly validate them).[52] Although it seems correct to see the *Statesman's Manual* and *The Friend* as relating in explicit ways to the *Biographia* and as connecting it to the *Aids to Reflection* (a later, more orthodox work), *The Friend* and the *Aids* seem nevertheless to group themselves together stylistically and by content, the *Biographia* and the *Statesman's Manual* forming a contrasting pair. Both the former two are specifically philosophical and theological in formulation, as is suggested by the heavy preponderance in them of the reason/understanding distinction, which expresses the active–passive dichotomy in the mental faculties. This bias toward philosophical formulation is evidenced again in the stylistic conception, which is in general more treatise-like. Both, also, deal specifically, – if briefly, – with the concept of polarity.

The *Biographia* and the *Statesman's Manual*, on the other hand, seem to lack this predominant treatise-style, as well as the usual explicit philosophical language for the most important themes, offering a more poetic formulation and style. The central theme of the *Biographia*, the distinction between the active and passive faculties, is expressed throughout in terms of the imagination and fancy and *never* in terms of the reason and the understanding. Moreover, the style is far from treatise–like; Coleridge has in fact achieved his most sustained level of 'metaphoric situations' and indirect communication in this work. Even the *Statesman's Manual*, though it uses the reason/understanding distinction, does so to relate the reason to the imagination, and seems to have as one of its primary concerns the relation of symbols to ideas, as distinct from allegory. Furthermore, the most stringently philosophical sections of the *Biographia*, the ten theses, for example, are presented in the poetic style of metaphoric situations, as we have tried to show above.

In considering the precise nature of this distinction between the two groups of works, one could suggest that in some sense the *Aids*, while being a work of great achievement, nevertheless looks back to previous thought, and is as a result less poetic, innovative, or imaginative, than the *Biographia*, especially in terms of style and method of composition. Certainly it offers its own rewards, however, in its preponderance of the 'philosophic intelligence'. It is heavily laden with Coleridge's earlier thought, yet organizes it in a more conventionally acceptable format, at the expense however of imaginative power and effect. In genre it veers towards the German Romantic fragment-form, however. The 1809–10

Friend, on the other hand, functions in an opposite sense from the *Aids* in relation to the *Biographia,* in that it is a tentative, probing, and struggling effort toward the achievement of a method sustainedly artistic and dramatic, the originality and innovation of which *The Friend* gives promises, as in 'Essays on Method' but never realizes in as sustained a way as the *Biographia. The Friend* and the *Aids* can also be distinguished from the *Biographia* and the *Statesman's Manual* in another respect. In the former two Coleridge does not hesitate to adopt German philosophic language to express 'true' opposition. He uses the metaphor of polarity freely and with purpose (as he also does in *Church and State,* a work which could be classified with this 'philosophy-laden' pair as well). But 'polarity' does not occur once in either the *Statesman's Manual* or the *Biographia;* Coleridge's rejection of this terminology is consistent with his preference for the use of more familiar English terms in making the passive/active faculty distinction. When, in the *Biographia,* he wishes to discuss the concept of opposition, Coleridge uses the much freer, more ancient and universal formulation of the unity or reconciliation of opposites, or the related metaphor of contraction and expansion.

This clear contrast in terminology between the two groups of works occurs at two crucial points, (1) where the 'seminal' ideas of opposition and (2) where the active nature of the mind's participation in the construction of experience are being discussed. In the works which we have thought to be more artistically innovative and original, Coleridge has preferred the non-Schellingian, non-German, and less philosophical expressions, choosing the freer, more universally known formulation of the reconciliation of opposites, and the more poetic, more English, active/passive distinction of imagination and fancy. The derivative formulations occur in the works which are less of an *artistic* achievement (as opposed to a discursive, philosophical genre), but which look forward or hark back to work of greater artistic accomplishment. A substantial aspect of their philosophic importance is the conventionality of method and organization to conform with the preponderance of an arrangement more conventionally and philosophically systematic, especially in the *Aids.* The sustained imaginative method of the *Biographia* spilled over into large parts of the *Statesman's Manual* and gave both works an 'airy brightness' which was surpassed only in the poetry.

IRONY IN 'THE ANCIENT MARINER' AND 'KUBLA KHAN'

The quality of airy imagination of the *Biographia* mentioned briefly above (which distinguishes the *Biographia* from any of Coleridge's other prose works, and especially from those employing the reason/

understanding distinction) we may, in view of our analysis in chapter four above, name 'high irony'. This pervasive irony lends the *Biographia* that imaginative dimension and playfulness which it of Coleridge's prose works best employs. And it connects the *Biographia* to the two poems which are most in the mind of all Coleridge's readers, 'The Ancient Mariner' and 'Kubla Khan'. This imaginative context of irony constituted by the pervasiveness of the 'reading analogy', is achieved in the poems in part by the fascinating relationship of the gloss to 'The Ancient Mariner' and of the preface to 'Kubla Khan'. The 'metaphoric situations' which act as the connecting links of the *Biographia* are another aspect of its relation to these two poems, in that those situations are also more products of the 'pure imagination' than any other of Coleridge's prose writings, except for scattered passages in the *Statesman's Manual*, the 'Essays on method' in the 1818 *Friend*, and a few instances in other works. Structurally the gloss and the preface act in similar ways to the crucial structural achievement of the *Biographia* in, for example, chapter twelve, accomplished by means of the letter, the missing chapter, the references to the missing essay on the supernatural supposedly affixed to 'The Ancient Mariner', and the missing prospectus of this 'missing' treatise on imagination. These are a few examples of the techniques of awakening the reader to the self-consciousness of the reading process as an important subject matter of the work.

'Kubla Khan' was published in May–June 1816 with the text of 'Christabel' (and 'Pains of Sleep'). The *Biographia* at that time had been finished and was awaiting publication, as was *Sybilline Leaves*, containing the new 'Ancient Mariner', with which the gloss was appearing for the first time. Hence 'Kubla Khan', with its extraordinary preface, and the *glossed* 'Ancient Mariner' were being prepared for publication close to the time of the writing of the *Biographia* (and the *Statesman's Manual*). It is hardly surprising that the same sublime playfulness of irony should have illuminated all of these works. It is not possible here to indicate fully the irony of the gloss and the preface, but a few general remarks will suggest its function. The gloss may *in part* be understood as the parody of a highly educated, intelligent, and even poetic, but nevertheless reductionist reader who fails to achieve the imaginative level of self-conscious participation which the poem invites.[53] For example, such a reader may externalize the action by adding geographical information and time-space observations in the gloss which nowhere occur in the poem.[54] He excludes himself most entirely from participation in the imaginative achievement of the poem through his conventionally moralistic response to the poem, by interpolating guilt, blame, remorse, superstitious signs, bad and good omens, cause and agency, sin, and retribution, etc., into the action of the poem by means of the gloss, while in the *poem* the level of moralizing is specifically and markedly excluded.[55] Nor is this conventional moralizing in the gloss consonant with Coleridge's own insistence, in reply to a comment by a reader that the moral was not emphasized enough, that, on the contrary, the moral intruded too much upon the reader.[56] How accurately Coleridge assessed the response of posterity and the pressing need for such a safeguard as the gloss is clear from a wealth of secondary literature about the poem charting the literal and unimaginative responses, which suggest the action to be wholly external and unrelated to a psychomythological experience,[57] and to a far greater 'cosmic' moral significance than can be expressed in the conventional terminology which the writer of the gloss imposes upon the poem.

Another way of interpreting the gloss to 'The Ancient Mariner' would be in terms of the conflict between pantheism (or paganism) and Christianity, which was discussed above in the second section of this chapter. It was suggested there that the related conflict between a pagan imagination and a Christianized reason eventually led to a suppression of the former faculty, so that the *Biographia* contrasts markedly with both the earlier prose (e.g. *The Friend*) and the later prose (such as *Aids to Reflection*) in the virtually unfettered activity of the paganistic element of imagination. In nearly all the other prose, excepting parts of the *Statesman's Manual*, the restraining forces of a rather conventional morality and religion were apparently more operative. Hence it is possible that the gloss of 'The Ancient Mariner' was added as a Christianizing, constraining commentary upon a poem which had escaped the controls and inhibitions of Coleridge's uncertainties more than any other work. Although we can see the gloss as an ironic *process* of a most powerful type operating successfully upon the reader to catapult him into that self-conscious imagination which was beyond the control of a traditionally religious 'reason', some readers may nevertheless remain uncertain as to Coleridge's participation in this ironic process.

The same hesitancy would apply to the preface of 'Kubla Khan' – Coleridge was only too aware of the implications of the last eighteen lines of the poem. Perhaps by means of the preface he hoped somehow to eschew conscious responsibility for them, or at least to hide the implications somewhat from his readers, as if the poem were a mere fantasy or poetic reverie with no important philosophic or religious implications to be read into its sheer poetic purity. Nevertheless, the preface to 'Kubla Khan' has also been singularly interpreted in a narrowly literal sense, as the quantity of literature exploring its historical-biographical accuracy testifies. But it, too, may function more importantly in an ironic way, as a mirroring situation in which the reader catches a glimpse of the tendency of his own mind toward a narrow, information-oriented response. Only by means of self-awareness is the reader able to see the metaphorical mode in which 'Kubla Khan' is a fragment in Shelley's and in the German romantic sense of 'fragment'.[58] This fragment metaphor is suggested by lines in the poem when it describes fragments which 'vaulted like rebounding hail' amid a seething fountain. Yet the poem even seems to be complete in any literal sense of the word – it does not appear to break off unfinished, for it reaches a highly integrated finale. Nor is it unlikely that the vision or dream, in which 'Kubla Khan' was supposed to have originated, might have been meant primarily as a metaphor for the state of imaginative inspiration, as something other than ordinary consciousness.[59] The song of the Abyssinian maid which the speaker-poet wishes to revive also occurred in a vision, and though the source of the song is the maid as she plays on her dulcimer, she is clearly an intermediary for the speaker himself. He ultimately is the original creator of that music, since it was in his vision that the maid played the song. She perhaps acts as a metaphor for the faculty of imagination in the way that Coleridge often described it, as a 'mediating' faculty, of which 'Kubla Khan' is the revived song.[60] The poem, and the aesthetic experience which results, is his dome, 'that sunny dome! those caves of ice!' which he wished to build with 'music loud and long'. 'That sunny dome! those caves of ice!' is a paradigmatic instance of the tension of oppositions which Brooks, Richards, Empson, and the German Romantics see as the constituents of ironic, imaginative poetry,[61] and which Coleridge saw theoretically – though whether he acted upon that theory or was acted upon by it is to ask whether irony was a process only, or a method. With its emphasis upon a method of metaphor and a method or process of irony, and with a theme of imagination as the primary faculty of perception and creative activity, the *Biographia* more closely resembles 'The Ancient Mariner' and 'Kubla Khan' than is generally supposed, and the features of the text are illuminated by the same spirit of inspiration which informs these two poems of 'pure imagination'.

Conclusion

✥

The *Biographia*'s readers

In the foregoing discussion it has been suggested that the *Biographia* contains a level of discourse which involves a consciousness of the reading process as a subject matter of the work in addition to the more explicit subject matter, which is the analysis of imagination. (By reading process is meant all the thinking, organizing, activated prejudices, habits, expectations, judging, perceiving, and values imposed unconsciously, which go into making a 'picture' or having an experience of a text.) Such a submerged level of discourse is necessary if even the more explicit level is to be properly understood. For it is the avowed character of imagination that it cannot be known merely discursively, and must be recreated – but by whom, if not by the reader? Imaginative reading and the hindrances and instruments to this achievement become the underlying, present concern of the *Biographia*.

The 'metaphoric situations' are carefully designed occasions of a more formal nature for stimulating imaginative reading. They are embedded within the surface as links to the pervading analogical level of reading as the hidden subject matter. But they are also symbols and models of this general level of metaphor which informs the discursive prose linked by these intense moments of poetic achievement. Thus, though they occur only unevenly scattered throughout the *Biographia*, they nevertheless can be construed as models of the method of the *Biographia*, a method designed to stimulate the reader to self-knowledge and to an apprehension of his thinking, judging and response generally. This method remains however at a submerged level, since to stimulate the reader to imaginative reading requires imaginative situations, metaphors. If it were a matter simply of telling the reader to think about thinking, a surface of discourse would be enough. But the reader must catch himself in the act of thinking and imagining, hence the necessity for indirection, or for leading the reader out of himself so that he can then turn and see himself from the needed distance. While the metaphoric situations are visable at the surface level from stylistic properties, their significance leads into the buried levels of meaning, first where the various and miscellaneous subject matter of the surface is perceived as different parts of a continuing analysis of imagination, and second, where this homogeneous subject matter is perceived imaginatively in its analogy with the reading process. Thus there are two distinguishable levels below the surface, one requiring attention, the other requiring thought, or the 'voluntary production in our own minds of those states of consciousness, to which, as to his fundamental facts, the Writer has referred us' (*Friend*, 1, 16). Both are active relative to the passivity of a surface reading which perceives only diversity and miscellany in the subjects proposed and discussed. Attention is called for at the first stage of submerged discourse: 'Attention has for its object the order and connection of Thoughts and Images, each of which is in itself already and familiarly known.' But to remain at this level is to understand imagination only as an abstraction of generalized thought, not to experience it as a form or mode of thought. The metaphors act as conductors towards these levels which lie behind the most discursive passages, such as the discussion of associationism in chapters four to nine.

Such a submerged level of discourse constitutes the underlying method of the *Biographia* and its unity, and this continuity is allowed to show growth and development. For example, the chapters on associationism can be understood as implying the metaphor of the reading process as subject matter and of the analysis of imagination as related subject matter when one considers that which is at issue in the distinction between a passive and an active faculty. For these chapters form the basis for the necessity of the fancy/imagination distinction, and as such, lead up meticulously to the demonstration of the faculty of imagination as the means of self-knowledge in chapters twelve and thirteen. The implication throughout those chapters is that a passive reading, like a passive faculty, must be shown to be insufficient for an understanding of the reading process, and analogously, of experience in general. A more active participation by the reader is implied in the analysis of associationism, if the reader is to grasp fully the reason for the inadequacy of a passive theory of mind, rather than merely to see it stated by an author.

Coleridge lays the groundwork for the possibility of this fuller appreciation of imagination and for a self-experiencing, through the self-analysis of the first few chapters, where he gives the example by analysing his own compositions – the most explicitly autobiographical section of the *Biographia*. The general point of this analysis is that the work needed for the growth of the mind is of an autobiographical nature, for both author and reader, that is, a constant effort at self-analysis and self-experiencing precisely in order to escape the limitations of the ego as product of unconscious assimilation. An uncritical acceptance of the self as it is is the true tyranny of egotism. The full import of Coleridge's decision to write his metaphysics 'as my Life and in my Life' is understood only when the necessity for self-criticism is realized as the touchstone and constant point of reference for the growth of the philosophic mind. The choice of the biographical genre indicates both the goal of thought and the means: self knowledge through self criticism. Specifically for the reader, the genre by analogy implies that his work in reading is to produce an autobiographical work in which his own consciousness and mind is the subject of analysis. By discovering the accidents of personal taste, prejudice, and values which overlay the individual mind, one may hope to discover the more essential laws or ideas which constitute the structure of mind as mind in a generic sense. The mistaken notion, that because of a preoccupation with self, the Romantic poets were egotists, results from the failure to distinguish as objects of their attention the individual self and a representative or universal concept of the 'person'.

The progression of these chapters, then, from autobiography and self-analysis up to the final gesture of irony in chapter thirteen, is hardly unsystematic. It is a mapping of the successive steps which the mind must surmount in order to reach the vantage point from which, as in volume two, it is able to engage in imaginative criticism. For the prerequisite of any serious thinking seems, according to Coleridge, to be an ability to think about one's own thinking. This constitutes the first and necessary step toward a more philosophical attitude. Yet within this philosophical arena are pitfalls which the reader is warned against, as e.g. mistaking the part for the whole, or more specifically, mistaking passive association for the whole of mental activity. The main hindrance to intellectual growth is brought into full view for the reader, namely, the passive theory of mind. Coleridge's task is to assist the reader beyond the limitations of this passive mechanical philosophy, and another stage of growth is thus indicated. A further hindrance involved in mistaking the part for the whole is mistaking as the goal of knowledge the individual self as opposed to the self as a representative concept. The chapters on self-consciousness strive to lift the reader to this awareness of a more generic level of being – which can only be grasped by an active faculty of intuition. That the critical analysis of poetry and its relations to prose and philosophy occurs only in the second volume after this development may suggest that Coleridge viewed the rigorous development of the philosophic mind as a prerequisite for sound criticism.

The reading analogy constitutes the unity of the work as an expression of the primary/secondary imagination distinction – that is, the relation of aesthetics to perception, of art to reality. It is established by metaphor, but it also constitutes the irony of the work, in two senses. It indicates the necessity for the ironic detachment of a self-conscious and critical reader who can observe his own reading and composing of the text. In addition, irony is inherent in the failure to become conscious of the metaphor of the reading process as a subject matter. For without this awareness of the method and unity of the work, its obscurity and miscellaneous character is a reflection of the reader's confused outlook, and of his naive belief that in reading he does not 'alter', that he can describe an objective text without interpreting, and that a discoverable text somehow exists to which he can refer as a stable entity when trying to determine meaning. What must be realized is that even at the most superficial, narrative level, the literal meaning, the text itself indeed, is not stable, but a potentiality for interpretation in diverse ways. Irony as a technique seeks to incorporate this paradox into the text in a self-conscious way, to intensify and heighten the effect upon the reader.

Romantic Irony is an analysis of self-consciousness in art – of the spectator's relation to a work of art and his mode of experiencing it. The concept of irony can be understood as a transcendental deduction of mind in aesthetic terms. Irony as a principle of structure requires a design which is unified but open-ended – closure would exclude the crucial level of metaphor and self-criticism. The organic/mechanical distinction is instructive for understanding how a work can be unified but nevertheless changing, growing, and incomplete in being open-ended: the *Biographia* leaves room for its own growth in the reading experience, its 'involucrum, for the antennae yet to come'. Romantic irony is not an account of ironic works, but of works of art as inherently ironic, in the 'high' German and Socratic sense.

Irony as self-consciousness requires the detachment which allows a commitment to activity, but not to the specific products of that activity, not to the stages of thought and interpretation as ends, but as means to further activity. Thus the *Biographia* is not merely a point of departure for reflection by the reader about issues raised; it is an arena in which the struggle toward the dynamic solution of these issues can be waged. To use a more apt metaphor, it is a continuing dialogue, for the reader's responses and difficulties are anticipated and dealt with as the narrative unfolds. This description may to some extent account for the deceptively comfortable conversational style of the work, which is a measure not of a carelessness or of casual, unsystematic lucubrations, but which is a measure of Coleridge's effort to engage the reader in a genuine dialogue as a fellow-labourer – and as a friend.

MODERN CRITICAL THEORY

Modern critical theory has only recently begun to formulate for itself adequate descriptions of the way in which works of art function in experience. Structuralism makes several gestures toward approaching the reading experience, through its questioning of the nature of communication (as indirect, for example), when it discusses language as a sign, and not the signified, or when it brands the literal imprisoning. Formalism had broached some of these issues too, particularly when it advised the breaking up of habitual, literal responses by shock techniques and 'defamiliarization'.

But one of the most important explicit statements of the reading process as a point of reference for critical procedure came from Georges Poulet, in the 'Phenomenology of Reading'.[1] Poulet discusses the concepts of surface text and 'interior' text, and he explores the relation of the reader as 'subject' to the work of art as 'object'. His terminology is clearly appropriate as a critical apparatus for reading Coleridge. In the same vein, R. H. Jauss, in 'Literary History as a Challenge to Literary Theory',[2] and Stanley E. Fish, in 'Literature in the Reader: Affective Stylistics',[3] followed Poulet's lead in making the consciousness of reading a pivotal point for critical reflection.

Fish's writing is the most sustained and clear account amongst English and American critics of the reader's role, and is at the same time the most useful in a discussion related to Coleridge. Fish uses terms such as 'progressive decertainizing', 'expectations of clarity thwarted', and 'purposeful disorientation', all of which are descriptions of stylistic characteristics in the *Biographia*. In discussing Plato's *Phaedrus*, he finds coherence not in a 'self-contained work', but in a work opening out to include the reader's participation in it. Predictably, Fish uses the metaphor of levels of discourse applicable to the *Biographia*: 'the real issues exist at a higher level of generality [than the surface issues]', (p. 136). It is of course amongst the 'real issues' that one requires unity and coherence, and disorganization at the surface would involve the sort of 'purposeful disorientation' which would lead the reader to look for the depth, the 'real issues'. In reference to the *Biographia*, one might say that associationism and imagination are not real issues until they are genuinely 'realized' by the reader. That is, as abstract concepts not experienced they are mere counters to play with, fixities and determinates which have no 'power of truth'. Fish makes a prediction peculiarly apt for the *Biographia* when he says that the method of including the reader's experience may 'result in the rehabilitation of works like *The Faerie Queene* which have been criticised because their poetic worlds lack "unity" and consistency' (p. 138).

Fish himself acknowledges a tradition from which his views develop, and he includes though not without reservations such obvious sources as Richards, Empson, and Riffaterre. Richards is particularly notable in view of his interest in Coleridge. Certainly his book *Coleridge on Imagination* (1934) seems to be pointing toward such a view of the usefulness of gaps, flaws and fragments which demand completion by imaginative acts, and of the importance of depth discourse as opposed to surface appearance. But in Richards these ideas are not explicitly referred to the reading process as a crucial element in the structure of a work, or as a force affecting the narrative technique.

Fish continued to develop his position in *Self-Consuming Artifacts* (Berkeley: 1972) and in other articles.[4] At the same time, translations have become available of another major theorist of the reading process, Wolfgang Iser. Iser's *The Implied Reader* (Baltimore: 1974) discusses the reader as an operative element in literature 'from Bunyan to Beckett'. He has explored the idea in numerous articles such as 'The Reading Process: A Phenomenological Approach', and earlier, in 'Indeterminacy and the Reader's Response in Prose Fiction'.[5] In the latter article he describes the purpose of gaps and flaws in a narrative as leaving room for imaginative acts, and he makes a typically Romantic statement in the former that 'the efficacy of a literary text is brought about by the apparent evocation and subsequent negation of the familiar' (p. 295). His latest translated book, *The Act of Reading* (1976) continues to develop the critical implications of a theory which includes the reading as an essential part of the unity of a text.

There has still not been an adequate appreciation of the similarity of these critical developments with the theories of the German Romantic Ironists. Aside from the theoretical similarities of modern critical theory to Coleridgean practice, this historical dimension would strengthen and elucidate the parallels, since it is related both to Coleridge and to modern critical theory. There have, however, already been tentative efforts to discuss Coleridge in terms of the reading process, as e.g., M. G. Cooke, in 'Quisque sui Faber: Coleridge in the *Biographia Literaria*' (1971), and Richard Mallette, in 'Narrative Technique and Structure in the *Biographia Literaria*' (1975).[6] Owen Barfield in *What Coleridge Thought* does not explicitly develop the reader's role as a critical technique, but it is everywhere implied in his discussion of Coleridge's commitment to a creative theory of mind in his metaphysics and his aesthetics. The present study is perhaps best described as an effort to bring together the direction of thought of such critics as Barfield and Stanley Fish, to offer a reading of the *Biographia* based firmly upon Coleridge's philosophy.

As is well-attested, the reception given the *Biographia* by Coleridge's contemporaries was nearly total rejection and ridicule. One of the most important reasons for this may have been the overwhelming and irrational suspicion of anything remotely connected with German thought.[7] Kant's system was, for one of Coleridge's reviewers, the 'most wilful and monstrous absurdity that was ever invented'. Coleridge's exposition of his own metaphysics is decribed as 'the formidable ascent of that mountainous and barren ridge of clouds piled on precipices and precipices piled on clouds...'[8] Another reviewer contended that the *Biographia* exposed a 'decrepitude of genius' in the author.[9] John Wilson in *Blackwood's* writes that 'the work is most execrable...he has...little or no real feeling'. Coleridge is accused in the most malicious terms of egotism for presuming to write an autobiography at all.[10] Most of the reviewers hardly discuss the work in terms of the ideas expounded. Their articles tend to be rambling and unfocused personal attacks upon the author; as one reviewer notes, 'We have felt it our duty to speak with severity of this book and its author' for fear of Coleridge's immorality and irreligion corrupting the 'rising generation'![11] One reviewer finds the 'Critique of Bertram' the most interesting part of the work.[12] There is almost no engagement with the issues nor any effort to grapple with the style, genre, or narrative techniques of the *Biographia*. The only occasion of an intellectual engagement with the work during this early period is Hazlitt's discussion of Hobbes's law of association;[13] most other comments are simply miscellaneous opinions of the reviewers, short, ridiculing, and undeveloped, on Coleridge's life and other works. Indeed the character of the reviews so openly displayed is a direct substantiation of the justice of Coleridge's complaints in the first chapters of the *Biographia*.[14] No doubt the reviews had a strong influence on the reading of the work.[15]

Amongst Coleridge's intimate friends the response may have been considerably different. Wordsworth did not seem, however, to appreciate the *Biographia*; he seems to have 'contented himself with skimming parts of it', and Crabb Robinson reports of him that 'Coleridge's book has given him no pleasure, and he finds just fault with Coleridge for professing to write about himself and writing merely about Southey and Wordsworth. With the criticism of the poetry too he is not satisfied. The praise is extravagant and the censure inconsiderate.'[16] Coleridge's German friend Ludwig Tieck had a different view: 'Your Biographia Literaria utterly enchanted me, instructed me, and amused me; I should think, however, that for the greater number of English readers it is too weighty and profound.'[17]

Coleridge describes the abuse from reviewers at length in a letter to his friend Thomas Allsop in December 1818, in which he says that these 'have joined with the frivolity and party spirit of "the Reading Public" in checking and almost in preventing the sale of my Works'. He then ponders which has been his worst enemy, 'the broad predetermined Abuse of the Edinburgh Review &c, or the cold and brief compliments with the warm *regrets*, of the Quarterly?'[18] But not all the reviews were hostile; in July 1819, J. G. Lockhart published favourable comments about Coleridge's works generally in a three volume work,[19] and he specifically attacked the malicious reviews of the *Biographia* published in *Blackwood's Magazine* in Oct. 1817. He may also have been the author of a review in *Blackwood's* in Oct. 1819 which was very enthusiastic about Coleridge.[20] The 1817 publication of the *Biographia* in America seems to have gone unnoticed by the reviewers only in the 1830s did the American Transcendentalist movement arouse an interest in Coleridge, and especially with the 1829 publication of *Aids to Reflection*.[21] By 1833 an article in the *Christian Examiner* was praising Coleridge's abilities as a thinker in preference to his poetry and criticism.[22] But this was the exception.[23]

For by the time of the publication of the *Biographia* in 1817, Coleridge was already established as a poet of genius, albeit 'wild, erratic genius', with 'wings but no hands'. With the third edition of *Poetical Works* in 1834 the reviewing climate seems to have changed to a less vicious mood, though Coleridge's reputation was certainly growing. Yet the effects of the first reviews on the *Biographia* continued to plague its sales. The first edition never sold out during Coleridge's lifetime. The second edition, of Sara and H. N. Coleridge, in 1847 was much less bitterly received, but with hardly more understanding or appreciation of the issues with which the *Biographia* grappled. Other editions appeared in England in 1866, 1884 and 1905, but none of these were annotated. Shawcross's edition in 1907 seems to mark a rise in interest in Coleridge as a critic and thinker in the early part of the twentieth century, which culminated in Richards's appreciative response in *Coleridge on Imagination* in 1933.

It seems correct to surmise however that Coleridge has rarely found 'fellow-labourers' amongst his readers of the *Biographia* until recently, for the general attitude toward the *Biographia* has been uncomprehending and rather severe on a number of points, from charges of obscurity, disorganization, and misuse of sources to qualified approval, at least of the criticism of volume two, but with little appreciation of the work's literary contribution as a 'Work per se'.[24] Sales had never been high throughout the nineteenth century. While the *Biographia* continues to irritate modern readers, it has also intrigued them, more probably than it had in the past with a few exceptions. It is gradually finding its readership, notably amongst those with an appreciation for theoretical and philosophical levels of discourse. While it continues to be vulnerable to attacks of plagiarism and more subtle forms of detraction, it is gradually gathering around itself a body of readers. It may be no accident that this appreciation is developing contemporaneously with the upsurge in a literary theory which invokes the centrality of the reading process or the spectator's role in art.

Notes

INTRODUCTION:

DIVERSE READINGS OF THE 'BIOGRAPHIA LITERARIA'

1 See Aristotle, *Poetics*, ch. 7, for the classic definition of an artistic whole.
2 Humphry House, *Coleridge: The Clark Lectures* (London: 1953), p. 16.
3 Basil Willey, 'Coleridge and Religion', *Writers and their Background: S. T. Coleridge*, ed. R. L. Brett (London: 1971), p. 221.
4 On the difference between copy and imitation see *BL*, II, 30, *CL*, III, 501, and see *CN*, II, 2274, Dec. 1804. Coleridge is correcting the continuing misunderstanding of Plato by contrasting copy and imitation. As E. A. Havelock has shown in his *Preface to Plato* (Oxford: 1963), Plato was objecting to the practice of art as copying, as a mirror of nature at its surface level. In this sense it is clearly accurate to talk of art as a third remove from nature. The integrity of the metaphor of art as a mirror derives from art as a reflection of mind. Sidney, in his *Defence of Poetry*, ed. J. A. Van Dorsten (Oxford: 1966), pp. 57–60, corrects the mistaken interpretation only very generally, though he hits upon the essential matter in insisting that Plato objected to the *abuse* of poetry as copying. Coleridge's imitation/copy distinction suggests the true sense of the ancients' use of the word 'imitation' to mean originality, while 'imitation' to us now implies mere copying.
5 Stephen Potter, *Coleridge and S.T.C.* (London: 1935): 'There is not in Coleridge any precise doctrine made clear for the sake of intelligibility.'
6 For an account of the meaning of the idea that both art and knowledge are experience, see John Dewey's *Art as Experience* (London: 1934), especially chapters 3, 4, and 5.
7 Dorothy Emmet, 'Coleridge and Philosophy', *Writers and their Background*, ed. Brett, p. 197.
8 *Ibid.*, 220.
9 J. H. Muirhead, *Coleridge as Philosopher* (London: 1930), pp. 98–9.
10 *BL*, I, 98.
11 Kathleen Coburn, in the introduction to *Coleridge: A collection of critical essays* (Englewood Cliffs: 1967), p. 4.
12 George Whalley, 'On Reading Coleridge', *Writers and their Background*, ed. Brett, p. 2. Professor Whalley's quotation of Coleridge is from *CN*, II, 2526.
13 Thus Coleridge says in the preface to 'Kubla Khan' that the poem is a

fragment and the connecting lines in the poem suggest a metaphorical meaning of 'fragment':

> A mighty fountain momently was forced:
> Amid whose swift half-intermitted burst
> Huge fragments vaulted like rebounding hail...

See chapter eight below for a discussion of 'Kubla Khan' as in part an ironic gesture. Shelley refers to all poems as fragments of one great poem in the 'Defence of Poetry'. It is a popular theme amongst the German Romantic poets, especially Friedrich Schlegel. See for example his *Athenäums-Fragmente* in *Prosaische Jugendschriften*, ed. J. Minor, 2 vols. Vienna 1882 and the 'Gespräch über Poesie'.

14 Whalley, 'On Reading Coleridge', p. 24.

15 *CL*, II, 1194 to Thomas Clarkson, 13 Oct. 1806.

16 Whalley, 'On Reading Coleridge', pp. 34–5. Professor Whalley explores this aspect of the *Biographia* in 'The Integrity of the *Biographia Literaria*', *Essays and Studies by Members of the English Association*, 6 (1953), 87–101. But see J. R. de J. Jackson, *Method and Imagination in Coleridge's Criticism* (Cambridge, Mass. and London: 1969), p. 15, for a firm appreciation of the philosophic core of the *Biographia*.

17 J. A. Appleyard, 'Critical Theory', *Writers and their Background*, ed. Brett, p. 135.

18 See for example *CN*, III, 3246 and 3290.

19 Appleyard, 'Critical Theory', pp. 135–6.

20 See Coleridge's comment on the letter: 'I met Dr Gooch...He consulted me about studying Schelling, in consequence of having read my Biographia Literaria – & asked me whether *Robinson* was not the writer of the dissuasive Letter!!! It is so like him, I suppose.' *CL*, V, 191 to Green, 8 Dec. 1821. See also *CL* IV, 728 to Thomas Curtis, 29 Apr. 1817.

21 Appleyard, 'Critical Theory', pp. 136 and 138 (my italics).

22 Coleridge seems to be making use of Kant's characterization of time as well as space as the subjective form of sensuous intuition, when he calls time a mere condition of association for finite minds. The realization that time as well as space is a subjective category of experience was one of Kant's advances beyond Berkeley. See chapter two below.

   Coleridge was of course an enthusiastic and avowed associationist in the mid-1790s. Though he did not publicly repudiate Hartley (or Locke and Newton) until 1801, his study of Kant from 1796 and throughout the sojourn in Germany in 1798–9, must have been steadily shaking his faith in Hartley.

23 This is certainly the Hegelian tone of the *Philosophical Lectures*, and it suggests the importance of both Coleridge's and Wordsworth's efforts to trace the growth of the individual poet's mind. The long introduction of Hegel's to his *Lectures on the History of Philosophy* can function as a fascinating elaboration of Coleridge's own 1818–19 lectures. See Hegel's *Lectures on the History of Philosophy*, translated by E. S. Haldane, 3 vols. (London: 1892–6). These lectures were also put together from the notes of students and auditors, as were Coleridge's in part.

24 On depth or inwardness as an object of the reason, see *BL*, I, 90, and see *LS (CC)*, 69, *T of L*, 53–5, and *CN*, I, 1125.

25 *LS (CC)*, 114, an example of Coleridge's thoroughly Socratic posture, which explains the method of many of Plato's dialogues. Socrates avoids ending a con-

versation with a dogmatic, linguistic rendering or solution to the concepts under discussion, such as justice, knowledge, perception, friendship, etc. He is rather seeking to shake his listener's faith in unexamined and unthinkingly accepted conventional views, by 'making the familiar unfamiliar'. Socrates seeks not to fill the mind with 'answers' but to clear space for reflection.

26 *LS* (*CC*), 97–8, but see also 27, n.1, *CN*, 1, 276 and 383n.

I. SOURCES OF THE 'BIOGRAPHIA LITERARIA' IN NOTEBOOKS AND LETTERS

1 Appleyard, 'Critical Theory', p. 125.
2 For this ascription by Coleridge himself see Shawcross, *BL*, 1, xcii and see below note 11; the epithet has been adopted with vigour. No notice has been taken of the possibility that Coleridge might have been expressing not *his* view of the *Biographia*, so much as the response from his audience: it *appeared* immethodical to *them*.
3 *CL*, iv, 578–9 to Brabant, 29 July 1815. See also the notes, which explain the errors Shawcross and Campbell were led to concerning a preface for the *Biographia* itself. On the *BL* beginning as a preface, see Professor Bate's *Coleridge* (London: 1969), pp. 130–1, for a sensitive handling of this issue. See also Jackson, *Method and Imagination*, pp. 12–14; see also pp. 53–7 for further observations on the *Biographia's* origins.
4 *CL*, iv, 578–9 note. The origins of the *Biographia* and its order of composition have been explored by several critics over the past eighty years. Shawcross offered his interpretation of the development of the *Biographia* in the introduction to his 1907 edition, which was based on the researches of J. Dykes Campbell. George Watson followed Shawcross's interpretation fairly closely in his edition of 1956. Both Shawcross and Watson assume that by July 1815, volume one had essentially been written and that Coleridge then set out to write a preface to *volume one*. This preface grew into volume two. Griggs challenged this apparently mistaken interpretation which was based on punctuation errors in a letter of Coleridge's. He reverses the order of composition and claims that the *Biographia* as a whole was the preface which grew into a 'work per se' (see the introduction to *CL*, iii and iv).

The most recent and detailed account of the development of the *Biographia*, primarily from March 1815 up to publication in July 1817, is D. M. Fogle's account, 'A Compositional History of the *Biographia Literaria*', in *Studies in Bibliography*, 30 (1977), pp. 219–34. Fogle's researches substantiate Griggs's interpretation in somewhat more explicit discussions of chapter developments. That is, the criticism of Wordsworth's poetry preceded the chapters on associationism and philosophy generally, though chapters one to four may precede all of these. Chapter four and the fancy/imagination distinction seem to have been the point of departure for the philosophical discussion.

George Whalley, in 'The Integrity of the *Biographia Literaria*', *Essays and Studies*, 6 (1953), 87–101, added another aspect to the genesis of the *Biographia's* construction by exploring Coleridge's early plans for a Life and an Essay on Poetry, from 1800 onwards. Kathleen Coburn's textual notes to the *Notebooks* act also to point out the numerous notebook passages throughout the 1800–15 period which were incorporated into the *Biographia*. This chapter seeks to discuss all three of these areas of the *Biographia's* development more extensively and in an integrated way. In addition, many of the early letter and notebook passages worked into the *Biographia* are shown to be important as types and examples of the method of the work.

5 For the elaboration of this objection see Appleyard, 'Critical Theory', and the introduction above on various readings of the *BL*.

6 *CL*, IV, 561 to Lord Byron, Mar. 1815.

7 See Shawcross's account in *BL*, I, xci–xcii. He includes the 'Critique on Bertram', though he says that even these pages are 'not wholly out of place; for they illustrate the continuity of his opinions'.

8 It is not absurd to think that Coleridge's conception of the role of the philosophical part might have undergone reassessment during the elaboration so that it came to have greater weight. Far from disturbing the design of the whole, it could be seen to have improved its symmetry. The appropriate relationship of parts in a whole may often become clear only during the execution.

9 *CL*, IV, 579 to Brabant, 29 July 1815. Note the humour of the last sentence and the teasing of the passage. A few sentences about his latest work to a friend hardly constitutes 'running on'. We are apt to take Coleridge's jibes at himself somewhat too seriously, overlooking a certain gracefulness and courteousness of expression. His comment relative to Wordsworth has often been cited as proof of an insensitivity (see e.g. Shawcross's *BL* Supplement), though his discussion of Wordsworth's poetry (tempered as it always was by reference to his excellencies, and set forth with the prime purpose of showing the theory alone to be erroneous in principle) pales in comparison with the cruel and thoughtless remarks which Wordsworth made and *published* with the poetry in *Lyrical Ballads*. See *CL*, I, 602n.

10 It is sobering that while Griggs corrects one misunderstanding of Shawcross and Campbell, caused by punctuation errors (see *CL*, IV, 578n), he propagates a similar error by removing context – and can only have done so because he *read* without carefully noting the punctuation. This long sentence of Coleridge's, part of which I have italicized, is an excellent example of his syntax in general. It often has the effect, because of its complexity, of pulling up the reader in his headlong dash, or, causing him, like a 'Skaiter [to] strike a Stop with [his] heel', to disentangle the organization of the clauses which is not immediately clear. Significant misreading can result from the failure to take the time to assess the connections of the parts. This may be an apt emblem of the process required in reading the *Biographia* as a whole.

11 Shawcross additionally hypothesizes in his Supplement to the 1907 edition, page xcii: 'The circumstances of its production are thus sufficient to explain why the *Biographia Literaria* should be the "immethodical miscellany" which Coleridge himself styles it. Further, we must remember that at the time of its composition Coleridge's health and spirits had sunk to their lowest ebb. Even if there was any definite project in his mind, he was hardly in a fit state to carry it out.' This claim has, as far as I know, never been challenged. It is taken up below.

12 Such a set of preconceptions and expectations, which are unconsciously mistaken as characteristics of the work itself, is almost always completely destructive of a fresh reading; this phenomenon is termed psychological projection. In reading no less than in philosophy, we may need to 'obtain entrance for the question, whether the truth of the Opinions in fashion...is quite so certain as [we] had hitherto taken for granted – ' *LS* (*CC*), 114n.

13 Cf. *The Friend* (*CC*), I, 450–7, for Coleridge's criticism of the immethodical,

unimaginative speech of the uneducated, which applies explicitly to Wordsworth's theory of low, rustic speech.

14 See *BL*, I, 193 for Coleridge's disagreement with Wordsworth on the imagination/fancy distinction. We anticipate a later section in noticing that this last part of chapter twelve on Wordsworth and the distinction between imagination and fancy looks forward not to any metaphysical disquisition written in philosophical style, as chapter thirteen *appears* to suggest to be the next step, but rather toward volume two. This is precisely what *does* follow, the continuity being interrupted only by the few pages in chapter thirteen on the 'two forces of one power'. To see that even this is not wholly unrelated, see *BL*, I, 8 on the two forces.

15 See above note 11 for Shawcross on this point.

16 Coleridge had stopped *The Friend* at number 27 in the spring of 1810, and though short of his projected number, this in itself was no small accomplishment. He took on every aspect of its publication except for the actual printing. He was not merely author, but proof-reader, editor, bookkeeper, publisher, distributor, seller, and collector. For a detailed account of the difficulties, see *The Friend* (*CC*), editor's introduction.

17 See the chronological table in *LS* (*CC*), xxiv–xxvi.

18 *Sybilline Leaves* and the *Biographia* were not finally published until 1817, due to delays in reaching agreements with publishers.

19 The lectures on the history of philosophy, collected and edited by Kathleen Coburn in *Philosophical Lectures 1818–19* have been widely underrated because of a conversational style which is deceptively easy, and which masks the compactness and penetration which a close reading brings out. Coleridge was also occupied with literary lectures in 1818, for a detailed account of which see Raysor's introduction in *Sh. C.*

20 The time of Coleridge's 'recovery' from the disappointments of the 'middle years' (the quarrel with Wordsworth in 1810, the loss of the Wedgwood annuity in 1812, and increased ill health perhaps partly due to opium) is generally put at April 1816 when he went to live with the Gillmans at Highgate. There is no doubt of the tremendous boost which this move must have been to his spirits; he had at last found a home after years of anguished wandering. The preparation of *Sybilline Leaves* and the two-volume *Biographia* are evidence, however, that Coleridge was not always paralysed by personal matters.

21 There are those who still seriously maintain that favourable circumstances are not the right milieu for creative activity. See e.g. Stephen Potter, who claims that 'the Wedgwood annuity was the most unfortunate circumstance of Coleridge's life'. *Coleridge and S.T.C.*, p. 86.

22 It is often difficult to know exactly how distinct from one another these early planned works were – sometimes they seem to have subsumed each other over the years, while at other times new boundaries were drawn to distinguish them. Sometimes a separate work became a preliminary to (or a part of) a greater plan, and vice versa. Sometimes different titles seem possibly to apply to the same work. Whatever the interconnections, the works mentioned in these early years are variously described as 'my curious metaphysical work' (*CL*, II, 776 to Poole, 1801), a 'History of Metaphysics in England' (*CL*, II, 927–8 to Samuel Purkis, 1803), and 'Organum verè Organum' (*CL*, II, 946–7 to Godwin, 1803) the last of which included a separate 'Organum verè Organum' stating Coleridge's own conception of logic rather than its history and development, as was to be done in the first section. Other works were the 'Comforts and Consolations' and the

'literary life', and finally the work to which he intended to devote the best of his life, 'On Man, and the probable Destiny of the Human Race' (*CN*, I, 1646). A close study of the history and development of Coleridge's plans makes it more clear how these various works are interrelated. It also shows which descriptions of plans seem to apply to the *MS Logic* and *Opus Maximum*, and how the plans were with some adjustments realized in the published works. On the *MS Logic* see Alice Snyder, *Coleridge on Logic and Learning* (Ann Arbor: 1929). The Malta–Italy trip and the years immediately following it seem to have marked a long period of dormancy, as if the plans had been blocked temporarily until Coleridge began *The Friend* in 1810. From then on they are once again taken up in ways very similar to the early descriptions. See e.g. *CL*, III 279 and 480.

23 *CN*, I, 1515, Sept.–Oct. 1803. George Whalley, 'The Integrity of the *Biographia Literaria*' points to even earlier material, such as plans to write 'An Essay on the Elements of Poetry' in 1800 (*CL*, I, 632), criticisms of Wordsworth in July 1802 (*CL*, II, 811–12 and 830) and at the same time a plan for Coleridge's own 'Preface'. A few months later he writes of his 'memorandum Book on the subject of poetry' (*CL*, II, 877). See above note 4.

24 Is it possible that the work, 'Comforts and Consolations', turned however into *The Friend*? Could a 'Soother of Absence' not be a friend? Thus the later chronology follows that of the 1803 projected order (*CN*, I, 1646), *The Friend* executed first, then the *Life*, that is, the *Biographia*. Perhaps the major plans which Coleridge mentions again and again throughout the early letters and notebooks actually were executed, but executed only some ten to fifteen years after these remarks were jotted down to himself or to friends. Some of these jottings seem to have been fully executed and published; others remain uncompleted, and in need of considerable editing. Nevertheless they exist in some salvageable form, namely as the *MS Logic* and the *Opus Maximum*. A number of the plans which come up in jottings in notebooks or letters were certainly executed in the lectures. Despite the efforts of friends, no one was able to produce a successful edition of Coleridge's literary lectures from notes, as did, e.g. Hegel's students for his *Science of Logic*, or his *Lectures on the History of Philosophy*.

25 *CL*, II, 1053 to Sir George Beaumont, 1 Feb. 1804. Coleridge seems already to have thoroughly assimilated Kant's use of 'Reason' and here connects it with his own 'Imagination', which is an important indication of how closely they are related (see below chapter eight). Coleridge also makes use here of the speculative/practical distinction in the context of feelings and imagination. This passage is a good example of the process of assimilation of ideas: the Kantian elements are unmistakable, but the Coleridgean application to new areas provides an exciting example of a mind in the act of transforming thoughts.

26 *CN*, I, 1646, Nov. 1803. At this time *The Friend* and the *Biographia* seem to be intertwined in Coleridge's thought.

27 *CL*, II, 1036 to Poole, 15 Jan. 1804. The last sentence is particularly relevant: the 'distracting Manifoldness' is an appearance only.

28 What the period between Spring 1804 and the end of 1808 must have been for Coleridge we hardly dare imagine. His taking up composition again shortly after his return to put together *The Friend* delayed his execution of the 'Literary Life' for several more years.

29 The several pages of Schelling passages in the *Biographia* were new not in the sense of ideas unfamiliar to Coleridge, but in the exciting formulation which captivated him, coupled with the fact that they were ideas of a contemporary

thinker. See chapter three below. Polarity itself was a new and exciting formulation and a metaphor of the ancient idea of the reconciliation of opposites: Blake's *Marriage of Heaven and Hell* is the first Romanticist expression, and the theme runs throughout his prophetic books. It takes the form of a ridiculing of the mind which sees only contraries because it uses merely the faculty of understanding. The understanding bows to the law of contradiction without the supervenience of the imagination to 'marry' contraries and change them into opposites. Reconciliation may also take the form of a male–female polarity (in a *humanizing* of the philosophical formulation, which is the poet's 'real' genius; cf. *CN*, III, 3246). The primary idea of polarity is opposition; contraries are a fiction of the abstracting understanding. Surely no one would claim that Blake got his *idea* from Schelling. Nor did Coleridge; it was the *metaphor* of polarity that fascinated him and which he took over, because he saw its relation to the idea of reconciliation which had interested him since 1796 or earlier. Polarity was an expression also of the discoveries being made in galvanism and electricity in Coleridge's time, an area in which he was greatly interested. To recognize that the value of polarity is in its being a new metaphor for an Idea (in the Platonic sense in which Coleridge used the word), is to realize also the centrality of metaphor for knowledge and dialectic, as all the Romantics saw it.

30 *CL*, III, 533 to Daniel Stuart, 12 Sept. 1814.

31 See p. 12 and note 24. The importance of this fact is incalculable for a reassessment of the *Biographia* as a whole, the metaphysical sections having been looked upon as a kind of unhappy afterthought and hence not an integral or important section. It is the re-evaluation of this judgment coupled with Coleridge's constant connecting of the poetic and philosophic which will form the foundation of a more appreciative reading of the *Biographia*.

32 *CL*, II, 671, to Humphry Davy, 3 Feb. 1801.

33 Although this passage does not appear in the *Biographia*, but only in *The Friend*, its early date is important in establishing the nature of Coleridge's use of his sources. This passage, like all the others quoted here, is important for what it says as a metaphor about thinking, in this case specifically about obscurity, profundity, and the necessity for a mode of communication which is indirect, – not only communication as indirect, however, but thought itself as indirect. That is, the highest objects of thought, ideas, can be immediately beheld only vaguely and through a mist; some clarity may be achieved in looking by means of a reflecting surface. The passage copied in German in May 1799 is translated:

> If ... the atmosphere is heavy with smoke and vapours which have not previously been dispersed by wind or waves or rarefied by the sun, then in this vapour, as on a screen extending along the canal some 30 [feet] high and near to the sea, the spectator may perceive the whole scene of those objects, both in the image reflected by the surface of the sea and, though not so clearly, in the atmosphere.
>
> Finally if the atmosphere is foggy and overcast, if at the same time it is wet and a rainbow appears, then the above-mentioned objects appear, as in the first case, only on the surface of the sea, but all in very vivid colours, and framed in red, green, and blue, or some other colour of the prism.

(*CN*, I, 431)

Five years later Coleridge experienced a related phenomenon of reflection on Rydal Lake, and reminded himself of the effect of a smoky atmosphere (*CN*, II, 1844, Jan. 1804). The corresponding passage in *The Friend* has been focused into a powerful, concise image, and connected directly to the issue of knowledge and communication:

> Were but a hundred men to combine a deep conviction that virtuous habits may be formed by the very means by which knowledge is communicated, that men may be made better, not only in consequence, but *by* the mode and *in* the process, of instruction...the promises of ancient prophecy would disclose themselves to our faith, even as when a noble castle hidden from us by an intervening mist, discovers itself by its reflection in the tranquil lake, on the opposite shore of which we stand gazing.   (*The Friend* (*CC*), I, 103.)

Coleridge strove, through the use of such extended metaphors coupled with the inherent philosophic analogy, to perfect such a mode of instruction by which the means and processes subsume the consequences. His collecting of these and the following exemplary passages or extended metaphors as early as 1799 suggests that he was already aware of their power of communicating his philosophical insights. For they combine sense and sensation or thought and feeling to produce an experience of knowledge.

34 Is this a hint ('...I applied this...') that Coleridge had written something on Wordsworth already? Could he have dictated the *Biographia* from notes more extensive and connected than anything which is found in the notebooks, notes which however were gathered and organized from these notebook entries on loose sheets?

The importance of this passage is once again the use of metaphor, in this case an organic metaphor of mind.

35 *CN*, I, 926, Mar.–Apr. 1801, and see note; and *BL*, II, 128–9, a reminder that for Coleridge philosophy interpenetrates poetry.

36 *CN*, I, 928, Apr. 1801. But see also *CN*, III, 4248, 1815, for an impassioned account of the unjustified accusations against men of genius because of the failure of readers to act upon this maxim.

37 Another fascinating example of an anecdote which seems hopelessly digressive occurs in chapter ten of the *Biographia*. Coleridge relates the tale about the spy who misinterprets Coleridge's mention of the name 'Spinoza' as evidence that he has been discovered and is being discussed as a 'nosy spy'. It is an instructive and delightful account of the misinterpretations that result from an ungenial posture in any situation of communication, particularly when the posture is additionally a non-participating, receptive one of passive audience. This instance is a case of 'psychological projection'. It serves one of the same functions as the situation Coleridge describes in reading Plato: to trick the reader into catching himself in the act, and to help him to readjust his approach. See below chapter five for a further account of the spy story.

38 *BL*, I, 160.

39 Compare this passage with *CL*, III, 278 to Lady Beaumont, 21 Jan. 1810, which seems to mention precisely this first case of the bewildered visionary:

> Of Jacob Behmen I have myself been a commentator,...It is a maxim with me, always *to suppose myself ignorant of a Writer's Understanding, until I understand his Ignorance*. This I have not yet decyphered to myself in the Teutonic Theosopher: yet I conjecture that being ignorant of Logic & not versed in the Laws of the Imagination, he rendered many *Intuitions* in his own mind, perhaps of very profound Truths, and, as it were, translated them into such *Images* and bodily feelings as by accident were co-present with his intuitions.

This passage certainly seems to be the link between the 1801 note and the final form it took in the *Biographia* in 1815.

40 *BL*, I, 160–1. Such a passage is another example of an exercise in irony and paradox at the expense of the reader who fails to initiate himself into the process of self-referral.

41 *CN*, I, 1622, Oct. 1803 and *BL*, I, 59–61, and see *The Friend* (*CC*), I, 109 and note. Cf. the marginal note to Fichte *Bestimmung des Menschen*, no. 2, hitherto unpublished: 'My main objection is that this [i]s not the [t]rue history [o]f the Process and Progress of a mind that instinctively feels and would fain, solve the Riddle of the World and of itself –.'

42 Cf. *CN*, II, 2535, Apr. 1805:

It is as trite as it is mournful, but yet most instructive and by the genius that can produce the strongest impressions of novelty by rescuing the stalest and most admitted Truths from the impotence caused by the very circumstance of their universal admission/(admitted so instantly as never to be reflected on, never by that sole key of Reflection admitted into the...effective legislative Council-chamber of the Heart) so true that they lose all the privileges of Truth, and, as *extremes meet*, by being Truisms correspond in utter inefficiency with universally acknowledged Errors...O to shew this, a priori by bottoming it in all our faculties/& by experience of touching Examples.

This last sentence is not an inadequate hint of the format and purposes of the *Biographia*: it abounds in the latter, i.e. 'touching examples', while only laying the ground for the former to be worked out in the *Opus Maximum*. Whether the examples provide enough material to make it possible to work out the super-structure theoretically is the context of the difficulty in reading the *Biographia*. In any case this last sentence is one more instance of the sense/sensation, thought/feeling, or word/experience conjunction: 'Bottoming it in all our faculties', is experience by example. See notes 44–7 below and the corresponding texts.

43 This passage is discussed in detail in chapter five below, as yet another early example of the extended metaphor which seems to be part of the method of the *Biographia*.

44 *CN*, I, 915, Jan.–Mar. 1801 and see note.

45 *CN*, I, 1620, Sept.–Oct. 1803 and 1643, Nov. 1803. See also *CN*, II, 2642, Aug. 1805.

46 *CN*, III, 3255, 1808. Cf. *BL* I, 52–3. And on bulls see *CL*, IV, 589 and 850, and VI, 632.

47 That is, the imagination/fancy distinction is likely to have the opposite effect upon the reader from that caused by the bull. The overcoming of either state is the union of sensation and sense (feeling and thought), which is knowledge. How to give the reader the sensation, the true grounding in experience, of the sense or idea, is a constant preoccupation of Coleridge. With particular reference to the statement of the imagination/fancy distinction as causing the opposite state from the bull, it will be suggested below that the *Biographia* becomes that treatise on imagination referred to in chapter thirteen as having been deleted, in so far as it seeks, in its constant reliance on metaphors to illustrate its philosophical ideas, to give the reader the sensation of imaginativeness by making him imaginative in his reading. The passage about the bull becomes yet another example of those extended metaphors which are the main constituents of the *Biographia*'s structural design, and which are the clues to an ongoing analogy

between the ostensive subject matter of the *Biographia* and the reading process as subject matter.

48 *CN*, I, 1678, Nov. 1803.

49 *CN*, I, 1678, Nov. 1803. See chapter five below for further comments on this passage as another example of Coleridge's method of capping discursive thought with a metaphor demonstrating that which was discussed, by giving the reader an immediate experience of that truth in the apprehension of the integrity of the metaphor used.

    For the corresponding passage see *BL*, I, 167.

50 *BL*, I, 167. For a clearly related source see *CN*, I, 1378, Mar.–July 1803, a detailed description of the transformation of the caterpillar into a butterfly.

51 *CL*, II, 1032 to Richard Sharp, 15 Jan. 1804. The butterfly–caterpillar images recur. Cf. e.g. *CL*, III, 542, V, 296–7, VI, 850, *CN*, II, 2556, III, 3247 and *P Lects.*, 387. The most closely related passage is in *CN*, III, 4088, f156, May–June 1811, on the chrysalis and the correspondent worlds: 'And what is Faith? – it is to the Spirit of Man the same Instinct, which impels the chrysalis of the horned fly to build its involucrum as long again as itself to make room for the Antennae, which are to come, tho' they never yet have been – O the *Potential* works *in* us even as the Present mood works *on* us!' Compare the continuation of the passage here with *BL*, I, 167: 'In short, all the organs of Sense are framed for a corresponding World of Sense: and we have it. All the organs of Spirit are framed for a correspondent World of Spirit: & we cannot but believe it. The Infidel proves only that the latter organs are not yet developed in him – .'

52 *CL*, II, 1034. This long discussion is another example of the connection in Coleridge's mind of any treatment of metaphysics as involving for him a philosophical and poetic content. The two volumes of the *Biographia* are not only *not* absolutely separate, but are intimately related. See *CL*, II, 671 to Humphry Davy, 3 Feb. 1801.

53 *CL*, II, 865–6 to William Sotheby, 10 Sept. 1802. The historical origins of the reason/understanding distinction run back through philosophy to Plato's νοῦς/διάνοια pair. See e.g. John Muirhead, *Coleridge as Philosopher* (London: 1930) p. 65, and John Barth, *Coleridge and Christian Doctrine* (Cambridge, Mass.: 1969), 17. Muirhead traces it in Bacon, Milton, Shakespeare and the Cambridge Platonists as the distinction between the intuitive and discursive, or *intellectus* and *ratio*. For Coleridge on the origins see *AR*, aphorisms CV and CVIII, 3.

    Barth seems to think that the imagination/fancy distinction did not grow out of the former distinction, though he grants the possibility that Coleridge's reading of Kant may have been the occasion for a fuller realization of its importance (Barth, *Coleridge and Christian Doctrine*, 23). The real difficulty is to establish precisely the relation of the two distinctions to each other, which will be discussed in chapter eight. It is impossible that Coleridge was unaware even at this early date of the discursive/intuitive distinction, which he would have known not only from reading Plato, Bacon, Milton, Shakespeare, Plotinus, etc., but perhaps more importantly from his own experiences.

54 The relation of imagination to passion is not entirely clear, but cf. *CN*, III, 3611, f17, 1809. This entry is an example of a passage which not only carries the import of the imagination/fancy distinction into religion, but also, as a result, suggests the close relation of 'Imagination' to Coleridge's 'Reason'. The 'one Life' theme expressed here is an early formulation of the part/whole relationship

which is involved both in the definition of the symbol (see below) and in the fancy/imagination distinction. The organic metaphor was a later, more German formulation of the same idea, which Coleridge elsewhere toys with in the formula 'unity in multeity' or 'involution of the particular in the universal'. He was also fond of the same biblical phrase which Berkeley kept quoting, 'In God we live and move and have our being' (cf. Acts 17.28), a phrase which also expresses the part/whole, finite/infinite relation. All of these formulations express the idea of a living, integral relation between parts and wholes, but from varying perspectives or in the terms of different discourses. The idea of the reconciliation of opposites, which will be discussed in chapter three, is yet another, ancient formulation of the idea of relationship, expressed in perhaps more abstract terms than the dichotomies between part/whole, individual life/one life, fancy/imagination, mechanic/organic, arrangement/method, etc. All of these dualities, however varied their applications, have in common the essential concern of expressing the nature of relationship and its central role in knowledge experience.

55 Cf. *LS* (*CC*), 30 for Coleridge's definition of symbol.
56 Compare the long note in *CN*, III, 3247, Spring 1808–18 and see 3290, f14.
57 *BL*, II, 11.
58 *CN*, III, 4015, f26, 1810. But see also *CN*, I, 609, Dec. 1799 for an early appreciation of

> the Serpent by which the ancients emblem'd the Inventive faculty [which] appears to me, in its mode of motion most exactly to emblem a writer of Genius. He varies his course yet still glides onward – all lines of motion are his – all beautiful, & all propulsive – ...So varied he & of his tortuous train
>   Curls many a wanton wreath;
> yet still he proceeds and is proceeding. –

Such an entry makes it very clear how early Coleridge was seeing these images as metaphors for the faculties of mind and its acts, an idea which he may have culled from his reading of the ancients in specific cases. But it is clear too that he was able to apply the metaphors to himself, as writer; as applied to reader the step is a short one.

This may also be an appropriate description of Coleridge's purposes (as well as the results) in the *Biographia*: the narrative appears to wander and be a miscellany of topics, but is actually 'propulsive' and proceeding by means of inherent connections, which are charted by the metaphors on the main course. It is not an accident that the Imagination is said to connect the most unusual and diverse elements; Coleridge has brought them into connection for us, but we must reconnect them if we are to comprehend the connection, or have the sense as well as the sensation.

59 *BL*, I, 85–6. This entry is similar enough to these pages to have been the source of the insect metaphor.
60 *BL*, II, 16.
61 *CN*, III, 4115, f27ᵛ, Oct.–Nov. 1811. Coleridge has previously (see above) used 'passion' for the imagination; the word itself is a fine example of the paradoxical relation between the passive and the active faculties, and of the integration necessary for imagination; with its etymological associations 'passion' expresses the dispute in philosophy as to whether 'suffering' or 'feeling' is purely receptive or a participatory, constructive experience.

But it also suggests the paradox that activity may appear at surface to be passivity, and vice versa. Many of the foregoing passages have raised precisely this issue. Thus, in the moments of silence and apparent vacancy the mind in its depths is preparing an effusion of inspired productions or intuitions and insights. The 'busy-ness' of the superficial consciousness can inhibit this deeper productivity, hence Coleridge talks of a 'sleep of the senses', or swoons and trances. He takes note more explicitly of this when he discusses the nature of genius and the relation of instinct to judgment, intention to inspiration, or conscious to non-conscious forces.

62 *CN*, III, 3708, Mar. 1810. Coleridge here uses imagination very loosely, to mean, in fact, fancy only. He almost always coupled the memory with fancy. See also *CN*, III, 4059, Mar.–Apr. 1811 on the passive and active memory and Hartley's false associationism. Coleridge only finally publicly rejected Hartley in 1801. See *CL*, II, 706 to Thomas Poole. But he certainly seems to have begun to have misgivings about his system considerably earlier.

63 *BL*, I, 85–6. Since the entire passage is quoted at the beginning of chapter five below, it is not repeated here.

64 *BL*, II, 10, 49, 53.

65 *CN*, III, 3611, f16ᵛ, 1809.

66 A careful examination of *BL*, II, chapters seventeen and eighteen, especially pages 41, 44, 49–53 will show that the germs of the chapters were in passages such as the 1809 notebook entry quoted above.

Even earlier germs occur in the letters right after 1800 when Coleridge was discussing the defects and beauties of Wordsworth's poetry. See e.g. Whalley, 'The Integrity of the *Biographia Literaria*' on these very early sources for the *BL*.

67 *CN*, III, 3615, 1809.

68 *CN*, III, 3827, f115, 1810.

69 *BL*, II, 12.

70 *CN*, III, 4111, Oct.–Nov. 1811.

71 See especially Coleridge's criticism of Wordsworth's 'state of excitement', *BL*, II, 41–2.

72 *CN*, III, 4112, Oct.–Nov. 1811.

73 See *CN*, III, 4113–15 and *BL*, II, chapter fourteen.

74 *CN*, III, 4186, 1813–15 and *CN*, III, 4265, Sept. 1815.

75 The index to the *Notebooks* under Coleridge, Samuel; PROSE, *Biographia Literaria*, provides a limited means of tracing the obvious connections and germs or early sources of the *Biographia*. There is no aid of comparable thoroughness in the letters, and they must be gone through individually. For the less obvious coincidences, the reader himself will in most cases be the sole resource. A thorough account of the *development* of Coleridge's thought in its main formulations based on the letters and notebooks is still to be written.

76 *CL*, IV, 758 to Lord Liverpool, 28 July 1817.

77 For Coleridge on Schelling's error see *CL*, IV, 874 and the continuation of this passage: 'it did not require the subtlety of Hume's Logic to demonstrate, that no cement can hold together Pious conclusions and Atheistic premises'.

78 See below, chapter two, p. 44, for the account of Coleridge's resistance to this deviation in Schelling from the 'perennial' philosophy.

79 Cf. *BL*, I, 98 which indicates the importance of the tree-sap imagery as a metaphor for the presence of imagination. Coleridge, being a true organicist, was fond of the tree as a symbol of thinking, knowledge, etc. Some of his most interesting uses of the image are *Friend* (*CC*), I, 458, *LS* (*CC*), 21, 32, 110, *AR*, 2, and

CL, II, 961, 1198, IV, 758, VI, 968. And see above on Wordsworth's genius as compared to a tree growing in rich soil, page 14 and note 34.

80 *CL*, IV, 874 to J. H. Green, 30 Sept. 1818. Coleridge goes on to explain that at the time of the *Biographia* he had only read the *System des transcendentalen Idealismus*, but that upon reading further he saw clearly that Schelling had erred. This suggests that Coleridge's own position in the *Biographia* was not so much erroneous to his mind in looking back upon it. It was simply incomplete and a misunderstanding of Schelling, Coleridge taking Schelling to be in agreement with himself when he actually was not. Cf. *CN*, III, 4424 on Schelling's whole philosophy as anticipated by Zoroaster.

81 *CL*, IV, 925, to J. Britton, 28 Feb. 1819. Compare Professor Whalley's conclusions: 'There is no sign that this was Coleridge's considered view at the end of his life, and few Coleridgeans would agree with him even if it were.' 'On Reading Coleridge', p. 34.

82 *TT*, 28 June 1834.

83 They would have misled the reader, for example, by apparently endorsing Schelling's system as he further developed it beyond the *System des transcendentalen Idealismus*.

84 *LS* (*CC*), 114n.

85 Cf. R. H. Fogle's assessment in *The Idea of Coleridge's Criticism* (Berkeley and Los Angeles: 1962), p. xi: 'As a philosopher he does not rival Kant or Schelling in sustained and systematic thought because it is not at bottom his purpose to do so; he is a poet–philosopher–critic...a genuinely organic thinker, whose mind is a totality and who aims always at synthesis.' George Whalley and Dorothy Emmet reach similar estimations in their articles in *Writers and their Background*, ed. Brett, which suggests Coleridge's own remark: 'Hints and Materials for Reflection/The Object too was to rouse and stimulate the mind – to set the reader a thinking.' *LS* (*CC*), 114n.

2. PHILOSOPHICAL SOURCES OF THE 'BIOGRAPHIA LITERARIA'

1 Marginal note to Kant, *Critique of Pure Reason*, MS no. 5, unpublished marginal comment.

2 *P Lects.*, lect. iii, 116.

3 *P Lects.*, lect. iv, 145: the fundamental paradox for dualism. Cf. a marginal note to Kant's *Logik*, MS no. 9 and published H. Niedecker, 'Coleridge: ses notes en marge de Kant', *Revue de littérature comparée*, 7 (1927), 139–40: 'Heterogenes can not be opposed, the one to the other. – Ergo, opposita semper unigena. Opposites must be one in a suppositum – or Thesis = Antithesis in the Prothesis. Two terms that have no equation in a common Root, cannot stand in opposition to each other.'

4 *P Lects.*, lect. iii, 114 and see lect. ii, 106.

5 *P Lects.*, lect. iii, 114. This view is explored throughout Coleridge's writings, and most often takes the form of the correlation of Idea to Law. See e.g. *C&S* (*CC*), 11–16, especially 13. And see *Friend* (*CC*), I, 459 and note, for Coleridge's note written in Copy A; see also *Friend* (*CC*), I, 467 and 492–3.

6 *P Lects.*, lect. iv, 145.

7 *P Lects.*, lect. iv, 145.

8 See *P Lects.*, lect. ii, 106 and 96.

9 Cf. *CN*, II, 2541, Apr. 1805 in which Coleridge describes his purpose as a reconciler.

10 Coleridge says of materialism: 'In short you have precisely this: if only the world had been from the beginning, then it would be, for it is plain that all which is now in the world is presupposed to account for the world; so that in truth this is one of those numerous instances, in all books of materialists without exception, in which the solution is itself a part of the problem. Therefore I say I do not consider this as deserving the name of philosophy. It is an anti-philosophy arising out of a thorough coldness of the moral feeling, and the habit of looking so intensely at the external world with all the powers of the heart fixed upon it, that at last the man does not deserve to be considered merely as having self-love (that supposes a reflex); he becomes a mere lover of self.' *P Lects.*, lect. ii, 106–7. On materialism see also lect. iii, 131–2, lect. xiii, 372ff., 376–9 and 386. And compare *T of L*, 45–6, 51–7, and 60–4. See *CL*, IV, 758–61 to Lord Liverpool, July 1817 for an interesting discussion from the theological perspective.

11 *CL*, I, 294 to Thelwall, Dec. 1796.

12 *CL*, VI, 1036 to R. H. Brabant, June 1815 (?). Coleridge's early and somewhat harsh view of Locke is stated in the Locke–Descartes letters to J. Wedgwood in 1801. He there attempts to demonstrate Locke's dependence on Descartes's epistemology, a dependence which was radically overlooked in Coleridge's day, and which has become more fully appreciated only in recent years. See e.g. *CL*, II, 677n. Although it is true that Coleridge says in *P Lects.*, 376–80 that Locke was no materialist, and although Locke's empiricism is certainly distinguishable from materialism, from the point of view of the 'Constructive Philosophy' the consequences of both are similar enough not to require a distinction to be emphasized in the discussion.

13 *CN*, II, 3156, Sept. 1807 and cf. *CN*, I, 920, Feb.–Mar. 1801: 'Materialists unwilling to admit the mysterious of our nature make it all mysterious – nothing mysterious in nerves, eyes, &c. but that nerves think &c!! – Stir up the sediment into the transparent water, & so make all opaque.' See also *LS (CC)*, 96.

14 *P Lects.*, lect. iii, 115. The sense of touch is explored by Coleridge throughout the notebooks via his distinction between single and double touch. See e.g. *CN*, II, 2399, Jan. 1805 on double touch, and see 2405, Jan. 1805, and 3215, 1807–8. Touch would be the sense of which sight, sound, smell, and taste are all variations, hence the possibilities of 'correspondence' and of such extraordinary occurrences as Coleridge reports in *CL*, IV, 774 to C. A. Tulk, Sept. 1817. On single and double touch, see John Beer's *Coleridge's Poetic Intelligence* (London: 1977), pp. 81–8 and see *CN*, I, 1827.

15 *AR*, 364 and cf. 353–4. See also *CN*, I, 328 and note, Dec. 1797, on the despotism of the senses, and *LS (CC)*, 89 on the tyranny of the eye specifically. And see *P Lects.*, lect. xiii, 374.

16 On the inadequacy of juxtaposition to express true synthesis see *Friend (CC)*, I, 94: 'It is the object of the mechanical atomistic Philosophy to confound Synthesis with *synartesis*, or rather with mere juxtaposition of Corpuscles separated by invisible Interspaces. I find it difficult to determine, whether this theory contradicts the Reason or the Senses most: for it is alike inconceivable and unimaginable.' See also *CN*, III, 451, May 1815.

17 On recent physics as showing the inadequacy of the atomic metaphor as a model see David Bohm, *Causality and Chance in Modern Physics* (London: 1957), and

on the dangers of taking models in science literally see Colin Turbayne, *Myth of Metaphor* (Columbia, SC: 1970).

18 *LS (CC)*, 89 and cf. 96. Dead nature was for Coleridge a contradiction in terms. Lifeless, cold matter was a fiction of the abstracting faculty. The *Theory of Life* is a concerted effort to bridge the false chasm between death and life (*T of L*, 21–38), as Coleridge shows in exposing the inadequacy of every definition of life. Cf. *CN*, III, 3632, Sept.–Nov. 1809. The one life theme expresses this reconciliation of death and life, and is basically a variation of the Platonic theme that all Being participates in vitality to some degree. See e.g. A. O. Lovejoy, *The Great Chain of Being* (Cambridge, Mass.: 1936). On matter see a marginal note to Kant, *Metaphysische Anfangsgründe der Naturwissenschaft*, MS no. 8, published W. Schrickx, 'Coleridge's Marginalia on Kant's *Metaphysische Anfangsgründe* . . .', *Studia Germanica*, 1 (1959), 170. See also *CN*, III, 4412, May 1818.

19 *T of L*, 45.

20 *CN*, I, 328, Dec. 1797, and see note. Cf. *LS (CC)*, 4n.

21 *CL*, I, 354 to Thomas Poole, Oct. 1797.

22 *BL*, I, 76–7.

23 *BL*, I, 81.

24 *BL*, I, 81.

25 *BL*, I, 177–8.

26 See e.g. *P Lects.*, lect. iii, 119–20. Berkeley's position is a highly problematic one. It seems that Berkeley was anticipating Kant's formalizing of the subjectivity of space when he put everything in the mind, hence his preoccupation with distance in *A New Theory of Vision*. When he brought in the Supreme Mind to preserve the world, he was interpreted as introducing a crass hypostasization, when what he was surely trying to suggest was that space (i.e. the condition of outness, of externality) was subjective not merely for the human *qua* individual, but as generic percipient being. The external world was subjective because it was only appearance. Kant was able to apply this subjectivity not only to space, but also to time. He could then show the 'internal world' of thoughts and sensations to be equally of the status appearance, and talk of Mind as more than merely the particular individual instances of minds. That Berkeley's Supreme Mind or Being was precisely this sort of generic transcendent concept seems fairly certain. His error was in not clearly elucidating the equal subjectivity of time and hence of the external *and* internal aspects of consciousness. To take Berkeley as a solipsistic subjective idealist is utterly to misconstrue his most important insights and his anticipations of Kant, and to miss his method of ironically parodying two apparently irreconcilable points of view, as in *The Three Dialogues*. Solipsism is the state of a mind which is imprisoned in its own individual ego and personality, which sees itself as nothing more than a particular existence, failing to realize that this very individuality is the symbol of a whole generic level of being. See my 'Berkeley's Ironic Method', *Philosophy and Literature*, 4 (1980), 18–32.

27 *P Lects.*, lect. iii, 120 and cf. xiii, 370–2. For Coleridge on the error of materialists see *CN*, III, 4087, May–July 1817. Coleridge's early enthusiasm for Berkeley in the 1790s is problematic because it is uncertain how he was reading him. That he later came to see him as a more Kantian idealist, with Platonic views about the nature of 'Ideas', seems likely.

28 Cf. *CN*. III, 3605, f120ᵛ, Aug.–Sept. 1809 on that which the philosophers Descartes, Berkeley, Hume, and Kant have in common.

29 Marginal note to Kant, *Critique of Pure Reason*, MS no. 5, unpublished marginal

comment. Cf. *P Lects.*, lect. xiii, 372, and cf. marginal note MS no. 7 in Kant, *Vermischte Schriften* (Copy A), published Niedecker, 'Coleridge', 342–3. And see *LS* (*CC*), 18n. Coleridge remarked of Fichte's philosophy that 'I sometimes imagine that I am reading a theory of Dreams – and that the philosophy is true and applicable to me only when I am asleep.' Marginal note to *Grundlage der gesammten Wissenschaftslehre*, MS no. 2, published W. Schrickx, 'Unpublished Coleridge Marginalia on Fichte', *Studia Germanica Gandensia*, 3 (1961), 184–6.

30 Coleridge formulates his specific view of the relation of mind and matter in, e.g., *CL*, III, 484 to Joseph Cottle, late Apr. 1814. On the mind as nature see *LS* (*CC*), 79 and *AR*, 57. See also *CN*, III, 4397, f52, Mar. 1818, and 4412, May 1818.

31 *CL*, III, 483 to Cottle, Apr. 1814.

32 *P Lects.*, lect. iv, 146. The *deus ex machina* is analogous to the literal interpretation of Berkeley's Supreme Mind in *The Three Dialogues*. On the *deus ex machina* see also *CN*, III, 4483.

33 *P. Lects.*, lect. xiii, 377. The ancients had always viewed nature as vital and animated, though not necessarily as a hylozoic nature.

34 *BL*, I, 88.

35 Cf. *LS* (*CC*), 74n.

36 MS no. 22, published W. Schrickx, 'Coleridge's Marginalia on Kant's *Metaphysische Anfangsgründe* . . .', *Studia Germanica*, 1 (1959), 182. Cf. the previous marginal note: 'Honor and Thanks are due to Kant for this first attempt. Even tho' the success had been less than it is, the attempt, the Idea, would have demanded the admiration and gratitude of every Philosopher: – The defects may all be traced to the barren Dualism of the Reflective System.' MS no. 21, and Schrickx, 'Coleridge's Marginalia', 181.

37 Whether the difference between mind and nature is an absolute and fundamental division, such that the two are finally heterogeneous substances, is a question the possibility of which suggests that 'facts of experience' are themselves 'appearances'. They constitute a *starting* point for investigation, not a conclusion or solution. But see below on '*essential* dualism' for the continuation of this dualistic interpretation which begins as barren and ends as generative.

38 *AR*, 17 and see 18. For Coleridge on distinguishing versus dividing see also *LS* (*CC*), 62, *T of L*, 22 and 25. On the relation of definitions to this distinction see *CL*, VI, 635–6 to Gillman, Oct. 1826, and *CN*, II, 2406, Jan. 1805.

39 *BL*, I, 88–9.

40 *BL*, I, 89–90.

41 *BL*, I, 94.

42 See for instance the first dialogue of *The Three Dialogues* of Berkeley, in which Philonous seeks to prove to Hylas the non-corporeality of qualities on the basis of the variability of their presence in 'abnormal' states of the perceiver, one of the most sustained accounts of the subjectivity of perception on these grounds.

43 On this point, Coleridge explains, all serious philosophies have agreed (*CN*, III, 3605, Aug.–Sept. 1809). It is in the controversy about the extent of this dependence that branches shoot out in opposing directions. The result for most schools was the positing of the reality *behind* the subjective qualities, a notion which Kant made it his object to explode and expose in all its self-contradiction. Nevertheless, the tenacity of the image of space in the words 'behind appearance' has proven generally unassailable not only for the layman.

44 For Coleridge on the noumenon/phenomenon distinction as age-old see a note

on Tenneman, *Geschichte der Philosophie*, MS no. 24, unpublished marginal comment, annotated about 1818 in preparation for the philosophical lectures: 'Never, surely, was a Ph. History composed under a stronger *Warp* of Pre-determination, that the elder Philosophers *must have* been – ignorant of Kant's Cr. d. r. Vernunft!!' See also Coleridge's remark in *CL*, VI, 896 to W. R. Hamilton, Apr. 1832, on 'Kant's *revival* of the distinction between Noumenon = nomen, Intelligible, Numen – and the *Phaenomenon* – both *potential* Entities, that *are* only in and for the mind or the sensation.'

45 The doctrine of primary and secondary qualities was fully explored by the seventeenth and eighteenth century philosophers in an attempt to distinguish the sensible and accidental aspects of experience from those with a law-like character or a necessity. The error lay in placing the law-like character wholly in the external and failing to see the correlation of the law and the idea which discovered the 'primary quality' (Bacon sought to correct this error in the *Novum Organum*). Thus the mind was divided from itself and, while satisfied in its need to distinguish accident from law, it created a sensible world and a world of objective laws, both separate from the perceiving mind. In the *De mundi* of 1770, Kant corrected this error and re-established the law-idea relation which Coleridge developed in *The Friend*'s 'Essays on Method'. Coleridge also attributes this correlativity of law and idea to Pythagoras in *P Lects.*, lect. iii, 114.

46 For Coleridge on innate ideas see *P. Lects.*, lect. xiii, 377. On Locke's criticism of innate ideas, see *CN*, III, 4180, Nov. 1813.

47 See Locke, *Essay Concerning Human Understanding*, ed. P. H. Nidditch (Oxford: 1975), vol. I, bk. I, chs. 2–4, on his rejection of innate ideas. In *The Philosophy of the Enlightenment*, trans. F. C. A. Koelln and J. P. Pettegrove (Princeton: 1951), p. 100, Ernst Cassirer encapsulates what would constitute Coleridge's rejection of 'empirical philosophy, which represents a series of attempts to minimize the difference between sensation and reflection and finally to wipe it out altogether. French philosophical criticism of the 18th century hammered at this same point in an attempt to eliminate the last vestige of independence which Locke had attributed to reflection.'

48 *CL*, II, 677–703, especially 691ff, where Coleridge criticizes Locke for a naive use of 'innate' as synonymous with 'connate'. He also points out Locke's error in his concept of abstract ideas, which Coleridge, Hume, and Berkeley all equally reject. See e.g. Hume, *A Treatise of Human Nature*, ed. C. Mossner (Baltimore, Md.: 1969) part II, section i. In part I, sec. i Hume criticizes Locke's misuse of 'ideas' in general, much as Coleridge did. See also George Berkeley, *Principles of Human Knowledge*, vol. 2: *Works*, ed. A. A. Luce and T. E. Jessop, 9 vols. (London: 1948–57), paragraphs 6–10 and 11 on Locke's error of abstract ideas.

49 For some interesting thoughts of Coleridge's on parts of speech as a reflection of common-sense views of perception see *CL*, VI, 817 to Hyman Hurwitz, Sept. 1829, and see *AR*, 157n.

50 *CN*, III, 3605, Aug.–Sept. 1809. Coleridge here uses 'know' in the sense of empirical knowledge or, with Kant, as knowledge of appearance. Whether we can know anything of this noumenon over and above sensuous experience is the issue which forces Coleridge and Plato to part ways with Kant and Aristotle.

51 These primary qualities should never have been hypostasized outside of mind.

52 *AR*, 199 and cf. 61 and *CN*, III, 3605, f120ᵛ–f117. And see *BL*, I, 93, for a similar comment on Leibniz and Locke.

53 That is, the distinction becomes an intellectual distinction, not a distinction

founded on experience, and seems to be a mere habituation to the mistaking of degree/kind-differences, which is precisely opposite to the state described in non-reflective world descriptions, as e.g. dualism.

54 See Kant, *Critique of Pure Reason*, trans. N. Kemp-Smith (London. 1929), 'Transcendental Analytic', on the thesis of the necessary unity of consciousness and the transcendent, unknowable ground of that consciousness, that is, the empirical self versus the transcendental unity of apperception. For a good account of this most difficult section see P. F. Strawson, *The Bounds of Sense* (London: 1966), pp. 24ff and 169ff.

55 This is the clue to the absurdity of a literalist reading of Berkeley, which must assume that 'inner consciousness' is infallible and real to a higher degree than the external world. It *is* more real within the limited context of the single, individual self. See e.g. A. J. Ayer, *The Problem of Knowledge* (London: 1956). But from the context of the individual *qua* human or being, or the individual in his generic being, it is a contradiction of facts of experience, which need to be accounted for, and not arbitrarily rejected.

56 Any solipsistic idealism suffers from this one-sidedness, just as Hume's personal identity as a mere conglomeration of all that has ever been experienced is a jumble of sensations without a focus or a real, separate percipient. See Hume, *Treatise of Human Nature*, part IV, sec. v: 'our notions of personal identity, proceed entirely from the smooth and uninterrupted progress of the thought along a train of connected ideas, according to the principles above-explain'd . . . there is no such idea [of self]'. Hume was, however, paving the way for Kant's transcendental unity of apperception. For in his closing statement he says 'all the nice and subtle questions concerning personal identity can never possibly be decided'. He left it to Kant to prove the necessity of a unity for a perception of the world as a totality, just as, in showing that the ideas of cause and necessary connection could not possibly be derived from experience, he prepared the way for Kant's formulation of the doctrine of the categories of the understanding. See note 26 above on Berkeley's contribution to Kant.

57 *CL*, I, 624 to Godwin, Sept. 1800.

58 *CN*, II, 2370, Dec. 1804. See *CL*, I, 479 to Poole, Apr. 1799 in connection with Hume on the 'Essence of Identity as not lying in *recollective* Consciousness'. For an illuminating analysis of memory and personal identity see *CL*, VI, 598–600 to Edward Coleridge, Jul. 1826, especially the following: 'If there had been no self-*retaining* Power, a Self-finding would be a perpetual Self-losing . . . but a self-retaining Power supposes a self-containing Power – a self-conscious Being.'

59 The question of personal identity was at the core of Coleridge's moral and religious philosophy, and Coleridge followed Kant in the crucial distinction between the thing and the person. The person must always be conceived as a 'subject which is its own object' (*CL*, VI, 600) while a thing is only an object. Things can be instruments to be exploited; but persons are never merely instruments. They must be treated empathically as agents with inherent integrity, not *derived* integrity. See e.g. *AR*, 58, 119, 123, and esp. 156n. See also *CN*, III, 4195, 1814–15 on person.

60 *BL*, I, 82.

61 *BL*, I, 83.

62 *CN*, II, 2471, Mar. 1805 and *CL*, I, 479 (see above note 58).

63 *CN*, I, 921, Feb.–Mar. 1801. See also G. N. G. Orsini, *Coleridge and German*

Idealism (Carbondale and Edwardsville, III: 1969), chapter four on the transcendental unity of apperception.

64 *CN*, III, 3362, Sept. 1808. To unite the thought and the feeling would, as we will explore in chapter eight, constitute *full* awareness. It is interesting that in this notebook entry Coleridge makes the comment on personal identity in relation to a bull, and in the final and fullest formulation of a bull in *BL*, I, 52–3, he uses personal identity as the example: '*I* was a fine child, but they changed *me*.'

65 *CL*, II, 1197 to Thomas Clarkson, Oct. 1806. It is in such early, struggling thoughts as this that we can understand the impact which Kant must have had on Coleridge in helping him to articulate more precisely these issues.

66 This is the sophism which leads modern philosophers in the search of a proof of the existence of other minds. We begin by assuming that we cannot know for certain the existence of other minds, and find ourselves involved in a safari into the most dangerous of jungles. The premise is so correct that the opposite can never be deduced from it. Yet it is only correct for the understanding which fails to see the individual as representative or symbolic. We can have no fuller, qualitatively richer existential knowledge of our own being than of other beings, hence self and other are equally uncertain and unknowable.

67 See Coleridge's comment on the world as a dream in *CN*, II, 2537.

68 It is in the failure to clarify exactly which sense of 'individual' or 'subjective' is being used that Strawson founders in his treatment of Kant's refusal to give priority to either the inner or outer worlds of experience. See Strawson, *Bounds of Sense*, pp. 51–7. And see e.g. *CN*, III, 4225, 1814–15.

69 'On the Philosophic Import of the Words OBJECT and SUBJECT', *Blackwood's Magazine*, 10 (Oct. 1821), 247–50. The existentialist broadens our understanding of idealism's universal application and objectivity in the extension of man to his fullest nature as being *qua* being. See also S. Kierkegaard's *Philosophical Fragments*, trans. D. F. Swenson (Princeton: 1936), in which Christ is significant not only as a historical figure and individual man, or not *even*, but as the symbol of man's participation in divinity or being. Kierkegaard's *Concluding Unscientific Postscript*, trans. Swenson, ed. W. Lowrie (Princeton: 1968), bears out this interpretation.

70 See note 26 above. Coleridge's 'one life' theme developed most fully in *T of L* is an analogue of the Platonic 'participation' of all finite existence in one reality. See *CN*, II, 2330, 3223, III, 4319, 4333, the poem 'Eolian Harp', *CL*, II, 864–5 to Sotheby, Sept. 1802, and *LS* (*CC*), 31. It frees Coleridge's idealism from any taint of solipsism. But for continuing scepticism about the possibility of a non-solipsistic idealism see Strawson: 'This, he [Kant] claims with evident sincerity, distinguishes his idealism from that of Berkeley who "degrades bodies to mere illusion". But we may wonder whether the distinction is as clear as he thought... space and time, bodies and states of consciousness, are not really on the same footing at all. The point may be obscured for us (and for Kant) by his insistence that all things in space and time are equally appearances; but the doctrine has quite a different force in respect of these two classes of things.' Strawson, *Bounds of Sense*, p. 57. See note 68 above. This is the suspicion which will always prevent a thorough understanding of transcendental idealism, and cannot be dispelled except by insisting that although we see *through* our own individual minds, we see *with* Mind in a generic sense. We exist as individuals, but we 'live and move and *have* our Being' in Self and Life, or God. See *CL*, IV, 768. Existence itself is for Coleridge a symbol of *being* to the imaginative mind

71 *CL*, II, 1194 to Thomas Clarkson, Oct. 1806. Cf. *CL*, VI, 817 to Hurwitz, Sept. 1829. On thought and thing see *CN*, III, 4351, and on the relations of words to thought, not to things, see *CL*, VI, 630 to Gillman, Oct. 1826. See also *CL*, IV, 885 to Derwent Coleridge, Nov. 1818: 'to think is to thingify'.

The distinction, as opposed to a division, between thought and thing is a direct answer to Strawson's objection quoted immediately above: 'bodies and states of consciousness' *are* on the same footing (though the 'outness prejudice' must be overcome in order to realize this basic similarity), and 'the doctrine' does *not* have 'quite a different force in respect of these two classes of things'. This naive account of the nature of reality (instead of appearance) is precisely what Kant is trying to expose as a prejudice resulting from too great attention to externality. See above for Coleridge on this habitual preoccupation with the 'external'.

72 See Kant, *Critique of Pure Reason*, pp. 65–82.

73 Cf. Coleridge on Kant:

Kant's merit consisted (mainly) in explaining the ground of the apodeixis in Mathematics: which neither Leibnitz nor Plato had attained to – and this he did by proving that Space and Time were 1. neither general terms, 2. nor abstractions from Things, 3. nor Things themselves; but, 4. the pure a priori forms of the intuitive faculty: ... They are the Acts of the perceptive Power, of which all particular acts of perception are modifications, directions &c. Time = unity, the point, resistance – = Multëity, area, absence of resistance. In the circle all possible Truths are symbolized.

CL, IV, 852 to Mr Pryce, Apr. 1818. See *AR*, 156n on the meaning of subjective and objective in mathematics. See also *CN*, III, 3973, Sept.–Oct. 1810 for Coleridge's comments on sensuous intuition. And see *CN*, III, 4266, Sept. 1815.

74 Kant, *Critique of Pure Reason*, 'Transcendental Analytic', especially pp. 111ff. Coleridge adopted without reservation the view that concepts depend upon sensuous content to be experienceable, which Kant had stressed as early as 1770 in the 'Inaugural Dissertation', or *De mundi*. See *De mundi sensibilis atque intelligibilis forma et principiis. Kant: Selected Pre-Critical Writings and Correspondence with Beck*, ed. G. B. Kerferd and D. E. Walford (Manchester: 1968), pp. 45–92. This view is expressed in Coleridge's definition of the symbol in distinction from the idea. See *LS* (*CC*), 30–1 and 114.

75 See Kant, *Critique of Pure Reason*, pp. 67–82 and 244 on Kant's rejection of both the empirical self and the world of objects as any more than appearances of equal status.

76 The idea of metaphysics as 'negative and critical' appears again as early as 1770 in the *De mundi*, sections 8 and 9.

77 It is the unfortunate result of the fact that concepts and ultimately universal ideas can only be represented in forms of space and time that these space–time garbs should be, after habitual use, mistaken for that which is signified. In Coleridge's terms, the image is mistaken for the idea, or the metaphorical for the literal or the allegorical. See *CN*, III, 3954, 3973, 4247 and 4309 for Coleridge on the degeneration of language. Thus the noumenon as 'above' or 'behind' appearance is apt to mislead because of the tenacity of the prejudice of 'outness' (see *BL*, I, 177). Hence Kant's emphasis on the almost uncontrollable tendency of the speculative reason to transgress its bounds. See the *Critique of Pure Reason*, 'Transcendental Doctrine of Method', especially chapter two.

78 Kant and Coleridge were constantly warning against mistaking abstracting for conceptualizing. See e.g. the *De mundi*, section 6. And see *AR*, 198, *CL*, II, 693

to J. Wedgwood, 1801, and the marginal note to Kant's *Logik*, ms no. 9, published in Niedecker, 'Coleridge', 139: 'Abstractions descend into Images, or total Impressions; but... an Idea never passes into an Abstraction and therefore never becomes the equivalent of an Image;...there is no interspace between Abstr. and Image for the Idea to occupy. Therefore I. and A. *ipso genere diverse.*' And see the note to Fichte's *Bestimmung des Menschen*, ms no. 12, unpublished marginal comment: 'Why not begin with explaining the nature and *uses* of *Abstractions* as an Organon Scientiae – whence would follow of itself an Insight into its sophistic *Abuse*, when the Instrument is <1st> identified, with, and then substituted for, the Realities, which were to be understood by its help!'

79 Thus in the *Phenomenology of Mind*, trans. J. B. Baillie (London: 1931), Hegel chooses 'here' and 'now' as his points of departure for the transcendence to the absolute. See Part A: 'Consciousness', §i 'Sense certainty'.

80 *BL*, I, 85.

81 *BL*, I, 87 and cf. 90–2.

82 See Coleridge's analysis in *AR* of Aristotle's preference for the objective and the result, *AR*, 220n.

83 Cf. *BL*, II, 'On Poesy or Art', 263: 'The seeming identity of body and mind in infants...the commencing separation in boyhood...finally all that presents the body as body becoming of an almost excremental nature'. Cf. *CN*, III, 4398, Mar. 1818.

84 Cf. *BL*, 52–3 on the effects of long and habitual association.

85 *P Lects.*, lect. iv, 145.

86 *Friend (CC)*, I, 94.

87 On the distinction between syncretism and synthesis see *CN*, III, 4251, May 1815 and see above note 16. On plagiarism see W. J. Bate, *Coleridge* (London: 1969), pp. 131ff, for a sensible perspective.

88 See Coleridge's distinction between instance and illustration in *BL*, II, 15, 17.

89 See below chapters five and six.

90 *BL*, I, 196.

91 *BL*, II, 'On Poesy or Art', 257–8: 'In the objects of nature are presented, as in a mirror, all the possible elements, steps, and processes of intellect antecedent to consciousness, and therefore to the full development of the intelligential act; and man's mind is the very focus of all the rays of intellect which are scattered throughout the images of nature. Now so to place these images, totalized, and fitted to the limits of the human mind, as to elicit from, and to superinduce upon, the forms themselves the moral reflexions to which they approximate, to make the external internal, the internal external, to make nature thought, and thought nature, – this is the mystery of genius in the Fine Arts. Dare I add that the genius must act on the feeling, that body is but a striving to become mind, – that it is mind in its essence!'

92 See Thomas McFarland, *Coleridge and the Pantheist Tradition* (Oxford: 1969), p. 20. See also Stephen Prickett, *Coleridge and Wordsworth*: *The Poetry of Growth* (Cambridge: 1970), p. 78, on Coleridge reading the Germans to understand better and confirm what he already knew. But see Norman Fruman, *Coleridge, The Damaged Archangel* (London: 1972) for a different assessment.

93 *BL*, I, 198.

94 *BL*, I, 188.

95 On the regulative versus constitutive see e.g. *LS (CC)*, 114 and *P Lects.*, 426. The most extensive account of this Coleridge/Kant dispute on the nature of ideas

is to be found in Coleridge's marginalia to Tennemann's *Geschichte der Philosophie*, which will be published in the *Coleridge Marginalia* (*CC*). Some of the most interesting notes to the Tennemann volumes can be found in the *P Lects.* notes, but many notes on this dispute were omitted because of their length. The annotated copies are in the British Museum. Some notes on ideas occur in vol. vi nos. 2, 3–5, viii, i, nos. 1–5, viii, ii, nos. 1–4.

96 See *BL*, i, 191.

3. EARLY SOURCES OF POLARITY IN COLERIDGE'S THOUGHT

1 *Friend* (*CC*), i, 94.
2 *CL*, iv, 775. See also the notebook entry of 1815 on Heraclitus and opposition, *CN*, iii, 4244.
3 For a later discussion of Heraclitus's philosophy see *CN*, iii, 4351, f22, Apr. 1817. Coleridge says elsewhere that all of Schelling is contained in Zoroaster's Oracles. See *CN*, iii, 4424, 1818.
4 The *OED* suggests that the Latin and Italian would not have been much older. Cf. Owen Barfield, *What Coleridge Thought* (London: 1971), p. 262, note 16.
5 *CL*, iv, 775.
6 Barfield, *What Coleridge Thought*, p. 186.
7 *Ibid.*, p. 187.
8 Marginal note to Boehme's *Aurora*, quoted in Barfield, *What Coleridge Thought*, p. 264, note 21. Coleridge is supposed to have been familiar with this work in his schooldays. See *CN*, i, 174n.
9 Barfield, *What Coleridge Thought*, p. 186.
10 *Ibid.*, p. 189.
11 Barfield seems to say that imagination is polarity. *Ibid.*, p. 90. Hence I find it difficult to reconcile this tentativeness with respect to Cusa, Lull, and Bruno, except that he is perhaps focusing too literally on the metaphor of polarity instead of the Idea essential to it.
12 See e.g. the marginal notes to Kant, *Metaphysische Anfangsgründe*, ms nos. 17, 21, 22, published Schrickx, 'Coleridge's Marginalia', 161–87, and *CL*, iv, 808 to Tulk, Jan. 1818: 'This oversight of Kant (in his astonishing *prophetic work*, written in his 22nd year, entitled Himmels system (System of the Heavens) of which Laplace's Méchanique Céleste is an unprincipled Plagiarism) in the assumption of *two* Powers only, as Newton had done before him, was the occasion of all the errors and imperfections of his theory.' Coleridge refers to Kant's *Universal Natural History and Theory of the Heavens* (1755), a translation of which exists by W. Hastie (Ann Arbor: 1969), with an interesting introduction discussing the relation of Laplace to Kant.
13 Barfield, *What Coleridge Thought*, pp. 265–6, n31 part 3. Marginal note on Swedenborg's *De Infinito et Causa Finali* – from a transcript in the possession of Victoria College, Toronto.
14 Barfield, *What Coleridge Thought*, p. 187.
15 *TT*, 30 Apr. 1830.
16 *AR*, 204.
17 Quoted from Barfield, *What Coleridge Thought*, pp. 266–7.
18 On Baxter's importance in logic, note Coleridge's marginal note to Baxter's *Life of Himself* (in Barfield, *What Coleridge Thought*, p. 182):

Among Baxter's philosophical merits, we ought not to overlook, that the substitution of Trichotomy for the old and still general plan of Dichotomy in the method and disposition of Logic, which forms so prominent and substantial an excellence in Kant's Critique of the Pure Reason, of the Judgement, and the rest of his works, belongs originally to Richard Baxter, a century before Kant; – and this not as a hint, but as a fully evolved and systematically applied principle. Nay, more than this; – Baxter grounded it on an absolute idea presupposed in all intelligential acts: whereas Kant takes it only as a fact in which he seems to anticipate or suspect some deeper truth latent, and hereafter to be discovered.

On Baxter see also other marginalia quoted in Barfield, pp. 262 and 266.

19 Coleridge's reading of these logicians began very early as we know from note-books and letters. On Bruno see *CN*, I, 927, 1801, in which he says he has read two works with great difficulty; see also *CL*, II, 809, Jul. 1802, and *CN*, II, 2264, Nov. 1804. Boehme's *Aurora* he read at school (*CN*, I, 174n) but was interested in him again in 1801: *CN*, I, 1000E. Cusa he mentions in 1803, saying he definitely must read him: *CN*, I, 1379; Baxter he mentions with great familiarity as early as 1796 in *CL*, I, 245, which is an astonishingly early date for his awareness of the dichotomy/trichotomy problem, no matter how tentative and unarticulated. Again in 1802 Baxter is mentioned in *CN*, I, 1181, and then in 1803 to Southey in a letter, *CL*, II, 956. Such an early familiarity with exactly those men who formulated the logic of trichotomy is indubitable evidence for the belief that Coleridge was thoroughly immersed in the idea of which polarity was a metaphor as much as a decade before he knew Schelling first hand.

20 Exactly how early Coleridge decided to make his first major work an examination of the logic of trichotomy is uncertain. In *CL*, I, 519 to Wedgwood, May 1799, he mentions the 'one work, to which I hope to dedicate in silence the prime of my life.' Two years later he mentions his 'curious Metaphysical Work' in *CL*, II, 776 to Poole, for which he must spend a great deal of time reading in the *old* libraries. Then more specifically in Feb. 1803, he says to Purkis that he plans a history of metaphysics in England, *CL*, II, 927–8. Only four months later this work had expanded into the 'Organum verè Organum'.

21 *CL*, II, 947–8 to W. Godwin, June 1803. Note the significance of mentioning Lull.

22 *CN*, II, 2502, Mar. 1805. This passage clearly refers to Kant's essay 'Negative Quantities' in *Vermischte Schriften*, which Coleridge annotated, a source which went unmentioned in the *CN* notes.

23 Cf. *CN*, II, 2541, 1805.

24 *CN*, II, 2832, May 1806.

25 Cf. *CN*, II, 2631, Aug. 1805: 'O! the complexities and the *Ravel* produced by Time struggling with Eternity! – a and b are different, and Eternity or Duration makes them one – this we call modification, the principle of all greatness in finite beings, the principle of all contradiction *and absurdity*.' I.e., contradiction and absurdity for the understanding but the only mode by which reason can represent an idea. Cf. *CN*, III, 4186, 1813–15.

26 *BL*, I, 197.

27 *BL*, I, 188 and 195–6.

28 *BL*, I, 86.

29 *CL*, II, 865–6, 1802 for the imagination/fancy distinction. See also *CL*, II, 1034 where fancy is *opposed* to imagination. And see below chapter eight for further discussion.

30 *BL*, i, 85–6 and *BL*, ii, 11.
31 *CN*, iii, 4326, Jan. 1817.
32 *C & S (CC)*, 24.
33 *BL*, i, 86.
34 *LS (CC)*, 30 and for a further example note *CN*, i, 928, Apr. 1801.
35 *Friend (CC)*, i, 156 and *LS (CC)*, 69–70.
36 *LS (CC)*, 69 and 68 n3.
37 *CL*, ii, 857 to Sotheby, Aug. 1802.
38 *CN*, i, 1725, Dec. 1803. It is interesting to note that in both this and the letter to Sotheby the *Orestes* is mentioned in relation to 'Extremes meeting'.
39 *CN*, ii, 3156, Sept. 1807.
40 *Friend (CC)*, i, 110. Coleridge mentions the proverb in connection with truths 'so true that they lie side by side with error'. See also *Friend (CC)*, i, 205 and 529.
41 *LS (CC)*, 133, and *AR*, 327–8n. For later applications of 'Extremes Meet' see *CN*, iii, 3400, Sept.–Oct. 1808, 3405, 3726, Mar. 1810, and 4007 f9ᵛ, Nov. 1810.
42 *CL*, iv, 768 to Tulk, Sept. 1817.
43 *CL*, iv, 690 to Gillman, Nov. 1816, and see 809.
44 *CL*, iv, 874.
45 Marginal note to Kant's *Metaphysical Anfangsgründe der Naturwissenschaft*, pp. 82–4, BM C 126 H 8. See also *CN*, iv, 4445 and 4449 on Schelling's errors.

4. IRONY AND INDIRECTNESS: THE GERMAN PHILOSOPHY OF ART

1 See e.g. Cleanth Brooks and Robert Penn-Warren, *The Well Wrought Urn* (London: 1949), and Brooks, *Modern Poetry and the Tradition* (Chapel Hill: 1939), for his sketchy and occasional treatment of Keats, Wordsworth, and Shelley. Equally occasional are Empson's references to the English Romantic poets in *Seven Types of Ambiguity* (London: 1930).
2 In all of the major studies of irony in England and America, the Germans were mentioned in passing if at all, and then with pejorative connotations as to discourage any student from serious investigation. This narrowness occurs even in the best studies of irony such as G. G. Sedgewick's *Of Irony* (Toronto: 1948), and David Worcester, *The Art of Satire* (Cambridge, Mass.: 1940).
3 Ingrid Strohschneider-Kohrs, *Romantische Ironie in Theorie und Gestaltung*, *Hermaea*, 6 (Tübingen: 1960).
4 Almost no studies relating the English Romantic poets to irony have been written, with a very few exceptions such as the article by N. F. Ford, 'Paradox and Irony in Shelley's Poetry', *Studies in Philology*, 57 (October 1960), 648–62, and P. Williams, 'Duty in Blake's Chimney Sweeper', *English Language Notes*, 12 (December 1974), 92–6.
5 Leavis's well-known criticism of Shelley's imagery as not concrete enough is a glaring example of the imposition of notions antithetical to the way in which the text is meant to function. Shelley's images are often not concrete precisely in order to inhibit the fancy so that the metaphorical import of the image can penetrate through the descriptive. This is Shelley's way of impressing his reader with the Coleridgean distinction between the idea and the image, and of freeing the reader from the enslavement of the eye and the senses generally in order to think and to imagine. See Leavis on Shelley in *Revaluation* (London: 1969).

6 D. C. Muecke, *The Compass of Irony* (London: 1969), pp. 159–215 especially.

7 *Ibid.*, p. 171 (Shelley), pp. 126, 190 (Wordsworth), pp. 6, 41, 81, 165, 186 (Byron), pp. 141, 190 (Blake). And see Muecke's shortened study *Irony* (London: 1970), pp. 2–3, for his inclusion only of Byron among ironists of the Romantic period.

8 *Ibid.*, p. 195.

9 As Tieck says: 'Die Ironie... ist vielmehr der tiefste Ernst, der zugleich mit wahrer Heiterkeit verbunden ist' ['Irony... is rather the most profound seriousness, which at the same time is bound up with high spirits.'] *Nachgelassene Schriften*, ed. R. Köpke, 2 vols. (Leipzig: 1855), ii, pp. 238–9.

10 *Friedrich Schlegel: Literary Notebooks, 1797–1801*, ed. Hans Eichner (Toronto: 1957), p. 62.

11 Köpke, *Nachgelassene Schriften*, ii, p. 238. On Hegel's and Kierkegaard's interpretations of the German Romantic Ironists see Strohschneider-Kohrs, *Romantische Ironie*, pp. 215–22, and for Tieck on Hegel see Köpke, *Nachgelassene Schriften*, ii, 238–9. See also Oskar Walzel, 'Methode? Ironie bei Friedrich Schlegel und bei Solger', *Helicon*, i (1938), 33–50, esp. 46–8. For Solger on the 'grobe-höhere' distinction see *ibid.*, 47, where he uses the terms 'extrafeine' und 'redliche ironie'.

12 Walzel, 'Methode?', 35. Cf. Köpke, *Nachgelassene Schriften*, ii, pp. 238–9, and see K. W. F. Solger, *Vorlesungen Über Aesthetik*, ed. K. W. L. Heyse (Leipzig: 1829), p. 245.

13 Strohschneider-Kohrs, *Romantische Ironie*, p. 131, from *Schriften*, 20 vols. (Berlin: 1828–46), vol. vi, pp. xxviii–xxix.

14 Søren Kierkegaard, *The Concept of Irony*, trans. L. M. Capell (London: 1966), p. 292. Kierkegaard also makes this distinction between high and common irony in his own terms – he contrasts irony as a figure of speech and irony as a standpoint, a leap of faith being required to achieve the latter (*ibid.*, p. 410 n35, and see p. 293). He distinguishes irony from satire and hypocrisy (*ibid.*, p. 273) and he discusses irony in the eminent sense as opposed to irony as an expression (*ibid.*, p. 271).

15 Kierkegaard's leap corresponds in some cases to my use of 'perspective flip', within the narrow limits of perceptual analysis.

16 See also Kierkegaard's statement on ironic orientation as essentially critical, in *The Concept of Irony*, p. 293.

17 Cleanth Brooks has shown the value of such a critical posture in his use of the metaphor of 'context' in discussing the meaning of irony. See e.g. *The Well Wrought Urn*, p. 171, and see also his 'Irony as a Principle of Structure', *Literary Opinion in America*, ed. Morton D. Zabel rev. ed. (New York: 1951), 729–41, esp. 738.

18 Strohschneider-Kohrs, *Romantische Ironie*, pp. 134, 136, and cf. p. 145.

19 Muecke, *Compass of Irony*, p. 3. See e.g. Solger, *Vorlesungen*, p. 170: 'Die Ironie ist keine einzelne, zufällige Stimmung des Künstlers, sondern der innerste Lebenskeim der ganzen Kunst.' ['Irony is no mere accidental mood of the artist, but the inner life of all art.']

20 Strohschneider-Kohrs, *Romantische Ironie*, 7.

21 See e.g. Muecke, *Compass of Irony*, p. 10.

22 Georges Palante, 'L'ironie: étude psychologique', *Revue Philosophique de la France et de l'étranger* (February 1906), 153; quoted in Muecke, *Compass of Irony*, p. 120.

23 F. Schlegel, *Literary Notebooks*, pp. 114, 84. Cf. Schlegel's statement in the *Marburger Handschriften*, Heft, I, 66, in Strohschneider-Kohrs, *Romantische Ironie*, pp. 22: 'Die Paradoxie ist für die Ironie die *conditio sine qua non*, die Seele, Quelle und Prinzip, was die Liberalität für den urbanen Witz.'
['Paradox is for irony the *conditio sine qua non*, the soul, source, and principle, what liberality is for the urbane.']

24 F. Schlegel, *Lyceums-Fragmente* 48, in *Prosaische Jugendschriften*, ed. J. Minor, 2 vols. (Vienna: 1882), II, p. 190. Kierkegaard also talks of irony as opposition in *The Concept of Irony*, p. 266, and says that 'irony asserts a relation of opposition in all its nuances' (*ibid.*, p. 272).

25 See e.g. F. Schlegel's *Lyceums-Fragmente* 47 and 54 and esp. 42, in *Prosaische Jugendschriften*, ed. Minor, II, pp. 189–91.

26 F. Schlegel, *Literary Notebooks*, p. 93. Cf. *Athenäums-Fragmente* 121, in *Prosaische Jugendschriften*, ed. Minor, II, p. 222, 'ein bis zur Ironie vollendeter Begriff, eine absolute Synthesis absoluter Antithesen, der stets sich selbst erzeugende Wechsel zwey streitender Gedanken'.
['a concept completed by irony, an absolute synthesis of absolute antitheses, the continual self-producing exchange of two conflicting thoughts'.]

27 Strohschneider-Kohrs, *Romantische Ironie*, p. 231, quoting Schelling's *System des transcendentalen Idealismus*.

28 *Ibid.*, p. 234.

29 *Ibid.*, p. 230, quoting Schiller.

30 Walzel, 'Methode?', 43.

31 Solger also uses the term 'Verschmelzung' in *Vorlesungen*, ed. K. W. L. Heyse (Leipzig: 1829), p. 187.

32 *Ibid.*, p. 123, and see pp. 127 and 129–31. See *CN*, III, 4384, 4388, and 4498 f139^{v} for Coleridge's response to F. Schlegel's definition of allegory as opposed to symbol.

33 Solger, *Vorlesungen*, p. 129.

34 Solger, *Erwin*, ed. Kurtz (Berlin: 1907), p. 199 and Solger, *Vorlesungen*, p. 187.

35 Solger, *Vorlesungen*, 123 and *Erwin* (Berlin: 1815), pt. II, 14.

36 Köpke, *Nachgelassene Schriften*, II, p. 238.

37 Kierkegaard's *Philosophical Fragments* is the most sustained, artistic representation of this duality reconciled. Cf. Solger, *Vorlesungen*, 241–2.

38 On 'Uebergang' see e.g. Solger, *Vorlesungen*, pp. 109, 221.

39 Cf. e.g. Coleridge on the finite permeated by the infinite, *CL*, VI, 897 to W. R. Hamilton, Apr. 1832.

40 See Solger, *Vorlesungen*, p. 247. Thus Coleridge, following Berkeley, repeatedly says, 'In God we live, and move, and have our being.' (Cf. Acts 17.28.)

41 *Ibid.*, pp. 67–8.

42 Strohschneider-Kohrs, *Romantische Ironie*, p. 235 and cf. pp. 225–6.

43 See *Prosaische Jugendschriften*, ed. Minor, II, 186–8, and see p. 198.

44 The importance of reflection acting synthetically with imagination is shown in Schlegel's emphasis upon the ultimate unity of philosophy and poetry; see e.g. *Lyceums-Fragmente* 115, in *Prosaische Jugendschriften*, ed. Minor, II, p. 200. For Solger on the 'Verstand' and imagination see *Vorlesungen*, pp. 220–21. Schlegel expresses the intimate relation of art and science and philosophy in *Athenäums-Fragmente* 255, in *Prosaische Jugendschriften*, ed. Minor, p. 246; 'Je mehr die Poesie Wissenschaft wird, je mehr wird sie auch Kunst. Soll die Poesie Kunst werden, soll der Künstler von seinen Mitteln und seinen Zwecken,

ihren Hindernissen und ihren Gegenständen gründliche Einsicht und Wissenschaft haben, so muss der Dichter über seine Kunst philosophieren.'

['The more poetry becomes science, the more it also becomes art. If poetry is to become art, if the artist is to have real insight and knowledge of his instruments, his goals, the hindrances to them, and their objects, then the poet must philosophize about his art.']

45 Strohschneider-Kohrs, *Romantische Ironie*, pp. 88 and 90.

46 *Lyceums-Fragmente* 37, in *Prosaische Jugendschriften*, ed. Minor, II, pp. 178–9.

47 *Lyceums-Fragmente* 37, in *Prosaische Jugendschriften*, ed. Minor, II, pp. 178–9. See Coleridge *Sh. C*, I, 194–8, on Shakespeare's judgment related to his genius, that is, his intention and his instinct. See below for discussion.

48 *Lyceums-Fragmente* 37, in *Prosaische Jugendschriften*, ed. Minor. See Coleridge's quote from Plotinus in *BL*, I, chap. xii, 167 for a similar insistence on submission to forces greater than his conscious control.

49 *Marburger Handschriften*, Heft, III, 52, in Strohschneider-Kohrs, *Romantische Ironie*, p. 32.

50 On thought and feeling see Tieck, *Lebenserinnerungen und Briefwechsel*, ed. F. Raumer, 2 vols. (Leipzig: 1861), II, p. 291. Muecke and Strohschneider-Kohrs both make the error of seeing irony as pre-eminently intellectual. See Muecke, *Compass of Irony*, pp. 29 and 220, and see Strohschneider-Kohrs, *Romantische Ironie*, p. 226, who sets 'Empfindung' against 'Besonnenheit' and opts for the latter as the character of irony. It ought to be the synthesis of the two. How else could one talk about the union of philosophy and art? See Kierkegaard, *The Concept of Irony*, p. 407, n15. See also Walzel, 'Methode?', pp. 36–7, and Solger on 'Begeisterung', *Vorlesungen*, p. 242, and p. 200 on 'Empfindung'.

51 See e.g. Schlegel's statement in *Prosaische Jugendschriften*, ed. Minor, I, p. 154: 'Auch der modernen Poesie würde Ihre Individualität unbenommen bleiben, wenn sie nur das Griechische Geheimnis entdeckt hätte, im Individuellen objecktiv zu seyn'.

['For modern poetry her individuality would have remained free, if she had only discovered the Greek secret, to be objective through the individual.']

This echoes very closely Coleridge's description of Shakespeare's genius of involuting the universal in the particular. The fact that this also constitutes the 'Greek secret' suggests why Friedrich Schlegel came to be dissatisfied with his opposition between classical and modern art, and finally pronounced that irony was not the characteristic of Greek literature, but of all great art.

52 Walzel, 'Methode?' 43 and cf. Strohschneider-Kohrs, *Romantische Ironie*, pp. 23–4 and 28–9.

53 See Coleridge's appreciation of Fichte in *BL*, I, 101–2.

54 See e.g. *CL*, IV, 898–900n.

55 *Sh. C*, I, 197–8, and *BL*, II, 'On Poesy or Art', 258. Cf. *CN*, III, 4397, f51–2.

56 *Coleridge on Shakespeare*, ed. R. A. Foakes (London: 1971), p. 82. For Tieck on the integration of thought and feeling see above note 50.

57 This relation of spectator to work of art was touched upon in the German observations on the technique of 'Illusionsstörung', by means of which the boundary between art and reality was radically threatened, in order that the spectator be awakened to his role in the drama. On 'Illusionsstörung', see e.g. Strohschneider-Kohrs, *Romantische Ironie*, pp. 153–4, for an incomplete understanding of the role of this technique: she fails to see it in relation to the spectator, and in fact this error is the weakness which underlies the entire work

and leads to her misapprehension of Jean Paul and others. As an example of the practical application of 'Illusionsstörung', Tieck's 'Gestiefelter Kater' is the obvious case. We might point to this technique of the ironist as the one most frequently employed by Coleridge, in his constant asides, both direct and indirect, to the reader, as we hope to show.

Eichendorff also makes use of the technique, and one might maintain that Friedrich Schlegel's *Lucinde*, in its style and form, is a gesture at 'illusionsstörung'. It is an ancient technique, employed e.g. in Sanscrit drama of the fifth to seventh centuries AD. See Bhasa's *Rama's Later History* for a fine example. And see below page 159 and note 5.

58 Solger, *Nachgelassene Schriften und Briefwechsel*, ed. L. Tieck and F. Raumer, 2 vols. (Leipzig: 1826), I, p. 117. And see *Tieck and Solger*, ed. Percy Matenko (New York and Berlin: 1933), p. 342.

59 Solger, *Vorlesungen*, pp. 505, and see Matenko, *Tieck and Solger*, p. 344.

60 Cf. Donald Sultana, *Coleridge in Malta and Italy* (Oxford: 1969), 387: 'As a close friend of Schelling [Tieck] was subsequently represented by Coleridge as exulting in the "identity" of Schelling's system of philosophy with that of Jacob Boehme, whose mysticism had earlier influenced Coleridge', and Ludwig Tieck; see below.

61 Solger, *Nachgelassene Schriften*, I, p. 17, and on mysticism see Matenko, *Tieck and Solger*, p. 486.

62 Matenko, *Tieck and Solger*, p. 66, and see 362–3.

63 Solger, *Vorlesungen*, I, pp. 144–5 and 157, and Matenko, *Tieck and Solger*, p. 39.

64 *Ibid.*, I, pp. 131–2 and 134.

65 Solger, *Vorlesungen*, p. 506.

66 *Ibid.*, pp. 506–7.

67 *Ibid.*, pp. 52–6.

68 *Ibid.*, pp. 59–65.

69 Josef Heller, *Solgers Philosophie der ironischen Dialektik* (Berlin: 1928), pp. 196–9.

70 Solger, *Vorlesungen*, pp. 111–16, and Solger, *Nachgelassene Schriften*, I, p. 360.

71 Solger, *Vorlesungen*, pp. 125–7.

72 *LS (CC)*, 30 and see note.

73 Solger, *Vorlesungen*, p. 127.

74 Cf. Thomas Mann, *The Transposed Heads*, trans. Lowe-Porter (New York: 1959), pp. 14–15: 'For there is not only the truth and knowledge of the understanding, but also the insight of the human heart, which sees as in an allegory and knows how to read the handwriting of all phenomena, not only in its first and simple sense, but also in its second and higher one, using it as means whereby to look through at the pure and spiritual. How will you arrive at a perception of peace, and feel the joy of cessation from conflict, unless you have a Maya-image to give you a hold on it – though in itself a Maya-image is by no means peace and joy! It is granted and vouchsafed to man to make actuality serve him to see the true by [*sic*]; language has coined the word "poetry" to express this boon'.

75 Solger, *Erwin* (Berlin: 1907), p. 199; Solger, *Vorlesungen*, pp. 186–7.

76 Solger, *Vorlesungen*, p. 205.

77 *Ibid.*, pp. 187–95.

78 See *Ibid.*, pp. 202–10.

79 *Ibid.*, pp. 242–5.

80 *Ibid.*, pp. 220–5.
81 *Ibid.*, pp. 224–5, 236.
82 *Ibid.*, p. 247.
83 See for example *BL* ii, 19 and *CL*, ii, 810 to William Sotheby, July 13 1802: 'You will agree with me that a great poet must be, implicité if not explicité, a profound metaphysician'.
84 Solger, *Nachgelassene Schriften*, i, pp. 381–2.
85 Matenko, *Tieck and Solger*, p. 225.
86 *Ibid.*, 95. See also Tieck's rejection of Hegel's systematizing preoccupations (Köpke, *Nachgelassene Schriften*, ii, 70) and his criticism of Friedrich Schlegel with the Coleridgean comment on the tendency of the mind to seek wisdom in superstition instead of sensing the divine in the actual world (Matenko, *Tieck and Solger*, 73).
87 Matenko, *Tieck and Solger*, p. 312.
88 Coleridge's personal and intellectual relation with Tieck is discussed in my article 'Coleridge's Friendship with Ludwig Tieck', in *Biographical and Critical Essays on Coleridge*, ed. Donald Sultana (New York: 1980).
89 See e.g., Matenko, *Tieck and Solger* and Walzel, 'Methode?', pp. 37–41, on A. W. Schlegel's weakened version.
90 Schlegel, *Prosaische Jugendschriften*, ed. Minor, ii, p. 426.
91 *Ibid.*, ii, p. 200.
92 *CL*, v, 190–1, Coleridge criticizing Kleist's studied 'lack of sentimentality', that is, his detachment and irony.
93 Schlegel, *Prosaische Jugendschriften*, ed. Minor, ii, p. 177.
94 *Ibid.*, ii, pp. 368–73.
95 *Ibid.*, ii, p. 220.

5. METAPHOR: PROCESS AND METHOD IN 'BIOGRAPHIA' I

1 General accounts of the reader phenomenon occur in Stanley E. Fish, *Self Consuming Artifacts* (Berkeley: 1972), and for a more recent account see Wolfgang Iser, *The Implied Reader* (Baltimore: 1974).
2 See above chapter four for a discussion of the genre of the *Biographia* as fulfilling Friedrich Schlegel's description of what a 'modern' work of literature ought to be.
3 For the account of Coleridge's early intentions to write his metaphysics as a Life, see above chapter one. This intention may be another example of his recognition of the importance of unifying thought and feeling (philosophy and life) through a self-criticism.
4 Coleridge's use of Schelling has already been briefly mentioned in the final section of chapter two. A considerable portion of the several pages in the *Biographia* borrowed from Schelling are less metaphorical in function than discursive. Rosemary Ashton, in *The German Idea* (Cambridge: 1980) reveals the almost fanatical distaste in Coleridge's time for anything German. This may be a primary reason why Coleridge disguised Schelling as a 'continental philosopher'. He hoped to gain a fairer hearing for the ideas presented by obscuring their origins, and by setting them, merely as of continental origin, amongst the more English background of his own thought and conversational style. Until one is familiar with the reviews of the time, it is impossible to appreciate the fanaticism of this hatred of German thought. When considering the charge of plagiarism, it

would be well to keep in mind this aspect of the times as a factor in Coleridge's secretiveness about his sources. He was not trying very hard to hide his sources from anyone open-minded enough and serious enough to glance at the first page of Schelling's most famous work, *System des transcendentalen Idealismus*, from which he borrowed an extensive passage of several sentences. His obfuscations seem more designed to blind the ignorant and not very well-read detractors of German literature. Thus he mentions Schelling for the sake of the interested reader, but just not in precise connection with his ideas, in order to confuse and thwart the detractors.

5 *BL*, I, 85–6.
6 On 'dead metaphors' see the first few paragraphs of Shelley's 'Defence of Poetry'. Coleridge refers to the degeneration of language in *CN*, I, 1835 and III, 3973.
7 *BL*, I, 167. Note that the philological basis of the passage is ψυχή, meaning butterfly, soul, or psyche.
8 *BL*, I, 167.
9 *BL*, I, 167.
10 Throughout the early chapters of the *Biographia* and *The Friend* Coleridge bares the complex of fear and arrogance that such uncertainty and doubt breeds. It should be noted that these theses are borrowings from Schelling, a fact which has been used as the 'explanation' for their obscurity. It is more likely that they are obscure because they direct the reader's mind to a level of intellectual self-investigation, thinking about thinking, to which he is unaccustomed, and which is one of the most difficult of activities. Cf. *The Friend* (*CC*), I, 106: 'reserve the deep feelings...to those obscure ideas...which their very sublimity renders indefinite'. These borrowings from Schelling function like those discussed above in the final section of chapter two, significant not as containing dogma or content but in so far as they are effective as metaphoric situations. See note 26 below. For further discussion of the ten theses, see Jackson, *Method and Imagination*, pp. 68–71.
11 This sort of 'identification process' is typical of the Romantic style, and we can see it operating dramatically in a poem such as Blake's 'Lamb', where Christ, child, and lamb are merely different aspects of being.
12 See the note on the bull, *BL*, I, 52–3. And see Richard Mallette, 'Narrative Technique and Structure in the *Biographia Literaria*', *Modern Language Review* 70 (Jan. 1975), 32–40, for an emphasis on the importance of the relation between reader and author. He says: 'Coleridge's attitude towards his audience nevertheless remains the determining factor in his choice of narrative technique' (p. 40).
13 Cf. *BL*, I, 153: 'For it is one contradistinction of genius from talent, that its predominant end is always comprized in the means; and this is one of the many points, which establish an analogy between genius and virtue...I would advise every scholar, who feels the genial power working within him, so far to make a division between the two [genius and talent].' 'Genial' here corresponds to the German usage.
14 *BL*, I, 198.
15 *BL*, I, 196. There are several indications in the *Biographia* that Coleridge regarded it as his own account of the growth of a poet's mind. This passage is one such hint; another occurs on page 129, lines 3–30.
16 *BL*, I, 200.
17 *BL*, I, 200. The idea of a method of metaphor constructed by means of a constant analogy of reading to the labour of composition, which focuses the 'fragments'

and supports the 'gaps' in the text, is an effort to go beyond either the mosaic method of Thomas McFarland in *Coleridge and the Pantheist Tradition* (Oxford: 1969) or the 'marginal method' of J. C. Christensen in his 'Coleridge's Marginal Method in the *Biographia Literaria*', *Publications of the Modern Language Association* 92 (Oct. 1977). Neither seems to see the use of sources as primarily either metaphorical or as functioning as 'reader recipes'. Christensen essentially denies that there is any method; to him the *Biographia* seems to be merely a random collection of marginalia to the authors discussed.

18 *Friend (CC)*, I, 103.

19 *Friend (CC)*, I, 106. The source of the distinction made here between ideas, concepts, and images is more properly Platonic than Kantian. Indeed, the exhortation to expect clarity only for certain types of conceptions is patently Aristotelian.

20 Once again the connection between Coleridge's anti-materialist philosophy and the designs of his works of art emerges.

21 *BL*, I, 90.

22 Shelley, 'Mont Blanc', *The Complete Poetical Works of Percy Bysshe Shelley*, ed. N. Rogers (Oxford: 1975), II, p. 80, lines 139–44.

23 See M. G. Cooke, 'Quisque Sui Faber: Coleridge in the *Biographia Literaria*', *Philological Quarterly* 50 (1971), 208–29, on the role of the reader and his obligation to participate.

24 *BL*, I, 173.

25 *BL*, I, 198.

26 *BL*, II, 127–8. This passage is also important as a demonstration of Coleridge's use of sources: the sources are used not for the sake of content or dogma, but for their role in his method of producing metaphoric situations. See above chapter two on Schelling and below, chapter six for further examples.

27 The resistance to this type of 'reader response' interpretation stems from the abhorrence of subjectivism. But as I have pointed out above in chapter two, this can never be the result either of Coleridge's position or of the proper reader-response position. The preoccupation of self, as selfhood, becomes inversely proportional to self-consciousness. The feelings of the man of genius 'have been habitually associated with thoughts and images, to the number, clearness, and vivacity of which the sensation of *self* is in an inverse proportion'. The conquering of selfhood is an outcome of the challenge to unthinking authority, and must be, for 'the lust of rule is grounded in this very craving for selfness', but so is the lust to be ruled. In defying outside authority, we dare not make the mistake that might seem to be a consequence, namely raising the selfhood to the position of ultimate authority. Nor is the only kind of knowledge left to us a purely subjective kind; see *The Friend (CC)*, I, 97: 'For that must appear to each man to be his reason which produces in him the highest sense of certainty: and yet it is not reason, except as far as it is of *universal validity and obligatory on all mankind*' (my italics).

28 *BL*, I, 63.

29 *BL*, I, 60.

30 *BL*, I, 133.

31 *BL*, I, 178.

32 *BL*, I, 173–4.

33 *Friend (CC)*, I, 16.

34 *BL*, I, 106–7. Cooke, 'Quisque Sui Faber', 215 also points out the relation of the

reader's role to Coleridge's comments on 'genial criticism': 'The standard of "genial" criticism that is a motif in the *Biographia* puts a positive obligation on the reader...rendered explicit and formidable in Coleridge's "golden rule" [on understanding an author's ignorance]'.

35 *BL*, I, 73–4.

36 *BL*, I, 166, and see 164–5.

37 Coleridge quotes Hooker on his readership: Hooker 'saw nevertheless occasion to anticipate and guard against "complaints of obscurity" as often as he was about to trace his subject "to the highest wellspring and fountain". Which, (continues he) "because men are not accustomed to, the pains we take are more needful a great deal, than acceptable; and the matters we handle, seem by reason of new-ness (till the mind grow better acquainted with them) dark and intricate".' *BL*, I, 64–5.

38 Cf. the coincidence in J. E. Irby's introduction to J. L. Borges's *Other Inquisitions* (New York: 1968), p. xv:

> The activation of thought, shared by author and reader, miraculously effected over fatal distance and time by works whose sense alters and yet lives on, is the real secret promise of the infinite dominion of mind, not its images or finalities, which are expendable. This is the method of Borges' essays, the process both examined and enacted in them...Hence the essay on Whitman, hence the final epigraph from the seventeenth-century German mystic Angelus Silesius:

> > Freund, es ist auch genug. Im Fall du mehr
> > willst lesen,/So geh und werde selbst die
> > Schrift und selbst das Wesen.

> > [Friend, it is surely enough. If you wish
> > to read further,/Then go and become yourself
> > the Writing and the Being.]

Coleridge and Borges share a great deal more than simply a common interest in German mysticism. The more this similarity in method and subject as well as the attitude to art and to readership is understood, the better Coleridge's method will be appreciated.

39 See note 15 above.

40 Borges expounds upon this theme throughout his essays in *Other Inquisitions*. See especially 'The Flower of Coleridge' and 'The Dream of Coleridge'. Shelley speaks of it in 'A Defence of Poetry', not only in the sense that all men are poets and that language is poetry, but in the sense that Coleridge refers to frequently in the *Statesman's Manual*, of the one activity of imagination ('Reason' for Coleridge) as the essence of human mental life.

41 *BL*, I, 168. See also *BL*, I, 65, 80, 100, 162–3, 164, and 200. See also note 37 above.

42 *BL*, I, 169–70. See also pages 109, and 148.

43 *BL*, I, 199.

44 *BL*, I, 162, and see 160–1. See also pages 99, 106–7, 166–7, and 200.

45 Coleridge achieved what Friedrich Schlegel rhapsodized about as one of the central purposes of the Romantic poet, the overthrowing of the traditional boundaries of genre, with the *Biographia* as the most sustained instance of a hybrid, synthetic achievement. See above chapter four. See Jackson, *Method and*

Imagination, pp. 61–73 on the structure of the *Biographia* and Coleridge's synthetic method.

46 *BL*, 1, 200. Again the use of the 'fragment' form connects Coleridge with the Schlegelian tradition. See e.g. the *Athenäums-Fragmente*, *Lyceums-Fragmente*, in Schlegel, *Prosaische Jugendschriften*, ed. Minor.

47 *BL*, 1, 52–3.

48 *BL*, 1, 199.

49 As was mentioned before, one of the most important emblematic passages of the *Biographia* is located in a note, another detail pointing to thoroughness of contemplation and reading required. Coleridge also has the curious habit of placing his asterisks in the middle of a phrase or a sentence and thus breaking up the unity of a thought, so that the reader must reread the sentence after the note, and apply the note's relation to it.

50 For the importance of this I/Me or subject/object distinction see Coleridge's article 'On the Philosophic Import of the Words OBJECT and SUBJECT', *Blackwood's Magazine*, 10 (Oct. 1821), 247–50.

51 *BL*, 1, 60. Cf. Shelley's 'A Defence of Poetry', *Selected Poetry and Prose of Percy Bysshe Shelley*, ed. Carlos Baker (New York: 1951), pp. 501–2: '[Poetry] awakens and enlarges the mind itself by rendering it the receptacle of a thousand unapprehended combinations of thought. Poetry lifts the veil from the hidden beauty of the world, and makes familiar objects be as if they were not familiar...' And see *ibid.*, 519: '[Poetry] purges from our inward sight the film of familiarity which obscures from us the wonder of our being... It creates anew the universe, after it has been annihilated in our minds by the recurrence of impressions blunted by reiteration.'

52 *BL*, 1, 62. According to Peter Hoheisel, Coleridge also admired Shakespeare 'on principle'; he sees the fragments of criticism as instances illuminating certain general principles. See 'Coleridge on Shakespeare: Method amid the Rhetoric', *Studies in Romanticism*, 13 (Winter 1974), 15–24, where he explains that Coleridge's 'critical technique is to search for the controlling idea which both transcends the play and is incarnated in it' (p. 23).

53 *BL*, 1, 9.

54 *BL*, 1, 21–2n.

55 J. S. Mill, 'Coleridge', *Mill on Bentham and Coleridge*, ed. F. R. Leavis (London: 1950), 103ff.

56 *BL*, 1, 23–4.

57 *BL*, 1, 26.

58 *BL*, 1, 30. This important distinction seems to have been missed by J. C. Christensen, in his misdirected article, 'The Genius in the *Biographia Literaria*', *Studies in Romanticism*, 17 (Winter: 1978), 215–31, an unfortunate example of the 'hypopœēsis' which it ascribes to Coleridge. See *The Friend*, 1, 478n, for the distinction between hypothesis and hypopœēsis, or supposition and subfiction.

59 See e.g. *BL*, 1, 31. A quick perusal of a list of his works will dispel any charge of laziness. Furthermore, when Coleridge undertook to publish *The Friend*, he was not only its author, but did literally everything up to the actual printing, and was his own collector, distributor, bookkeeper, etc.

60 *BL*, 1, 32.

61 *BL*, 1, 42, Coleridge describing Southey's *Cid*.

62 *BL*, 1, 35.

63 *BL*, 1, 39.

64 *BL*, I, 37.

65 *BL*, I, 57.

66 *BL*, I, 59–60.

67 *BL*, I, 61.

68 *BL*. I, 98. This is another example of a metaphor capping a discursive argument. Coleridge's philosophy comes closest to the atraditional reading of Plato, which is suggested though not elaborated in Havelock's *Preface to Plato*, and which is usually branded mysticism.

69 Cf. the passage from 'On the Philosophic Import of the Words OBJECT and SUBJECT', *Blackwood's Magazine*, 10 (Oct. 1821), 247–50: 'The immediate *object* of the mind is always and exclusively the *workings* or *makings* above stated and distinguished into two kinds...Outness is but the feeling of otherness (alterity), rendered intuitive, or alterity visually represented.' And further: 'Since both then, the feelings of my own existence and the feeling of the existence of things without, are but this sense of an acting and working – it is clear that to exist is the same as to act or work...'

6. PROCESSES AND METHODS IN 'BIOGRAPHIA' II

1 Cf. Coleridge's comment on dialectic in *CN*, III, 4418, f13, Aug. 1818: 'Dialectic, or the evolution of Truth by means of logical Contradictions'. Dialectic is at the heart of the dynamic philosophy or reconciliation of opposites.

2 Cf. Hegel: The reading mind must 'resolve, in science, not to deliver itself over to the thoughts of others on their mere authority, but to examine everything for itself, and only follow its own conviction, or, still better, to produce everything itself and hold only its own act for true'. *Phenomenology of Mind*, trans. J. B. Baillie (London: 1931), p. 136. Coleridge's unsympathetic reading of Hegel's *Wissenschaft der Logik* (the only work of Hegel's which Coleridge read) reflected in the marginal comments is strangely at odds with the many points of method and self-conscious composition which they both shared. Hegel's introduction to his *Lectures on the History of Philosophy*, trans. E. S. Haldane (London: 1892–6) is particularly revealing of their shared views.

3 On distinctity see e.g. *CN*, II, 2406, Jan. 1805 and *CL*, VI, 897 to W. R. Hamilton, Apr. 1832, and 961 to Green, Sept. 1833.

4 *BL*, II, 216.

5 The closeness of Shelley's imagination/reason distinction and Coleridge's reason/ understanding is remarkable in the following passage from the 'Defence of Poetry', *Shelley*, ed. Baker, p. 494: 'According to one mode of regarding those two classes of mental action, which are called reason and imagination, the former may be considered as mind contemplating the relations borne by one thought to another however produced; and the latter, as mind acting upon those thoughts so as to colour them with its own light, and composing from them, as from elements, other thoughts, each containing within itself the principle of its own integrity. The one is the τὸ ποιεῖν, or the principle of synthesis, and has for its objects those forms which are common to universal nature and existence itself; the other is the τὸ λογιζειν, or principle of analysis, and its action regards the relations of things, simply as relations; considering thoughts, not in their integral unity, but as the algebraical representations which conduct to certain general results. Reason is the enumeration of quantities already known; imagination is

the perception of the value of those quantities, both separately and as a whole. Reason respects the differences, and imagination the similitudes of things. Reason is to the imagination as the instrument to the agent, as the body to the spirit, as the shadow to the substance'. The closeness of Shelley's theories of art and language to Coleridge's are further suggested by Shelley's enthusiastic response to the *Biographia*, which he had read by Dec. 1817. For this source, and numerous other references to flattering remarks about Coleridge, see J. B. Beer, *Coleridge the Visionary* (London and New York: 1959), 344 n42.

6 *BL*, II, 6 (these are two distinct statements).

7 *BL*, II, 98. Cf. *CN*, III, 3973, f27, Oct. 1810, 4237, f41, Oct. 1814, and 4309, esp. f61. Coleridge says in the first entry: 'But we are too social – we become in a sort Idolators – for the means, we are obliged to use to excite notions of Truth in the minds of others or our own, we by witchcraft of slothful association, impose on ourselves for the Truths themselves – Our intellectual Bank stops payment – & we pass an act by acclamation that hereafter the Paper-Promises shall be the Gold & Silver itself – and ridicule a man for a dreamer, and reviver of antiquated Dreams, who believes that Gold & Silver exist – . This may do as well in the *market* – but O! for the universal, for the man himself, the *difference is woeful* – .'

8 *BL*, II, 121. Cf. *AR*, aphorism 1, and *CN*, III, 4016, 1810:
> Man of genius places things *in a new light* – this trivial phrase better expresses the appropriate effects of Genius than Pope's celebrated Distich –
>> What oft was thought but ne'er so well exprest –
> It has been *thought* DISTINCTLY, but only possessed, as it were, unpacked & unsorted – the poet not only *displays* what tho' often seen in its unfolded mass had never been opened out, but he likewise adds something, namely, Lights & Relations.

9 *BL*, II, 16.

10 *BL*, II, chap. xxiv, 216. *Cf. BL*, I, chap. xii, 180–2. This 'act of becoming' is central to Coleridge's philosophy. He equates Faith with ,Act in *LS* (*CC*), 90, *CL*, v, 48, with Prayer in *LS* (*CC*), 55n, God as Act in *CL*, II, 1195–6, *LS* (*CC*), 18, 48, with Will in *AR*, 76, 233n, and substitutes the Thing for the Act in *CL*, IV, 792, which is related to all his reflections upon the relation of Thing to Thought, for thought is also Act. Cf. *CN*, I, 923 on Hartley thinking. Note *CN*, II, 2342, Dec. 1804: 'To be and to act, two in Intellect, (that mother of orderly multitude, & half Sister of Wisdom & Madness) but one in essence = to rest and to move = ▢ and a ◯! and out of the infinite combinations of these, from the more and the less now of one now of the other all pleasing figures arise'.

11 On the duty of communicating aright see e.g. *The Friend* (*CC*), I, 9, 21, 48–9, and *P Lects.*, lect. iv, 164.

12 *CL*, IV, 768 to C. A. Tulk, Sept. 1817.

13 *BL*, II, 120–1. Coleridge does not illustrate this explanation with his own metaphor; he borrows Plato's pre-existence metaphor.

14 On esotericism see *P Lects.*, 159, 160, 164–5 and 426. See also *CN*, III, 3617, 1809, *Friend* (*CC*), I, 447 and 461 and *CN*, III, 4309, f61, Spring 1816: 'I have dwelt on this for more reasons than one – first, because a remark that seems at first sight the same – namely – that every thing clearly perceived may be conveyed in simple common language without thinking on – to whom? is the disease of the age. – an arrogant pusillanimity – a hatred of all information that cannot be obtained without thinking...The sum therefore is this: – The conveyal of Knowledge by Words is in direct proportion to the stores and

faculties of Observation (internal or external) of the person, who hears or reads them.'

15 *BL*, II, chap. xvii, 40. Keats uses a similar metaphor of the harvest for imaginative activity and its fruits, in 'La Belle Dame sans Merci', as well as in 'Ode to Autumn'.

16 Cf. *BL*, II, chap. xviii, 44, and *P Lects.*, lect. ii, 102: 'It was amongst the great Pythagorean symbols so to convey truth in part as that it might make the mind susceptible hereafter of another portion. To tell truth, but so at the same time to convey it as to prepare the mind for greater truths, was the grand maxim of what may be called moral politics.' And on the true object of reflection cf. *CN*, III, 3965, Jul. 1810: 'Wordsworth's enemies – especially that Mistress Bare and Bald – the reason – that his works make them restless by forcing them in on their own worthless Selves – and they recoil from their Heart, or rather from the place where the Heart ought to be, with a true *Horror Vacui*. – ' See also *CN*, III, 3946, June–Jul. 1810.

17 *BL*, II, chap. xvii, 32. The metaphor of 'contraction and hardening' is very appropriate for the closing up of the faculties into narrow chinks from which we view the world in 'ordinary consciousness'. Note the metaphor borrowed from Schelling in *BL*, I, chap. xiii, 195–6 on the two opposite forces of expansion and contraction. Blake uses the image throughout his prophetic books; see e.g. *The First Book of Urizen*, ch. 2, pt. 1: 'The will of the Immortal expanded/Or contracted his all flexible senses;/'.

18 Cf. *BL*, II, 64 and 85.

19 *BL*, II, 102. Coleridge is following Aristotle and Sidney (in *The Defence of Poetry*, ed. Van Dorsten, pp. 66–7), in his criticism of unreflective history in contradistinction from poetry. Coleridge uses personification here, which Blake considers to be the primary activity of imagination. The analogical basis of most of the metaphors discussed here functions like personification: the reader is constantly required to see himself in the objects or persons discussed. Thus, he is the traveller, for example, in the quotation above.

20 *BL*, II, 63.

21 *BL*, II, 65. Ludwig Tieck had made a similar claim for the laws of imagination. See Tieck's *Nachgelassene Schriften*, II, 132. And see above chapter four.

22 Cf. *BL*, II, 17 and 124.

23 *BL*, I, 199.

24 Cf. *Friend* (*CC*), I, 12–13, Coleridge ironically complaining: 'to fill up pleasantly the brief intervals of fashionable pleasures, and above all to charm away the dusky Gnome of Ennui, is the chief appropriate business of the Poet and – the *Novelist*!'

25 *BL*, II, 124.

26 Such as, e.g. 'The White Doe', *BL*, II, 127ff.

27 *BL*, II, 14.

28 *BL*, II, 12.

29 See *CN*, III, 3935, June–Jul. 1810 for an indirect description of the method of the *Biographia*: 'One excellence of the Doctrine of Plato, or of the Plotino-platonic Philosophy, is that it never suffers, much less causes or even occasions, its Disciples to forget themselves, lost and scattered in sensible Objects disjoined or *as* disjoined from themselves. It is impossible to understand the Elements of this Philosophy without an appeal, at every step & round of the Ladder, to the fact within, to the mind's Consciousness – and in addition to this, instead of lulling

the Soul into an indolence of mere attention (for a comparative *Indolence* it is, even as, relatively to mere passive amusement (a musâ) or positively passive affections of Sense & Sensation, it is likewise a comparative *Effort*) but rouses it to acts and energies of creative Thought, & Recognition – of conscious re-production of states of Being...no man...can read the many extracts... without an ahndung [*sic*], an inward omening, of a system congruous with his nature, & thence attracting it – /The boast therefore of the modern Philosophy is to me a decisive proof of its being an ₁Anti-philosophy...that it calls the mere understanding into exertion without exciting or wakening any interest, any tremulous feeling of the heart, as if it heard or began to *glimpse* something which had once belonged to it...'

30 See e.g. I. A. Richards, *Coleridge on Imagination* (London: 1934), p. 98: 'No description of imagination is of any use to those who do not otherwise sometimes know this way – as poets; or know when they are in it, as readers.' And note Coleridge's anticipation of his audience's response in *CN*, III, 3948, June–Jul. 1810. The intensity of his bitterness may be due in part to the response to *The Friend*, which had just been forced to cease publication. The section which most interests us here is the last few impassioned lines: 'I tell you, you are ignorant – & yet eager & always ready to judge & decide – ...Wretches! but do you not put the plain question to your own Conscience – or if you have none to your Memory & Consciousness – Is it, or is it not, true, that I am ignorant – that I have not studied this subject as it alone can be studied, namely, by steady meditation on the *facts* vitally present & distinctly felt?'

31 Cf. *AR*, 9 and 17 on meditation: 'Thy law is exceeding *broad* – that is, compre-hensive, pregnant, containing far more than the apparent import of the words on a first persual [*sic*]. It is my *meditation* all the day.'

32 *BL*, II, 18.

33 *BL*, II, Satyrane's Letters, 161. The simile reminds the reader of the special relationship between author and reader which constituted for Coleridge a friendship if realized.

34 *BL*, II, 11, and cf. *BL*, I, 86.

35 The coincidence of thought and feeling is one of the central formulations of intuitive and imaginative experience. See e.g. *CN*, III, 3362, 3246, 3287, and *CL*, II, 1034. Coleridge frequently speaks of the imagination as the power which supplies the passion, the unifying feeling which pervades the thought and gives it a ground in experience. This unity of thought and feeling is expressed by several metaphors recurring throughout Coleridge's writings, e.g., in his fondness for the union of head and heart, as in *CL*, II, 864, 1190, VI, 842 and *AR*, 88 and 167; in the image of the sun as the symbol of light and warmth, as in *CN*, III, 3379, and of course in his insistence on the ultimate union between philosophy and religion, as in *CN*, II, 2445, *CN*, III, 3813 and *P Lects.*, lect. xiii, 390.

36 *BL*, II, 19.

37 *BL*, II, 13, extract from 'Nosce teipsum' ('know thyself'), by Sir John Davies. Cf. the Milton passage prefixed to chapter thirteen of *BL*, I.

38 For Coleridge this relationship in the form of geniality was necessary to a thorough participation in his works. See above note 33.

39 Most of the Romantics recognized the importance of this 'flip of perspective' and the resulting identification which is the means of achieving self-conscious-ness. Blake uses it extensively in the *Songs*, as e.g. in 'The Lamb' and 'Infant Joy'. Keats comments upon his poem 'The Thrush' obliquely when he says:

'The setting sun will always set me to rights – or if a Sparrow come before my Window I take part in its existence and pick about the Gravel.' Letter to Benjamin Bailey, 22 Nov. 1817. 'Ode to a Nightingale' is a dramatization of the process of identification made possible by imagination, in this case the result being the transcendence of personal ego, and hence mortality. For Keats and Shelley participation in visionary poesis was a victory over death.

40 *BL*, II, 76. In citing 'Love Unknown' Coleridge remarks a few pages earlier (p. 73) that he has chosen the poem both to illustrate a specific point of style and also for 'the present purpose'. We may conjecture that this enigmatic present purpose is the awakening of the imaginative participation which would constitute a 'treatise on the nature and genesis of imagination', by means of jolting the reader into a self-consciousness about his reading as a creative, thinking, interpreting activity.

41 *LS (CC)*, 30.

42 Contrast Shawcross's views in his 'Supplementary Note' to the *BL*, I, xciii–v. As Professor Bate points out in *Coleridge* (London: 1969), 175, Wordsworth was not very happy about Coleridge's chapters on him in the *Biographia*.

43 Cf. Coleridge on 'book-learning' in *CL*, II, 962 to Southey, 7 Aug. 1803: 'I have observed, that great works are now a days bought – not for curiosity, or the amor proprius – but under the notion that they contain all the *knowlege* [*sic*] a man may ever want/and if he has it on his *Shelf*, why there it is, as snug as if it were in his *Brain*. This has carried off the Encyclopaedia.' For his views on the limitations of words and language see e.g. *LS (CC)*, 25 and 46 and *AR*, 87–8. The importance of the dialogue as a form of thinking is suggested by Plato's style of writing in which he mirrors the reader's relation to him as author in the relation of his characters to Socrates.

44 *BL*, II, 97.

45 See e.g. *BL*, II, 106, and *AR*, 2–3. In the *Songs*, Blake frequently uses the tree as a metaphor of mind.

46 *BL*, II, 65.

47 The 'spring' was another image of imaginative knowledge, particularly because of its remarkable double meaning as a fountain and a mechanical device. See e.g. *LS (CC)*, 20, 31, 91, *CN*, I, 980, *CN*, III, 3320, 4291, and various other references as in *Friend (CC)*, I, 65 and 432.

48 On the organic as opposed to the mechanical see e.g. *P Lects.*, lect. v, 175, *CN*, II, 2444, III, 4251, and *CL*, V, 47. Coleridge's frequent use of 'germ' is another organic image. See e.g. *LS (CC)*, 49, 51, etc. See further *LS (CC)*, 71–2 and note, and 89.

49 On arrangement distinguished from method see *Friend (CC)*, I, 457, and see *CN*, I, 531, Nov. 1799 and *CN*, III, 4313, Apr. 1816.

50 *BL*, II, 102.

51 Cf. *AR*, 2–3 on the tree as an image of the interrelatedness of the various branches of knowledge.

52 See for example *Friend (CC)*, I, 449 on 'a whole in every part'.

53 For a similar effect see Wordsworth's 'Yew-Trees' quoted in *BL*, II, 124–5.

54 See the introduction to J. L. Borges's *Labyrinths* (New York: 1962), p. xvi, for some fascinating accounts of Borges's work which seems to describe him as a modern Coleridge in method and style: 'Borges is skeptical as few have ever been about the ultimate value of mere ideas and mere literature. But he has striven to turn this skepticism into an ironic method, to make of disbelief an aesthetic

system, in which what matters most is not ideas as such, but their resonances and suggestions, the drama of their possibilities and impossibilities, the immobile and lasting quintessence of ideas as it is distilled at the dead center of their warring contradictions.' Or equally applicable: 'Any great and lasting book must be ambiguous, Borges says; it is a mirror that makes the reader's features known' (*ibid.*, p. x).

55 See *BL*, II, 215.
56 *BL*, II, 218.

7. STRUCTURAL UNITY IN THE 'BIOGRAPHIA'

1 See *CN*, I, 1835, Jan. 1804, *CN*, III, 3268, Feb. 1808, and *CN*, III, 3312, May 1808, on inventing new words and desynonymizing. And see *The Friend* (*CC*), I, 449.

2 *BL*, I, 194.

3 Coleridge can say, 'Thought is a laborious breaking through the law of association', *Misc C*, 389; and 'the streamy Nature of Association, which Thinking = Reason, curbs & rudders', *CN*, I, 1770, Dec. 1803.

4 Cf. I. A. Richards, *Coleridge on Imagination* (London: 1934), p. 77: 'Fancy indeed, is the mind's activity in so far as Hartley's associationism seems to apply to it.' See also the first section in chapter eight below, for a more detailed account of association and Coleridge's use of the term.

5 The materials for Coleridge's discussion of poetry in *BL*, II, are traceable in the notebooks and letters, often to a precise coincidence of phrases. Some of the related entries from the notebooks are *CN*, III, 3246, 3286, 3290 f16, 3247, 3573, 3611, 3615, 3632, 3827, 4111–12, 4115, and 4397 f48–9. All of the main features are contained in these passages such as the unity of thought and feeling, of the imagination as giving the predominant passion, and so on. See above chapter one for a fuller discussion.

6 *BL*, II, 8.

7 *BL*, II, 10.

8 This is the method of the dynamic or dialectic philosophy, hence the centrality of the idea of reconciliation and progression.

9 *BL*, II, 11.

10 Cf. *AR*, aphorism 1 for the similarity of the operation of the genius in the one and in the other.

11 *BL*, II, 19.

12 *BL*, II, 104. Cf. note 21 below on Keats.

13 Cf. Henri Poincaré, *Science and Method*, trans. Francis Maitland (London: 1914), pp. 62–3, on the sudden illumination in mathematics.

14 See e.g. Colin Turbayne, *The Myth of Metaphor*, on the role of metaphor in knowledge.

15 *BL*, II, 33 and see 'Satyrane's Letters', 158–9.

16 *BL*, II, 33.

17 *BL*, II, 187. Cf. *CN*, III, 4186, ff35–6, 1813–15 on true idealism.

18 For some interesting notebook entries on intuition see e.g. *CN*, III, 3801, 4186, 4351, and 4377.

19 On the relation of the experience of conscience to intuition or a testifying state see e.g. *AR*, 105ff, 304, and *CN*, III, 3591, Autumn 1809.

20 For the relation of intuitive truth and knowledge as faith see *LS* (*CC*), 18, 47,

96, *AR*, 6, 9, 183, 303ff, and *P Lects.*, lect. xiii, 374 and 389 for the faith of reason.

21 Although this distinctity in unity is everywhere understood in Coleridge's works by his synthesis of thought and feeling, head and heart, sense and sensation, and in his placing the moral at the root of all aesthetic, spiritual and intellectual experience, it is rarely as sublimely expressed as it is by Keats, in his letters on beauty and truth. See e.g. the letter to Benjamin Bailey, 22 Nov. 1817: 'What the imagination seizes as Beauty must be truth – ... for I have the same idea of all our Passions as of Love they are all in their sublime, creative of essential Beauty.' In the same letter he says 'I am certain of nothing but of the holiness of the Heart's affections and the truth of Imagination.' See also the letter to George and Georgina Keats, 16 Dec. 1818 – 4 Jan. 1819, and the letter to Benjamin Bailey, 13 Mar. 1818.

22 Cf. e.g. *LS* (*CC*), 67n, and *CN*, ii, 2445, Feb. 1805.

23 See *CL*, v, 327 to Tulk, 13 Feb. 1824: 'All real science is *mythological* – '.

24 That perception of the underlying principle is not to be mistaken for any 'thing-in-itself' however. The ground must remain the mystery; see e.g. *AR*, 121, *CN*, iii, 3973, Oct. 1810, 3878, June 1810.

25 See below the discussion of the distinction between the intelligential and the practical intuition.

26 On the necessity for paradox see *AR*, 6, *CN*, ii, 2631, Aug. 1805, and iii, 4183, 1813–15.

27 On the sacrifice of truth to expression see *CN*, iii, 3575, July–Sept. 1809. Coleridge's constant emphasis that Ideas cannot be 'comprehended' makes the same point. See e.g. *LS* (*CC*), 99 and *AR*, 152.

28 See *CN*, ii, 2502, Mar. 1805 and iii, 4326, 1816–17.

29 Cf. *CN*, iii, 4186 ff35–36ᵛ, 1813–15. And see *BL*, i, chap. xii, 178–9.

30 The German Romanticists theorized far more about irony than did the English. See for example Solger on irony in *Erwin* and *Philosophische Gespräche*, and Friedrich Schlegel, especially the *Athenäums-Fragmente* and *Lucinde*, as well as *Lyceums-Fragmente*, and the essay 'Über das Unverständlichkeit'. See also Kleist's 'Über das Marionettentheater'. Tieck's various dramas, esp. *Der Gestiefelte Kater*, were most intensely in the ironic mode, as was Eichendorff's *Aus dem Leben eines Taugenichts*. Coleridge drew not only on German philosophy, but also upon this rich literary movement; he was personally acquainted with Tieck, and knew at first hand Kleist's and Novalis's writings. Kierkegaard might be seen as the immediate inheritor on the continent of this highly self-conscious and Platonic irony in his writings under the pseudonym of Johannes Climacus. See above chapter four for an elaboration of the concept of irony as used in Germany. On metaphor as a form of irony and indirect communication, see Norman O. Brown, *Love's Body* (New York: 1966).

31 *BL*, ii, 12.

32 See Thomas McFarland, 'The Origin and Significance of Coleridge's Theory of Secondary Imagination', *New Perspectives on Coleridge and Wordsworth*, ed. G. H. Hartmann (New York: 1972), pp. 195–246, for a thorough account of the sources in Tetens's *Psychologie* and Coleridge's use of the distinction. McFarland does not touch upon the structural significance of the borrowings for the *Biographia*.

33 The threshold metaphor is one whose significance is beginning to be recognized among critics, though long used by poets. See e.g. Angus Fletcher, 'Positive

Negation', *New Perspectives*, ed. Hartman, pp. 133–64. As an example of a modern literary dramatization of threshold experiences see e.g. J. L. Borges's story 'The Man on the Threshold', *The Aleph and Other Stories: 1933–69*, ed. and trans. N. T. di Giovanni (London: 1971). In this case the reader is also the 'Man'.

34 Cf. Coleridge's comment, 'Consciousness being the narrow *Neck* of the Bottle', *Inquiring Spirit*, ed. K. Coburn (London: 1951), pp. 30–1.

35 On the deadening effects of custom cf. Shelley: '[The poet's] language is vitally metaphorical; that is, it marks the before unapprehended relations of things and perpetuates their apprehension, until the words which represent them become, through time, signs for portions or classes of thoughts instead of pictures of integral thoughts; and then if no new poets should arise to create afresh the associations which have been thus disorganized language will be dead to all the nobler purposes of human intercourse.' 'Defence of Poetry', ed. Baker, p. 496. Or see Keats: 'Memory should not be called knowledge – Many have original minds who do not think it – they are led away by Custom – Now it appears to me that almost any Man may like the Spider spin from his own inwards his own airy Citadel – ', letter to J. H. Reynolds, 19 Feb. 1818.

36 See e.g. Appleyard, 'Critical Theory', pp. 135–6.

37 Cf. Richards, *Coleridge on Imagination*, p. 77 on fancy and Hartley's association-ism, and note 4 above.

38 The three-fold distinction has the advantage of acting also as a sign for dialectical progression and polarity or the reconciliation of opposites, so that the reader is always reminded of the existence of not only the thetic text, volume one, or the antithetic, volume two, but of the prothetic or transcendent unity of both, as the higher *imagined* third. Thus Coleridge realizes on a practical level the results of his speculations in metaphysics: he presents in the structure of the *Biographia* the apparent duality of experience, and then shows the essential homogeneity as well as the means by which the appearance of duality is overcome.

See Cooke, 'Quisque sui Faber' for a similar view that the imagination as subject matter permeates the work and is not merely confined to chapter thirteen: 'A basis for identifying the imagination at its work, or in process, is diffused through the body of the *Biographia* and deserves to be recognized alongside the more prominent definition semi-crystallized in chapter thirteen' (p. 229).

39 Not of course in the sense in which the oracle is usually misunderstood to mean the personal, individual self, as we have emphasized in prevous chapters. See a fascinating description by Keats of the poet and man of genius as transcending self: 'As to the poetical Character itself, . . . it is not itself – it has no self – it is every thing and nothing – . . . A Poet is the most unpoetical of any thing in existence; because he has no Identity – he is continually in for – and filling some other Body – . . . the poet has . . . no identity . . . not one word I ever utter can be taken for granted as an opinion growing out of my identical nature – how can it, when I have no nature?' Letter to Woodhouse, 27 Oct. 1818. Keats is suggesting why neither the poet as individual nor the reader as individual is in any position to determine meaning or certainty in literature.

40 *BL*, I, 162. Cf. the missing chapter in *Tristram Shandy*.

41 This is a point which needs to be emphasized frequently, in view of the tenacity of the belief that immediate responses can somehow be measures of the work in a pure form, unalloyed by 'interpretation'.

42 *BL*, I, 160–1, 164–5, 166, 167–8.

43 *BL*, I, 169–70.

44 There is some danger that this statement could be mistaken for a description of a philosophy which is merely syncretic. But consider this notebook entry: ' "Eclectic Philosophy'; 'Syncretism'; 'Adoption of the Best', †and† or by whatever other phrases the same process of intellect may be represented, is the Death of all Philosophy. Truth is one and entire, because it is *vital*. Whatever lives is contradistinguished from all juxtapositions of mechanism, however ingenious, by its oneness, its impartibility; – and mechanism itself could not have had existence, except as a counterfeit of a living Whole – /. Suppose, that of the Alphabet of which I deem *true*, A. B. C. D. were to be found in Pythagoras; E. F. G. H. in Plato – I. L. M. N. in Aristotle – P. Q. R. S. in Epicurus; T. U. Y. X. †from† in Zeno or his followers – / – yet if indeed I have a *system*, these parts are not there on account of their having been in Pyth: Plat. Arist. Epic. or Zeno – but because B. is the necessary consequence of A... and so forth – O! this picking & choosing is a grievous evil. It comes at last to this – whatever – in whatever writer agrees with my... previous Thoughts & the fashion of the Age, I live in, that I select, – whence deduced I care not. – ' *CN*, III, 4251, May 1815.

45 There is a general consensus that Coleridge means by this 'future work' the work which he usually referred to as the 'Logos' or 'Logosophia'. He had mentioned the 'Logosophia' several times in volume one of the *Biographia*, in relation to the refutation of materialism (*BL*, I, chap. viii, 92, 'Productive Logos'), in relation to the detailed working out of the Dynamic or Constructive Philosophy (*BL*, I, chap. xii, 179, the 'Logosophia'), and in relation to the 'absolute thing' and Spinoza, versus Fichte's substitution of act for thing (*BL*, I, chap. xii, 182n, 'Logosophia'). At one point he says that he will announce the 'Logosophia', 'at the end of this volume', though I think it is fairly evident that he means 'at the end of this Work', for everywhere else he says he intends to announce it at the end of the *Biographia* (see *CL*, IV, 703 to J. Wedgwood, 6 Feb. 1817, and *BL*, I, 202). No doubt Coleridge *is* referring to this vast undertaking which eventually came to include the early *MS Logic* as well. See the detailed descriptions of it in *CL*, IV, 589–90 to John May, 27 Sept. 1815, 687 to H. J. Rose, 25 Sept. 1816, and later references in *CL*, V and VI: *CL*, V, 275, *CL*, VI, 773, 967. But it is clear from these descriptions that he intends far more by the 'Logos' than a treatment of the imagination, which is to compose only a small section of the larger work. It is unfortunate that, because the 'future work' has a literal referent, there is a general obstinacy to admit the irony operating especially throughout the last chapter (as well as in the rest of the *Biographia*, in its degressions and anecdotes). It is assumed that irony and the literal level must somehow exclude each other, but it should be clear that irony can only act in and through a literal level. The fact that an actual referent for the 'future work' exists hardly excludes the ironic level at which this other work is a joke on the attitude of the reader to wait for future enlightenment, instead of 'constructing' it for himself. Some substantiation for this view comes from *CL*, IV, 767 to Tulk, Sept. 1817, when Coleridge explains: 'In my literary Life you will find a sketch of the *subjective* Pole of the Dynamic Philosophy; the rudiments of *Self*-construction, enough to let a thinking mind see *what it is like*...'

46 *BL*, I, 202.

47 *LS* (*CC*), 81. This is not to deny that Coleridge may at one time have planned such an essay on the supernatural; he mentions such an essay to Lord Byron

(see *CL*, iv, 561, Easter Week 1815). But the *function* of the reference to it, and to the other unfinished or unrealized works, seems to be ironic in the context of the *Biographia*. See Barfield, *What Coleridge Thought*, page 74 on the significance of the missing chapter thirteen, and the importance of context, e.g., the *Biographia* as a whole, for a definition and analysis of imagination.

48 *Friend (CC)*, i, 542n.

49 *BL*, i, 180: 'To know is in its very essence a verb active' or see 166: 'How and whence to these thoughts, these strong probabilities, the ascertaining vision, the intuitive knowledge may finally supervene, can be learnt only by the fact.'

50 Cf. Borges, 'Garden of Forking Paths', *Labyrinths*, p. 20: 'Everything happens to a man precisely, precisely *now*.'

51 Cf. e.g. *AR*, 61 which describes nature and that which is above nature, namely reason and will – the logos.

52 The gloss of 'The Ancient Mariner' is another example of the ironic context which Coleridge has built around the poem dramatizing the obtuseness of literal mindedness and the reader who is always waiting to be told something, waiting for something to happen, so that all the while the 'happening' is passing him by. See chapter eight below on the gloss to 'The Ancient Mariner' and on the preface to 'Kubla Khan'.

J. L. Borges's story, 'The Man on the Threshold' delineates the experience of misguided expectations blinding the reader to what is going on in front of him.

53 For Coleridge on his works as fragments see *CL*, vi, 847–8 to H. F. Cary, 29 Nov. 1830. He insists that his principles have a 'continuous and systematic character'; what is at fault is simply the 'occasional & fragmentary way, in which they have hitherto been brought before the Public'. This latter point no longer applies, as we have all of Coleridge's works at hand which were published, and many more besides, such as the *T of L*, the *P Lects.*, and the notebooks and letters. His unconventional mode of integrating branches of knowledge and creating hybrid genres is offensive only to those who insist upon the conventional crutches of compartmentalization. But these crutches only too frequently stand in the way of a perception of the basic integration of knowledge important to Coleridge. See e.g. *P Lects.*, lect. v, 175.

54 Cf. the following notebook entry: 'The slave of custom is roused by the rare and accidental alone; but the axioms of the unthinking are to the philosopher the deepest problems as being the nearest to the mysterious root and partaking at once of its darkness and pregnancy.' *Coleridge: Select Poetry and Prose*, ed. S. Potter (London: 1962), 436–7.

55 Cf. *AR*, 197, and see *LS (CC)*, 69 note 3 for the original passage: 'It is wonderful, how closely Reason and Imagination are connected, and Religion the union of the two.'

8. IMAGINATION AND REASON, AND THE
CONFLICT OF PANTHEISM AND CHRISTIANITY

1 *BL*, i, 194. In the following discussion I rely upon Owen Barfield's discussion in *What Coleridge Thought*, especially chapter seven, as the most lucid account to date of Coleridge's aesthetic theories. For the eighteenth-century use of the two words see W. J. Bate and John Bullitt, 'The Distinction between Fancy and Imagination in Eighteenth Century English Criticism', *Modern Language Notes*, 60 (1945), 8–15.

2 Walter Pater, 'Essay on Wordsworth', *Appreciations* (London and New York: 1889), 37.
3 Cf. *BL*, 1, 60–1. Contemporaries both acclaimed and ignored the distinction; see e.g., Terry Otten, 'Macaulay's Critical Theory of Imagination and Reason', *Journal of Aesthetics and Art Criticism*, 28 (Autumn 1969), 33–44.
4 T. S. Eliot, *The Use of Poetry and the Use of Criticism* (London: 1933).
5 Livingston Lowes, *Road to Xanadu* (London: 1927), p. 103.
6 *Ibid.*, p. 44.
7 *Ibid.*, p. 48.
8 *Ibid.*, p. 37.
9 Cf. Richards, *Coleridge on Imagination*, p. 77. In this context it is noteworthy that in Hartley's *Observations on Man* (1749) the only mention of imagination comes in a chapter on dreams, in which it is merely indicated as a faculty requiring less attention in thinking than reverie; see pt. 1, prop. xci.
10 See e.g. *AR*, 199n.
11 I. A. Richards, in 'The Clark Lectures', 1974 (unpublished) sharply criticized the use of 'external' material to explain and interpret poetry.
12 Richards, *Coleridge on Imagination*, p. 31.
13 *Misc. C*, 42–3.
14 John Muirhead, *Coleridge as Philosopher*, p. 78.
15 *BL*, 1, 202.
16 J. V. Baker, *The Sacred River* (Baton Rouge, La.: 1957), p. 118. Baker's errors are repeated and exacerbated more recently by R. D. Hume, in his misguided article 'Coleridge and Kant on Imagination', *Journal of Aesthetics and Art Criticism*, 28 (1970), 485–96. Hume not only shows a failure to grasp the most basic contribution of idealism to epistemology. He also shows a crippling unfamiliarity with some of Coleridge's most important statements about imagination and genius. He claims that for Coleridge the secondary imagination is not subject to laws, when Coleridge time and again insists that the laws of imagination are as rigid as the laws of logic, and that they are laws originating in its own nature, which is why the organic metaphor is apt. These issues come up both in the *Shakespeare Criticism* and in the *Biographia*. See e.g. the remark when Coleridge speaks of genius: 'As it must not, so neither can it, be lawless! For it is even this that constitutes it genius – the power of acting creatively under laws of its own origination (*Sh. C*, 1 198). Mr Hume seems to think that because imagination is not mechanical (no rules given from *without*) that it must be lawless. But says Coleridge, 'The rules of the IMAGINATION are themselves the very powers of growth and production (*BL*, ii, 65). He misunderstands the relation of fancy to imagination because he fails to grasp that they are genuinely interrelated: he seems to think they work entirely independently of one another, so that he can conclude with the peculiar comment that works of fancy are different from, not inferior to works of imagination, and must not be judged by the same criteria! But how many times must Coleridge emphasize that it is the *integration* of the faculties that produces a work of genius, and that imagination (and reason) can work only in and through the fancy (and understanding)? The relation between primary and secondary imagination is hardly discussed, since Hume seems to think they are hardly related, and one must wonder what Coleridge's point was in distinguishing two aspects of imagination if there is no significant relation between these two activities.

Hume's error, which reveals his mistaken notion of idealism, has its roots in an inaccurately applied and wholly unanalysed distinction between the 'constructive' (which he seems to define as the mechanical, or operating according to rules from without) and the 'creative'. But Coleridge's use of the words 'constructive philosophy' should have warned Mr Hume that more was meant by Coleridge than Hume was understanding. His errors are understandable; the tone of his article less so. See his 'Coleridge's Retention of the Primary Imagination Distinction', *Notes and Queries*, 16 (Feb. 1969), 55–6 for the origins of this deceptive constructive/creative distinction, which repeats Baker's errors in failing to grasp that idealism characterizes perception as creative. It actually claims that externality and independence are *not* aspects of the real, and that the transcendental unity of apperception (working through the developing empirical consciousness) constitutes, constructs, or creates the known world according to laws of its own nature. Coleridge tries to explain why this concept of the creativity of perception is so difficult to grasp; it is one of the main themes of *BL*, chapters five to eight, and the 'outness prejudice' is his phrase for this difficulty. But just because of its 'hardness-to-be-understood', it should not be branded nonsense. Overcoming custom is always difficult, and new ways of seeing basic activities require effort. But they also reward it.

17 Baker, *Sacred River*, p. 120.
18 *Ibid.*, 118.
19 Richards, *Coleridge on Imagination*, pp. 58–9.
20 Cf. Kant's numerous related discussions throughout the *Critique of Pure Reason* on the transgressions of the reason as speculative.
21 Baker, *Sacred River*, p. 127. Yet see also page 69 on Plotinus and page 74 on Cudworth, and see page 81, where Baker seems to have grasped the creative nature of fundamental perceptive activity. See also indirect argument against Baker in Stephen Prickett's fine study, *Coleridge and Wordsworth*: pp. 71–9, esp. pp. 74–5.
22 See above on the analogy between poet and perceiver. See also the 'Defence of Poetry', ed. Baker, p. 496.
23 *BL*, I, 202. See S. V. Pradhan, ' "Coleridge's Philocrisy" and his Theory of Fancy and Secondary Imagination', *Studies in Romanticism*, 13 (Summer 1974), 235–54, for further discussion and on the unity of Coleridge's aesthetics and his philosophy.
24 Baker can say in the same breath that the unconscious and the passive are to be equated (Baker, *Sacred River*, pp. 128 and 191), and yet that the unconscious activity is the 'genius of the man of genius' (*ibid.*, p. 143, quoting Coleridge).
25 Richards, *Coleridge on Imagination*, pp. 58, 64, and chapter three in general, and see page 227: 'Poetry freed from a mistaken conception of its limitations will remake our minds and with them our world. Such an estimate of the power of poetry may seem extravagant; but it was Milton's no less than Shelley's, Blake's, or Wordsworth's.'
26 R. H. Fogle, *The Idea of Coleridge's Criticism* (Berkeley: 1962), p. 8.
27 Thus Berkeley's use of the language of nature as a metaphor for perception indicates this same awareness of the analogy between perception and poetizing as fundamentally creative. Perception, like language, is learned, determined by the two factors of the mind's structural laws and cultural rules, which take the form of values and in that way determine what we see by determining what we

attend to. Cf. Baker, *Sacred River*, pp. 36–8, and see also J. R. Barth, *Coleridge and Christian Doctrine* (Cambridge, Mass.: 1969), p. 19.

28 See the essay 'On Poesy or Art' in *BL*, II. See also the thirteenth of the 1818–19 lectures on literature in *Misc. C*, 204ff. See further McFarland, 'The Origin and Significance of Coleridge's Theory of Secondary Imagination', pp. 195–246.

29 Baker, *Sacred River*, p. 125, and see pp. 217 and 225. Note Wordsworth's comment in the 'Preface to the second edition . . . of the *Lyrical Ballads*', *Poetical Works of William Wordsworth*, ed. E. de Selincourt (Oxford: 1944), II, p. 386, that the primary laws of our nature are discoverable from the way in which we 'associate ideas in a state of excitement'.

30 *Friend (CC)*, I, 456; *Sh. C*, 188, 191; *BL*, I, 59–60; and cf. *BL*, II, 12, 16, 65. Again Owen Barfield's discussion of the reason, in *What Coleridge Thought*, chapters 8, 9, and 10, was extremely illuminating for the following discussion.

31 *LS (CC)*, 29.

32 *BL*, I, 86.

33 *Anima Poetae*, ed. E. H. Coleridge (London: 1895), p. 186.

34 *LS (CC)*, 30.

35 R. F. Brinkley, *Coleridge on the Seventeenth Century* (Durham, NC: 1955), p. 694. For a discussion of the reason/imagination distinction from a different perspective, see Elinor Shaffer, 'Coleridge's Revolution in the Standard of Taste', *Journal of Aesthetics and Art Criticism*, 28 (Winter 1969), 213–21. The relation of the sublime to the beautiful and Coleridge's advance beyond Kant and Schelling are examined.

36 *LS (CC)*, 69–70.

37 *LS (CC)*, 69 note 3.

38 *Friend (CC)*, I, 501.

39 See Barth, *Coleridge and Christian Doctrine*, pp. 19–22 on the idea as expressed in terms of the sensible and the role of symbol.

40 *LS (CC)*, 30. Notice the four-fold Platonic scheme of knowledge implied in the movement from the individual through the special and general up to the universal.

41 *LS (CC)*, 113–14.

42 *LS (CC)*, 29 n1. Cf. Prickett, *Coleridge and Wordsworth*, p. 79, on the closeness of the definition of symbol in the *Statesman's Manual* and imagination in the *Biographia*.

43 We might rather state the dichotomy as between poetry and science, as Shelley does in the 'Defence'.

44 *LS (CC)*, 73n.

45 On thought and feeling see *CN*, III. 3246, 3247 and 3290.

46 *BL*, I, 167.

47 It is crucial to notice that though apparently similar to the Kantian distinction between speculative and practical reason, this distinction is quite different. In the former, it is the presence or absence of will which is at issue. But in the Coleridgean distinction, will is present in both cases, while what is being emphasized is the preponderance of the linguistic, or thought element, over feeling, sensation, and aesthetic (in the narrow sense of aesthetic as applied to the fine arts). As Keats explains, in a broad application the common ground of the poetic and philosophic is re-emphasized as 'Beauty is Truth, Truth Beauty', suggesting the perfection of wisdom as the unity of thought and feeling.

48 The progression in contemplation from this point onwards seems more and more

towards silence, towards a state which, in our culture, is thought to be 'non-productive'. Certainly the artistic productivity drops, but Eastern philosophers offer an alternative view; that it is only with the eventual quieting of those activities which to us seem most valuable and creative that the individual progresses furthest to his potentiality as a spiritual being. Mind is simply *another* organ, a sixth sense to be overcome. On the Eastern view, the frequent occurrence of the zenith of poetic activity being achieved by a very early age would suggest that there is left room in the mind for a maturer development of genius – a more silent, solitary place. See e.g. D. T. Suzuki, *Outlines of Mahayana Buddhism* (London: 1907).

49 See Thomas McFarland, *Coleridge and the Pantheist Tradition* (Oxford: 1969), for a thorough investigation of this tension. See also W. J. Bate, *Coleridge* (London: 1969), p. 161, for another briefer account of this conflict in Coleridge between pantheism and Christianity.

50 *BL*, ii, 218.

51 See *P Lects.*, 425–9, for some of Coleridge's marginal notes on ideas in Tennemann's *Geschichte der Philosophie*.

52 See e.g. Imre Lakatos, 'Falsification and the Methodology of Scientific Research Programmes', *Criticism and the Growth of Knowledge*, ed. I. Lakatos and A. Musgrave (Cambridge: 1970), pp. 91–196.

53 See Lawrence Lipking, 'The Marginal Gloss', *Critical Inquiry*, 3 (Summer 1977), 609–56, esp. 613–25, for a profound and witty account of the gloss to 'The Ancient Mariner', and other glosses. For an insight into what 'gloss' meant for Coleridge, see the wavering between 'gloss' and 'paint' in 'The Night-Scene', and 'gloss' and 'feign' in 'Triumph of Loyalty', *Poetical Works*, ed. E. H. Coleridge, 2 vols. (Oxford: 1912), i, 422, lines 52ff, and ii, 1071, lines 310ff.

54 See Coleridge: 'You will take especial note of the marvellous independence and true imaginative absence of all particular space or time in the Faery Queen... It is truly...of mental space. The poet has placed you in a dream, a charmed sleep, and you neither wish, nor have the power, to inquire where you are, or how you got there.' *Misc. C*, 36. Cf.: 'We are also conscious of an "extraordinary sense of the mind's *very being*, in suspense, above time and space", that "arises in the poet himself in the act of composition".' A. R. Jones, 'The Conversation and other Poems', *Writers and their Background*, ed. Brett, p. 99.

55 See *CL*, ii, 864 on the 'bad trick of moralizing everything', and see *BL*, ii, 105 on moralizing: 'For the communication of pleasure is the introductory means by which alone the poet must expect to moralize his readers.' See the 'Defence of Poetry' for repeated insistence on this point by Shelley.

56 See *TT*, 31 May 1830.

57 For some consideration of the function of the gloss see George Watson's study, *Coleridge the Poet* (London: 1966).

58 Cf. John Beer on the fragment: 'the total poem may not be readily available in the immediate verbal structure which appears on the page. There *is* a fine poem on the page: it moves to the incantation of its own mazy rhythms and turns sinuously in mazes of bright enchantment. But the total poem which is revealed when we explore those images turns out to criticize the self-indulgence of incantation for its own sake and to accept that incantation only as the necessary context for the projection of a more exalted and inclusive view of art.' J. B. Beer, 'Poems of the Supernatural', *Writers and their Background*, ed. Brett, p. 69.

59 Note these scattered hints of Coleridge's: 'We are nigh to waking when we

dream, we dream.' *CN*, III, 4410. 'A poem may in one sense be a dream, but it must be a waking dream.' *Literary Remains*, ed. H. N. Coleridge (London: 1836–39), I, 173. And see note 54 above.

60 Cf. *CN*, III, 4022 on music as 'articulated breath'.

61 The sense in which ironic poetry makes self-consciousness its object, and the sense in which it should be understood as a mirroring of the reader's self is more frequently misunderstood than grasped. Coleridge explains:

> The causativeness hath not ceased, and what shall the product be? All power and all reality are already present...What then remains to be communicated? It must in some high sense be other and yet it must be a Self. For there is no other than Self...We must...proceed as if we substantiated Altereity itself... The altereity must have some distinction from the original absolute identity or how could it be contemplated as other, and yet this distinction must be such as not to contradict the other co-essential term. It must remain in some sense the Self, though another Self...a Self wholly and adequately repeated, yet so that the very repetition contains the distinction from the primary act, a Self which in both is self-subsistent, but which yet is not the same because the one only is self-originated. (*MS*, B3, ff242–6, 251, quoted in Barth, *Coleridge and Christian Doctrine*, p. 89.

CONCLUSION: THE 'BIOGRAPHIA'S' READERS

1 Georges Poulet, 'The Phenomenology of Reading', *New Literary History*, 1 (Oct. 1969), 53–68.

2 R. H. Jauss, 'Literary History as a Challenge to Literary Theory', *New Literary History*, 2 (Autumn 1970), 7–38.

3 Stanley E. Fish, 'Literature in the Reader: Affective Stylistics', *New Literary History*, 2 (Autumn 1970), 123–62.

4 See e.g. 'Facts and Fictions: A Reply to Ralph Rader', *Critical Inquiry*, 1 (June 1975), 883–91, and 'How Ordinary is Ordinary Language?', *New Literary History*, 5 (1973), 41–54. For a rather different view of the reader's role see Walter J. Slatoff, *With Respect to Readers: Dimensions of Literary Response* (Ithaca, NY: 1970).

5 Wolfgang Iser, 'The Reading Process: a Phenomenological Approach', *New Literary History*, 3 (Winter 1972), 279–300. And 'Indeterminacy and the Reader's Response in Prose Fiction', *Aspects of Narrative*, ed. J. Hillis Miller (New York: 1971), 1–45.

6 On these two writers see chapter five above.

7 See Rosemary Ashton, *The German Idea: Four English Writers and the Reception of German Thought 1800–1860* (Cambridge: 1980), pp. 27–56. Indeed it was Francis Jeffrey who in 1802 condemned German literature sweepingly and attacked the Lake poets' interest in it (p. 31). On Jeffrey see Erdman and Zall, 'Coleridge and Jeffrey in Controversy', *Studies in Romanticism*, 15 (Winter 1975), 75–83.

8 Hazlitt in the *Edinburgh Review* 1817, in *Critical Heritage*, ed. J. R. de J. Jackson (London: 1970), 301 and 303.

9 Anonymous, 'New Publications in August [1817]', *Monthly Magazine*, XLIV, 152–60 (in *Critical Heritage*, ed. Jackson, 1970).

10 John Wilson, 'Some Observations on the *Biographia Literaria* of S. T. Coleridge,

Esq. – 1817', *Blackwood's Magazine*, ii, 3–18 (in *Critical Heritage*, ed. Jackson, 1970). See M. Munday, 'John Wilson and the Distinction between Fancy and Imagination', *Studies in Romanticism*, 13 (Autumn 1974), 313–22.

11 *Ibid.*

12 Anonymous, 'Biographia Literaria', *Monthly Review*, 88 (1819), 124–38 (in *Critical Heritage*, ed. Jackson, 1970).

13 Hazlitt, *Edinburgh Review*, 1817.

14 See *BL*, i, chapter three especially, and see Jeffrey's response in a long, acrimonious footnote to Hazlitt's review of 1817 (also in *Critical Heritage*, ed. Jackson, 1970).

15 For more information see P. A. W. D'Itri, 'A Study of Samuel Taylor Coleridge's Critical Reception in Five Major Nineteenth Century Periodicals', Michigan State University Dissertation: 1968.

16 See George Whalley, 'The Integrity of the *Biographia Literaria*', *Essays and Studies by Members of the English Association*, n.s. 6 (1953), 100, and *Crabb Robinson's Diary*, 4 Dec. 1817. See J. O. Hayden, 'Coleridge, the Reviewers, and Wordsworth', *Studies in Philology* 68 (Jan. 1971), 105–19, for a strained attempt to suggest that Coleridge's Wordsworth criticism in the *Biographia* was nothing but a hodge-podge of comments collected from the periodicals of the day.

17 E. L. Griggs, 'Ludwig Tieck and Samuel Taylor Coleridge', *Journal of English and German Philology*, 54 (April 1955), 267. On German versus English readers see Carlyle's *Works*, ed. H. D. Traill, 30 vols. (Chapman and Hall, London: 1899), xxvi, 1–55, especially the first few pages.

18 *CL*, iv, 889, and see 938 on reviews of Wordsworth as equally malicious; and see also 947–9.

19 See *CL*, iv, 966–7 on Lockhart and for a letter of Coleridge's to him.

20 J. G. Lockhart, 'Essays on the Lake School of Poetry, No. iii: Coleridge', *Blackwood's Magazine*, iv (1819), 3–12 (in *Critical Heritage*, ed. Jackson, 1970).

21 *Critical Heritage* (ed. Jackson, 1970), 17.

22 *Christian Examiner* xiv (Boston and New York: 1833) 108–29.

23 See a later friendly review in *Literary World* x (New York: 1852), 404–6. There was another review of Coleridge in the same periodical in 1847; see *Literary World*, ii, 464, 503–4.

24 See the introduction for details of this mixed response amongst more recent readers and critics.

Bibliography

꙰꙰

All works quoted, cited, or mentioned, and many of the works consulted, are listed below: works by Coleridge first in alphabetical order of titles, then works by other authors in alphabetical order of authors' or editors' names, and finally a list of available critical bibliographies.

WORKS BY S. T. COLERIDGE

Aids to Reflection in the Formation of a Manly Character. Ed. Thomas Fenby. Edinburgh: 1905.
Anima Poetae. Ed. E. H. Coleridge. London: 1895.
Biographia Literaria; or Biographical Sketches of my Literary Life and Opinions. Ed. J. Shawcross. 2 vols. London: 1907.
Coleridge on the Seventeenth Century. Ed. R. F. Brinkley. Durham, NC: 1955.
Coleridge on Shakespeare. Ed. R. A. Foakes. London: 1971.
Collected Letters of Samuel Taylor Coleridge. Ed. E. L. Griggs. 6 vols. Oxford: 1956–71.
The Collected Works of Samuel Taylor Coleridge. General ed. Kathleen Coburn. 16 vols. London and Princeton: 1969– .
Confessions of an Inquiring Spirit. Ed. H. St. J. Hart. London: 1956.
On the Constitution of Church and State According to the Idea of Each with Aids towards a Right Judgement on the late Catholic Bill. Ed. John Colmer. Vol. 10 of *The Collected Coleridge.* London and Princeton: 1977.
Essays on His Times. Ed. David V. Erdman. 3 vols. Vol. 3 of *The Collected Coleridge.* London and Princeton: 1978.
The Friend. A Series of Essays in Three Volumes. To Aid in the Formation of Fixed Principles in Politics, Morals, and Religion, with Literary Amusements Interspersed. Ed. Barbara E. Rooke. 2 vols. Vol. 4 of *The Collected Coleridge.* London and Princeton: 1969.
Hints towards the Formation of a more Comprehensive Theory of Life. Ed. S. B. Watson. London: 1848.
Inquiring Spirit: A New Presentation of Coleridge from his Published and Unpublished Prose Writings. Ed. Kathleen Coburn. London and Princeton: 1951.
Lay Sermons. Ed. R. J. White. Vol. 6 of *The Collected Coleridge.* London and Princeton: 1972.
Lectures 1795: On Politics and Religion. Ed. L. Patton and P. Mann. Vol. 1 of *The Collected Coleridge.* London and Princeton: 1971.

'Lecture on the Prometheus of Aeschylus'. *Transactions of the Royal Society of Literature*, 11 (1834), 384–404.
Literary Criticism. Ed. J. W. Mackail. London: 1908.
Literary Remains. Ed. H. N. Coleridge. 4 vols. London: 1836–39.
Marginalia. J. G. Fichte's *Bestimmung des Menschen*. Berlin: 1800. *MS* in British Library.
Marginalia. J. G. Fichte's *Grundlage der gesammten Wissenschaftslehre*. Leipzig: 1794. *MS* in British Library.
Marginalia. On J. G. Fichte. Ed. W. Schrickx. 'Unpublished Coleridge Marginalia on Fichte', *Studia Germanica Gandensia*, 3 (1961), 184–6.
Marginalia. I. Kant's *Handbuch der Logik*. Königsberg: 1800. *MS* in British Library.
Marginalia. I. Kant's *Metaphysische Anfangsgründe der Naturwissenschaft*. Riga: 1787. *MS* in British Library.
Marginalia. I. Kant's *Vermischte Schriften*. 4 vols. Halle: 1799 and Königsberg: 1807. *MS* in British Library.
Marginalia on Kant. Ed. H. Niedecker. 'Coleridge: ses notes en marge de Kant', *Revue de Litérature Comparée*, 7 (1927), 135–40, 336–48, 521–30.
Marginalia on Kant. Ed. W. Schrickx. 'Coleridge's Marginalia on Kant's *Metaphysische Anfangsgründe der Naturwissenschaft*', *Studia Germanica*, 1 (1959), 161–87.
Marginalia. Karl Solger. *Erwin. Vier Gespräche über das Schöne und die Kunst*. 2 vols. Berlin: 1815. *MS* in British Library (Egerton).
Marginalia. Karl Solger. *Philosophische Gespräche*. Berlin: 1817. *MS* in British Library.
Miscellaneous Criticism. Ed. T. M. Raysor. London and Cambridge, Mass.: 1936.
The Notebooks of Samuel Taylor Coleridge. Ed. Kathleen Coburn. 3 parts in 6 vols. so far published. London and New York: 1957– .
'On the Philosophic Import of the Words OBJECT and SUBJECT'. *Blackwood's Magazine*, 10 (Oct. 1821), 247–50.
Philosophical Lectures of Samuel Taylor Coleridge 1818–19. Ed. Kathleen Coburn. London: 1949.
Poems. Ed. J. B. Beer. London and New York: 1963.
Poetical Works. Ed. E. H. Coleridge, 2 vols. Oxford: 1912.
Select Poetry and Prose. Ed. Stephen M. Potter. London: 1962.
Shakespearean Criticism. Ed. T. M. Raysor. 2 vols. London: 1930.
Specimens of the Table Talk of the Late Samuel Taylor Coleridge. Ed. H. N. Coleridge. London and New York: 1835.
Treatise on Method. Ed. A. D. Snyder. London: 1934.

II. WORKS BY OTHER AUTHORS

Adair, Patricia M. *The Waking Dream*. London: 1967.
Anonymous. 'Coleridge Biography'. *Literary World* (New York) 10 (1852), 404–6.
Appleyard, J. A. *Coleridge's Philosophy of Literature: the Development of a Concept of Poetry 1791–1819*. Cambridge, Mass.: 1965.
'Critical Theory'. *Writers and their Background: S. T. Coleridge*. Ed. R. L. Brett. London: 1971, pp. 123–46.
Aristotle. *The Art of Poetry*. Trans. I. Byswater. Ed. W. H. Fyfe. Oxford: 1940.

Ashton, Rosemary. *The German Idea: Four English Writers and the Reception of German Thought 1800–1860.* Cambridge: 1980.

Ayer, A. J. *The Problem of Knowledge.* London: 1956.

Bachelard, Gaston. *On Poetic Imagination and Reverie.* Ed. C. Gaudin. New York: 1971.

   Poetics of Reverie. Trans. D. Russell. New York: 1969.

   Poetics of Space. Trans. M. Jolas. New York: 1964.

   Psychoanalysis of Fire. Trans. A. C. M. Ross. London: 1964.

Bacon, Francis. *The Novum Organon.* Trans. G. W. Kitchin. Oxford: 1855.

Badawi, M. M. *Coleridge: Critic of Shakespeare.* Cambridge: 1973.

Baker, James V. *The Secred River: Coleridge's Theory of the Imagination.* Baton Rouge, Louisiana: 1957.

Barcus, J. E. *The Homogeneity of Structure and Idea in Coleridge's Biographia Literaria, Philosophical Lectures, and Aids to Reflection.* University of Pennsylvania dissertation: 1968.

Barfield, Owen. *Saving the Appearances: A Study in Idolatry.* London: 1957.

   What Coleridge Thought. London: 1971.

Barth, J. R. *Coleridge and Christian Doctrine.* Cambridge, Mass.: 1969.

   Symbolic Imagination. Princeton: 1977.

Bate, Walter Jackson. *Coleridge.* New York: 1968; London: 1969.

Bate, Walter Jackson and Bullett, John. 'The Distinction between Fancy and Imagination in Eighteenth Century English Criticism'. *Modern Language Notes,* 60 (1945), 8–15.

Beardsley, M. C. and Wimsatt, W. K. 'The Intentional Fallacy'. *Sewanee Review.* 54 (Summer 1946), 458–88.

Beckett, Samuel. *Waiting for Godot.* Ed. J. Fletcher. London: 1971.

Beer, John B. *Coleridge's Poetic Intelligence.* London: 1977.

   Coleridge the Visionary. London and New York: 1959.

   'Ice and Spring: Coleridge's Imaginative Education'. *Coleridge's Variety.* Ed. J. B. Beer. London: 1974, pp. 54–80.

   'Poems of the Supernatural'. *Writers and their Background: S. T. Coleridge.* Ed. R. L. Brett. London: 1971, pp. 45–90.

   'A Stream by Glimpses: Coleridge's Later Imagination'. *Coleridge's Variety.* Ed. J. B. Beer. London: 1974, pp. 219–42.

Berkeley, George. *An Essay towards a New Theory of Vision. Works.* Ed. A. A. Luce and T. E. Jessop. 9 vols. London: 1948–57. Vol. I, pp. 141–239.

   A Treatise Concerning the Principles of Human Knowledge. Works. Ed. A. A. Luce and T. E. Jessop. 9 vols. London: 1948–57. Vol. II, pp. 1–113.

   Three Dialogues between Hylas and Philonous. Works. Ed. A. A. Luce and T. E. Jessop. 9 vols. London: 1948–57. Vol. II, pp. 147–263.

Blake, William. 'The First Book of Urizen'. *Blake: Complete Writings.* Ed. G. Keynes. London: 1966, pp. 222–36.

   'The Marriage of Heaven and Hell'. *Blake: Complete Writings.* Ed. G. Keynes. London: 1966, pp. 148–58.

Bohm, David. *Causality and Chance in Modern Physics.* London: 1957.

Booth, Wayne C. *The Rhetoric of Fiction.* Chicago: 1961.

   A Rhetoric of Irony. Chicago: 1974.

Borges, J. L. *The Aleph and Other Stories: 1933–69.* Ed. and trans. N. T. di Giovanni. London: 1971.

   Labyrinths. Ed. D. A. Yates and J. E. Irby. New York: 1962.

Other Inquisitions: 1937–52. Introduction J. E. Irby. New York: 1962.

Bostetter, E. E. 'The Nightmare World of "The Ancient Mariner"'. *Studies in Romanticism,* 1 (Summer 1962), 241–54.

The Romantic Ventriloquist. Seattle: 1963.

Brandl, Alois. *Samuel Taylor Coleridge und die englische Romantik.* Berlin: 1886.

Brett, R. L. 'Coleridge and Wordsworth'. *Writers and their Background: S. T. Coleridge.* London: 1971, pp. 167–94.

'Coleridge's Theory of Imagination'. *English Studies,* 2 (1949), 75–90.

Brooks, Cleanth. 'Irony and "Ironic" Poetry'. *College English,* 9 (1948), 231–7.

'Irony as a Principle of Structure'. *Literary Opinion in America.* Ed. M. D. Zabel. Revised edn, New York: 1951, pp. 729–41.

Modern Poetry and the Tradition. Chapel Hill: 1939.

Brooks, Cleanth and Penn-Warren, Robert. *Understanding Fiction.* New York: 1943.

The Well Wrought Urn: Studies in the Structure of Poetry. London: 1949.

Brown, Norman O. *Love's Body.* New York: 1966.

Burke, Kenneth. 'Thomas Mann and André Gide'. *Literary Opinion in America.* Ed. M. D. Zabel. Revised edn, New York: 1951, pp. 243–52.

Burnet, John. *Greek Philosophy: Thales to Plato.* London: 1932.

Carlyle, Thomas. *Works.* Ed. H. D. Traill. 30 vols. London: 1896–1901, vol. xxvi.

Cassirer, Ernst. *The Philosophy of the Enlightenment.* Trans. F. C. A. Koelln and J. P. Pettegrove. Princeton: 1951.

The Platonic Renaissance in England. Trans. J. P. Pettegrove. Edinburgh: 1953.

Cherniss, H. F. *Aristotle's Criticism of Plato and the Academy.* Baltimore: 1944.

The Riddle of the Early Academy. Berkeley: 1945.

Christensen, J. C. 'Coleridge's Marginal Method in the *Biographia Literaria*'. *Publications of the Modern Language Association,* 92 (Oct. 1977), 928–40.

'The Genius in the *Biographia Literaria*'. *Studies in Romanticism,* 17 (Winter 1978), 215–31.

Coburn, Kathleen. 'Reflexions in a Coleridge Mirror'. *From Sensibility to Romanticism.* Ed. F. W. Hilles and H. Bloom. New York and London: 1965, pp. 415–30.

Cooke, M. G. 'Quisque Sui Faber: Coleridge in the *Biographia Literaria*'. *Philological Quarterly,* 50 (1971), 208–29.

Cudworth, Ralph. *The True Intellectual System of the Universe.* Ed. John Harrison. 3 vols. London: 1845.

Dewey, John. *Art as Experience.* London: 1934.

Diels, Hermann. *Die Fragmente der Vorsokratiker.* Ed. W. Kranz. 3 vols. Fifth edn, Berlin, 1934–7.

Eliot, T. S. 'The Function of Criticism'. *Selected Prose of T. S. Eliot.* Ed. Frank Kermode. London: 1975, pp. 67–76.

'Tradition and Individual Talent'. *Selected Prose of T. S. Eliot.* Ed. Frank Kermode. London: 1975, pp. 37–44.

The Use of Poetry and the Use of Criticism: Studies in the Relation of Criticism to Poetry in England. London: 1933.

Emmet, Dorothy. 'Coleridge and Philosophy'. *Writers and their Background: S. T. Coleridge.* Ed. R. L. Brett. London: 1971, pp. 195–220.

Empson, William. *Seven Types of Ambiguity.* London: 1930.

The Structure of Complex Words. London: 1951.

Erdman, D. V. and Zall, P. M. 'Coleridge and Jeffrey in Controversy'. *Studies in Romanticism,* 15 (Winter 1975), 75–83.

Findlay, J. N. *Plato, the Written and Unwritten Doctrine*. London: 1974.

Fish, Stanley E. 'Facts and Fictions: A Reply to Ralph Rader'. *Critical Inquiry*, 1 (June 1975), 883–91.

'How Ordinary is Ordinary Language?' *New Literary History*, 5 (1973), 41–54.

'Literature in the Reader: Affective Stylistics'. *New Literary History*, 2 (Autumn 1970), 123–62.

Self Consuming Artifacts. Berkeley: 1972.

Fletcher, Angus. 'Positive Negation'. *New Perspectives on Coleridge and Wordsworth*. Ed. G. H. Hartman. New York: 1972, pp. 133–64.

Fogle, D. M. 'A Compositional History of the *Biographia Literaria*'. *Studies in Bibliography*, 30 (1977), 219–34.

Fogle, R. H. 'Critical Practice'. *Writers and their Background: S. T. Coleridge*. Ed. R. L. Brett. London: 1971, pp. 147–66.

The Idea of Coleridge's Criticism. Berkeley: 1962.

Ford, N. F. 'Paradox and Irony in Shelley's Poetry'. *Studies in Philology*, 57 (October 1960), 648–62.

Freeman, K. *The Pre-Socratic Philosophers: A Companion to Diels, 'Fragmente der Vorsokratiker'*. Oxford: 1946.

Fruman, Norman. *Coleridge, the Damaged Archangel*. London: 1972.

Goodman, Nelson. *Fact, Fiction, and Forecast*. London: 1954.

Languages of Art. London: 1969.

Green, J. H. *Spiritual Philosophy; founded on the teachings of S. T. Coleridge*. Ed. J. Simon. 2 vols. London: 1865.

Griggs, E. L. 'Ludwig Tieck and Samuel Taylor Coleridge'. *Journal of English and German Philology*, 54 (April 1955), 262–8.

Grow, L. M. *The Prose Style of Samuel Taylor Coleridge*. Salzburg: 1976.

Hartley, David. *Observations on Man*. Introduction: T. L. Haguelet. 2 vols. in one. Gainesville, Florida: 1966.

Havelock, E. A. *Preface to Plato*. Oxford: 1963.

Haven, Richard. *Patterns of Consciousness: An Essay on Coleridge*. Amherst, Mass.: 1969.

Hayden, J. O. 'Coleridge, the Reviewers, and Wordsworth'. *Studies in Philology*, 68 (Jan. 1971), 105–19.

Hazlitt, William. 'Biographia Literaria'. *Edinburgh Review*, 28 (1817), 488–515.

Hedge, F. H. 'Coleridge's Literary Character'. *Christian Examiner* (Boston and New York) 14 (1833), 108–29.

Hegel, G. W. F. *Lectures on the History of Philosophy*. Trans. E. S. Haldane. 3 vols. London: 1892–6.

Phenomenology of Mind. Trans. J. B. Baillie. London: 1931.

Heller, Josef. *Solgers Philosophie der ironischen Dialektik*. Berlin: 1928.

Helmholtz, Anna A. *The Indebtedness of S. T. Coleridge to A. W. Schlegel*. Madison, Wis.: 1907.

Hempel, C. G. *Philosophy of Natural Science*. Englewood Cliffs, NJ: 1966.

Heraclitus. *Ephesius*. Ed. P. E. Wheelwright. Princeton: 1959.

Hesse, Mary B. 'The Explanatory Function of Metaphor'. *Logic, Methodology and Philosophy of Science*. Ed. Yehoshua Bar-Hillel. Amsterdam: 1965, pp. 249–59.

The Structure of Scientific Inference. London: 1974.

Hoheisel, Peter. 'Coleridge on Shakespeare: Method amid the Rhetoric'. *Studies in Romanticism*, 13 (Winter 1974), 15–24.

House, Humphry. *Coleridge: The Clark Lectures, 1951–2*. London: 1953.

Hume, David. *A Treatise of Human Nature*. Ed. C. Mossner. Baltimore, Maryland: 1969.

Hume, R. D. 'Coleridge and Kant on Imagination'. *Journal of Aesthetics and Art Criticism*, 28 (1970), 485–96.

'Coleridge's Retention of the Primary Imagination Distinction'. *Notes and Queries*, 16 (Feb. 1969), 55–6.

Iser, Wolfgang. *Der Akt des Lesens: Theorie ästhetischer Wirkung*. München: 1976.

The Implied Reader: Patterns of Communication from Bunyan to Beckett. Baltimore: 1974.

'Indeterminacy and the Reader's Response in Prose Fiction'. *Aspects of Narrative*. Ed. J. Hillis Miller. New York: 1971, pp. 1–45.

'The Reading Process: A Phenomenological Approach'. *New Literary History*, 3 (Winter 1972), 279–300.

D'Itri, P. A. W. A Study of Samuel Taylor Coleridge's Critical Reception in Five Major Nineteenth Century Periodicals. Michigan State University dissertation: 1968.

Jackson, J. R. de J. *Coleridge: The Critical Heritage*. London: 1970.

Method and Imagination in Coleridge's Criticism. Cambridge, Mass. and London: 1969.

Jauss, R. H. 'Literary History as a Challenge to Literary Theory'. *New Literary History*, 2 (Autumn 1970), 7–38.

Jones, A. R. 'The Conversation and other Poems'. *Writers and their Background: S. T. Coleridge*. Ed. R. L. Brett. London: 1971, pp. 91–122.

Kant, Immanuel. *Critique of Judgment*. Trans. James C. Meredith. Oxford: 1952.

Critique of Pure Reason. Trans. Norman Kemp-Smith. London: 1929.

De mundi sensibilis atque intelligibilis forma et principiis. Kant: Selected Pre-Critical Writings and Correspondence with Beck. Ed. G. B. Kerferd and D. E. Walford. Manchester: 1968, pp. 45–92.

Universal Natural History and Theory of the Heavens (1755). Trans. W. Hastie. Introduction: M. K. Munitz. Ann Arbor: 1969.

Keats, John. *Letters of John Keats, 1814–21*. Ed. H. E. Rollins. 2 vols. Cambridge, Mass.: 1958.

Kennedy, W. L. *The English Heritage of Coleridge of Bristol, 1798; the Basis in Eighteenth-Century Thought for his Distinction between Imagination and Fancy*. New Haven: 1947.

Kierkegaard, Søren. *The Concept of Irony*. Trans. L. M. Capell. London: 1966.

Concluding Unscientific Postscript. Trans. D. F. Swenson. Ed. W. Lowrie. Princeton: 1968.

Philosophical Fragments. Trans. D. F. Swenson. Introduced N. Thulstrup. Revised H. V. Hong. Princeton: 1936.

Knox, Norman. *The Word 'IRONY' and its Context 1500–1755*. Durham, NC: 1961.

Koch, Max. 'Ludwig Tiecks Stellung zu Shakespeare'. *Shakespeare Jahrbuch*, 32 (1896), 330–347.

Lakatos, Imre. 'Falsification and the Methodology of Scientific Research Programmes'. *Criticism and the Growth of Knowledge*. Ed. Imre Lakatos and Alan Musgrave. Cambridge: 1970, pp. 91–196.

Leavis, F. R. *Revaluation: Tradition and Development in English Poetry*. Harmondsworth: 1964.

Lipking, Lawrence. 'The Marginal Gloss'. *Critical Inquiry*, 3 (Summer 1977), 609–56.

Locke, John. *Essay Concerning Human Understanding*. Ed. P. H. Nidditch, Oxford: 1975.

Lockhart, J. G. *Peter's Letters to His Kinsfolk*. 3 vols. London: 1819.

Lovejoy, A. O. *The Great Chain of Being: A Study in the History of an Idea*. Cambridge, Mass.: 1936.

Lowes, J. L. *The Road to Xanadu: A Study in the Ways of the Imagination*. 2nd edn, London: 1927.

Lüdeke, H. *Ludwig Tieck und das alte englische Theater: Ein Beitrag zur Geschichte der Romantik*. Frankfurt am Main: 1922.

Mallette, R. 'Narrative Technique and Structure in the *Biographia Literaria*'. *Modern Language Review*, 70 (Jan. 1975), 32–40.

Mann, Thomas. 'The Art of the Novel'. *The Creative Vision*. Ed. H. M. Block and H. Salinger. New York: 1960, pp. 84–96.

The Transposed Heads: A Legend of India. Trans. H. T. Lowe-Porter. New York: 1959.

Marquardt, Hertha. *Henry Crabb Robinson und seine Deutschen Freunde*. Göttingen: 1964.

Matenko, Percy (ed.). *Tieck and Solger: The Complete Correspondence*. New York: 1933.

McFarland, Thomas. *Coleridge and the Pantheist Tradition*. Oxford: 1969.

'The Origin and Significance of Coleridge's Theory of Secondary Imagination'. *New Perspectives on Coleridge and Wordsworth*. Ed. G. H. Hartman. New York: 1972, pp. 195–246.

Mesmer, Franz Anton. *Mesmerism*. Ed. G. Frankau. London: 1948.

Mill, J. S. 'Coleridge'. *Mill on Bentham and Coleridge*. Ed. F. R. Leavis. London: 1950, pp. 99–168.

Muecke, D. C. *The Compass of Irony*. London: 1969.

Irony. London: 1970.

Muirhead, John H. *Coleridge as Philosopher*. London: 1930.

Munday, M. 'John Wilson and the Distinction between Fancy and Imagination'. *Studies in Romanticism*, 13 (Autumn 1974), 313–22.

Nethercot, A. H. *The Road to Tryermaine*. Chicago: 1939.

Orsini, G. N. G. *Coleridge and German Idealism*. Carbondale and Edwardsville, Illinois: 1969.

Otten, Terry. 'Macaulay's Critical Theory of Imagination and Reason'. *Journal of Aesthetics and Art Criticism*, 28 (Autumn 1969), 33–44.

Palante, Georges. 'L'ironie: étude psychologique'. *Revue Philosophique de la France et de l'étranger*, 61 (Feb. 1906), 147–63.

Parker, Reeve. *Coleridge's Meditative Art*. Ithaca, NY: 1975.

Pater, Walter. *Appreciations. With an Essay on Style*. London and New York: 1889.

Patrides, C. A. *The Cambridge Platonists*. Ed. and introduced C. A. Patrides. London: 1969.

Penn-Warren, Robert. 'Pure and Impure Poetry'. *Critical Essays in Criticism 1920–48*. Ed. R. W. Stallmann. New York: pp. 85–104.

The Rime of the Ancient Mariner. With an Essay by Robert Penn-Warren. New York: 1946.

Plato. *The Collected Dialogues of Plato*. Ed. E. Hamilton and H. Cairns. Princeton: 1961.

Poincaré, Henri. *Science and Method*. Trans. Francis Maitland. London: 1914.

Potter, Stephen M. *Coleridge and S.T.C.* London: 1935.

Poulet, Georges. 'The Phenomenology of Reading'. *New Literary History*, 1 (Oct. 1969), 53–68.

Pradhan, S. V. ' "Coleridge's Philocrisy" and his Theory of Fancy and Secondary Imagination'. *Studies in Romanticism*, 13 (Summer 1974), 235–54.

Preston, John. *The Created Self: The Reader's Role in Eighteenth Century Fiction*. London: 1970.

Prickett, Stephen. *Coleridge and Wordsworth: The Poetry of Growth*. Cambridge and New York: 1970.

Romanticism and Religion. Cambridge: 1976.

Pynchon, Thomas. *The Crying of Lot 49*. Philadelphia: 1966.

Read, Herbert. *Coleridge as Critic*. London: 1949.

'Existentialism, Marxism and Anarchism'. *Anarchy and Order: Essays in Politics*. Boston: 1971, pp. 141–60.

Ribbeck, Otto. 'Ueber den Begriff des εἴρων'. *Rheinisches Museum*, 31 (1876), 381–400.

Richards, I. A. *Coleridge on Imagination*. London: 1934.

Robinson, Henry Crabb. *Amatonda. A Tale from the German of Anton Wall. With Selections from Jean Paul Richter*. London: 1811.

Diary, Reminiscences, and Correspondences. Ed. T. Sadler. 3 vols. London: 1869.

Ross, William David. *Plato's Theory of Ideas*. Oxford: 1951.

Sartre, J. P. *The Psychology of Imagination*. London: 1950.

Schelling, F. W. J. von. *Bruno, oder über das göttliche und natürliche Prinzip der Dinge. Ein Gespräch*. Reutlingen: 1834.

System des transcendentalen Idealismus. Werke. Ed. Manfred Schröter. 13 vols. München: 1946–59. Vol. II, pp. 327–634.

Schlegel, Friedrich von. *Literary Notebooks 1797–1801*. Ed. Hans Eichner. Toronto: 1957.

Neue Philosophische Schriften. Ed. J. Körner. Frankfurt am Main: 1935.

Prosaische Jugendschriften. Ed. J. Minor. 2 vols. Vienna: 1882.

Schrickx, W. 'Coleridge and the Cambridge Platonists'. *A Review of English Literature*, 7 (1966), 71–90.

Sedgewick, G. G. *Of Irony, especially in the Drama*. Toronto: 1948.

Shaffer, Elinor S. '*Kubla Khan' and the Fall of Jerusalem; the Mythological School of Biblical Criticism and Secular Literature, 1770–1880*. Cambridge: 1975.

'Metaphysics and Culture: Kant and Aids to Reflection'. *Journal of the History of Ideas*, 31 (1970), 199–218.

'Postulates in Philosophy'. *Comparative Literature Studies*, 7 (1970), 297–313.

'Coleridge's Revolution in the Standard of Taste', *Journal of Aesthetics and Art Criticism*, 28 (Winter 1969), 213–21.

Shelley, Percy Bysshe. *The Complete Poetical Works of Shelley*. Ed. N. Rogers. 2 vols. so far published. Oxford: 1972–5.

Selected Poetry and Prose of Percy Bysshe Shelley. Ed. Carlos Baker. New York: 1951.

'A Defence of Poetry'. *Selected Poetry and Prose of Percy Bysshe Shelley*. Ed. Carlos Baker. New York: 1951, pp. 494–522.

Shibles, W. A. *Metaphor: An Annotated Bibliography and History*. Whitewater, Wisconsin. 1971.

Sidgwick, Arthur. 'On some Forms of Irony'. *Cornhill Magazine*, n.s. 22 (April 1907), 497–508.

Sidney, Sir Philip. *Defence of Poetry*. Ed. J. A. Van Dorsten. Oxford: 1966.

Slatoff, Walter J. *With Respect to Readers: Dimensions of Literary Response*. Ithaca: 1970.

Snyder, Alice D. *Coleridge on Logic and Learning*. Ann Arbor: 1929.

'The Critical Principle of the Reconciliation of Opposites as Employed by Coleridge'. *Contributions to Rhetorical Theory*, 9 (1918), 1–56.

Solger, Karl W. F. *Erwin, Vier Gespräche über das Schöne und die Kunst*. Parts I and II in one volume. Berlin: 1815.

Erwin, Vier Gespräche über das Schöne und die Kunst. Ed. W. Henckmann. Munchen: 1971. Reprint of the Berlin 1907 edition.

Nachgelassene Schriften und Briefwechsel. Ed. L. Tieck and F. von Raumer. 2 vols. Leipzig: 1826.

Philosophische Gespräche. Berlin: 1817.

Tieck and Solger: The Complete Correspondence. Ed. Percy Matenko. New York: 1933.

Vorlesungen über Aesthetik. Ed. K. W. L. Heyse. Leipzig: 1829.

Strawson, P. F. *The Bounds of Sense*. London: 1966.

Strohschneider-Kohrs, Ingrid. *Romantische Ironie in Theorie und Gestaltung*. *Hermaea*, 6. Tübingen: 1960.

Sultana, Donald. *Samuel Taylor Coleridge in Malta and Italy*. Oxford: 1969.

Suzuki, D. T. *Outlines of Mahayana Buddhism*. London: 1907.

Taylor, A. E. *Plato*. London: 1922.

Varia Socratica. Oxford: 1911.

Taylor, Thomas. *Thomas Taylor the Platonist; Selected Writings*. Ed. Kathleen Raine and G. M. Harper. London: 1969.

Thirlwall, Connop. 'On the Irony of Sophocles'. *Remains, Literary and Theological*. Ed. J. J. S. Perowne. 3 vols. London: 1878. Vol. III, pp. 1–57.

Thomson, J. A. K. *Irony – An Historical Introduction*. London: 1926.

Thorpe, C. D. 'The Imagination: Coleridge versus Wordsworth'. *Philological Quarterly*, 18 (Jan. 1939), 1–18.

Tieck, Ludwig. *Lebenserinnerungen und Briefwechsel*. Ed. F. von Raumer. 2 vols. Leipzig: 1861.

Letters, hitherto unpublished, 1792–1853. Ed. E. H. Zeydel, P. Matenko, and R. H. Fife. New York: 1937.

Nachgelassene Schriften. Ed. R. Köpke. 2 vols. Leipzig: 1855.

Tieck and Solger: The Complete Correspondence. Ed. Percy Matenko. New York: 1933.

Ludwig Tieck. Erinnerungen aus dem Leben des Dichters nach dessen mündlichen und schriftlichen Mittheilungen Ed. R. Köpke. 2 vols. Leipzig: 1855.

Werke. Ed. J. Minor. 2 vols. Vol. 144 of Deutsche National Literature. Berlin and Stuttgart [no date].

Turbayne, Colin. *Myth of Metaphor*. Columbia, SC: 1970.

Walsh, William. *Coleridge: The Work and the Relevance*. London and New York: 1967.

Walzel, Oskar. 'Methode? Ironie bei F. Schlegel und bei Solger'. *Helicon*, I (1938), 33–50.

Watson, G. G. *Coleridge the Poet*. London and New York: 1966.

Whalley, George. 'Coleridge Unlabyrinthed'. *University of Toronto Quarterly*, 32 (1962–3), 326–45.

'The Integrity of the *Biographia Literaria*'. *Essays and Studies by Members of the English Association*, n.s. 6 (1953), 87–101.

'On Reading Coleridge'. *Writers and their Background: S. T. Coleridge*. Ed. R. L. Brett. London: 1971, pp. 1–44.

Wheeler, Kathleen M. 'Berkeley's Ironic Method'. *Philosophy and Literature*, 4 (1980), 18–32.

'Coleridge's Friendship with Ludwig Tieck'. *Biographical and Critical Essays on Coleridge*. Ed. Donald Sultana. New York: 1980.

Wheelwright, Philip E. *Metaphor and Reality*. Blomington, Indiana: 1962.

Willey, Basil. 'Coleridge and Religion'. *Writers and their Background: S. T. Coleridge*. Ed. R. L. Brett. London: 1971, pp. 221–43.

Samuel Taylor Coleridge. London: 1972.

Williams, P. 'Duty in Blake's Chimney Sweeper'. *English Language Notes*, 12 (Dec. 1974), 92–6.

Wilson, John. 'Some Observations on the *Biographia Literaria* of S. T. Coleridge, Esq. – 1817'. *Blackwood's Magazine*, 11 (1817), 3–18.

Wimsatt, W. K. and Beardsley, M. C. 'The Intentional Fallacy'. *Sewanee Review*, 54 (Summer 1946), 458–88.

Winkelmann, Elisabeth. *Coleridge und die Kantische Philosophie: Erste Einwirkung des deutschen Idealismus in England*. Leipzig: 1933.

Worcester, David. *The Art of Satire*. Cambridge, Mass.: 1940.

Wordsworth, William. 'Preface to the second edition...of the *Lyrical Ballads*', *Poetical Works of William Wordsworth*. Ed. E. de Selincourt. 5 vols. Oxford: 1944–9, vol. II, pp. 384–404.

'Preface to the Lyrical Ballads'. *The Prose Works of William Wordsworth*. Ed. W. J. B. Owen and J. W. Smyser, 3 vols. Oxford: 1974. Vol. I, pp. 118–59.

Wright, John W. *Shelley's Myth of Metaphor*. Athens, Georgia: 1970.

Yates, Frances A. *Giordano Bruno and the Hermetic Tradition*. London: 1964.

Zeydel, E. H. *Ludwig Tieck, the German Romanticist: A Critical Study*. Princeton: 1935.

Ludwig Tieck and England. A Study of the Literary Relations of Germany and England during the early Nineteenth Century. Princeton: 1931.

III. BIBLIOGRAPHIES OF CRITICISM

Caskey, J. D., and Stapper, M. M. *S. T. Coleridge: A Selective Bibliography of Criticism 1935–77*. London and Westport, Conn.: 1978.

Haven, R. and J., and Adams, M. *S. T. Coleridge Annotated Bibliography 1793–1899*. London and Boston: 1976.

Index

This register does not include works listed in the bibliography but not mentioned or cited in the text.